SECRET HISTORY

SECRET HISTORY

Hidden Forces that Shaped the Past

Joel Levy

For Dawn

First published in 2004 by Vision Paperbacks,
a division of Satin Publications Ltd.
101 Southwark Street
London SE1 0JF
UK
info@visionpaperbacks.co.uk
www.visionpaperbacks.co.uk
Publisher: Sheena Dewan

A catalogue record for this book is available from the British Library.

ISBN: 1-904132-57-X

2 4 6 8 10 9 7 5 3 1

Cover and text design by ok?design
Printed and bound in the UK by
Mackays of Chatham Ltd, Chatham, Kent

Contents

Introduction

History is like a great river, rolling down through the ages. Its surface presents a story of dates, battles and treaties; kings, presidents and generals – the official story that you are taught at school. But much remains hidden from view: the murky depths that conceal history's true movers and shakers, the deceit and betrayal; the veiled currents of secret diplomacy and dark conspiracy that guide the course of events. This is the secret story of the past, exposed to the light in *Secret History: Hidden Forces that Shaped the Past*.

Secret History shows how hidden forces have always shaped the true course of history, from the mystery cults of the ancient world to the clandestine societies of Revolutionary Europe; from the nascent secret services of the 17th century to the sprawling espionage empires of the Cold War; from the lone genius of Archimedes to the vast military-industry complex of the Manhattan Project. Who were the powers behind the thrones? How many battles were decided before sword was drawn or shot ever fired? To what extent are great moments in history scripted and stage-managed by actors who never take the stage?

The role of history has always been to help us understand the present and think intelligently about the future. Today, as much as at any time in the past, the true forces that shape the course of events are hidden. Do countries go to war for the stated moral and political reasons, or to fulfil secret nexus of economic and strategic goals? What are the real relationships between America and the repressive regimes it counts as allies in the War on Terror? To what extent are Western democracies actually controlled by big business and special interests?

Perhaps a future historian will be able to answer these questions definitively. For now we must look to the lessons of the past to give us clues about the present. That's what this book aims to provide: episodes and incidents from history that shed light on the role of hidden forces in shaping that history. Perhaps they can shed a little light on the history that is being made today.

1

꧁

Conspiracies, Secret Societies
and Cults

꧂

The conspiracy theory of history has definite entertainment
appeal, and generally makes for more exciting reading than the
usual litany of economic forces, social trends and political
movements that constitutes the 'mainstream' version. But this
appeal, and the manifold excesses of the conspiracy movement, can belie its status as 'real' history. This chapter presents
a range of historical case studies, incidents and episodes that
illustrate the influence of the hidden hand of conspiracies,
cults and secret societies in real history. Given that the subjects
are clandestine, inevitably there is some speculation – but none
of it is unfounded. The topics covered range from the exercise
of cultural influence through a secret society in ancient times
(the Mystery religions of ancient Greece) to the complex web
of (mainly) right-wing parapolitics that has directed so much
of post-war history. The chapter closes with a look at the uses
of myth and conspiracy, which demonstrates how groups and
governments throughout history have used and abused stories
about secret plots and plotters for their own ends.

*

The Mystery religions – Ancient secret societies? c1500 BCE – 393 CE

Mystery religions, or Mysteries, were religious rites celebrated by the ancient Greeks, and later by other members of the Hellenised world. They differed from ordinary, public religious rites in that they could only be celebrated by initiates (in Greek, *mystes*, from which we derive the word 'mystery') – those who have undergone a special initiation process. Most of the Mysteries were similar in overall theme and content. They promised to free initiates of the fear of death by promising them a happy existence in the afterlife (in contrast to the dismal lot awaiting the uninitiated), based on the revelation of secret knowledge. Many scholars argue that Mystery religions formed the basis of Christianity. Might they also have served as a kind of ancient Freemasonry, a secret society offering social advancement through occult knowledge?

Among the most ancient and important Mysteries were the Eleusinian Mysteries, based around the cult site of Eleusis, close to Athens. The Eleusinian Mysteries told the story of Demeter and her daughter Persephone, agriculture gods who travelled to the underworld but then returned, bringing fertility to the earth and knowledge of agriculture to the people. Initiates celebrated their religion by processing to a temple where they were shown sacred objects and vouchsafed some sort of uplifting revelation, the exact nature of which was a closely guarded secret that remains a mystery to this day. It probably grew out of prehistoric fertility rites, and had an ancient history. Mysteries were celebrated at Eleusis every year for nearly two thousand years, from around 1500 BCE until the cult was finally suppressed by the Roman emperor Theodosius in 393 CE. The sacred site was razed to the ground three years after that by the invading Goths and Visigoths under Alaric.

During this period, the Eleusinian Mysteries had evolved from a local cult to an imperial secret society. To begin with membership was open to any Athenian, but barred to those with 'unclean hands' (murderers) and those who did not speak Greek (barbarians). As Greek influence spread around the ancient world, so membership of the Mysteries widened to include any 'civilised' peoples. They became popular with the cultivated classes of neighbouring societies; most importantly the Romans. Indeed, for the Romans, initiation became a mark of social standing and several emperors joined up, including Augustus, first and greatest of the Roman emperors, Nero and others. In joining, initiates experienced personal transformation and were subsequently expected to adhere to a certain code, known as a 'rule of life'.

The similarities with modern Freemasonry are numerous. Initiates shared secrets, and, in theory, a whole worldview, which were barred to the uninitiated masses. They started as equals, whatever their secular status, and had to progress through degrees of knowledge. Once the Mysteries became popular with the Roman elite, it is not hard to imagine that they began to fulfil a similar social function to Freemasonry, allowing behind the scenes networking and social climbing. The Mysteries also helped to bring initiates within the compass of Greek culture. While Rome eventually grew far more powerful than Greece had been, many aspects of her culture, particularly that of the Roman elite, were Hellenistic. Through the power of Rome, the influence of Greece permeated much of the ancient world. Greek values and culture propagated from Northern Britain to the Middle East. Did co-opting the Roman elite into a Greek secret society help to achieve this?

A claim often made for the Mystery religions is that they formed the basis of Christianity. There are certainly many similarities. Mysteries such as those of Eleusis, Bacchus and Orpheus, and similar eastern Mysteries like the Mithraic cult, are based on mythologies of 'dying-and-rising' gods: deities who die/pass into the underworld, but are then resurrected to bring salvation to mankind. Perhaps the Mystery religions shaped Roman culture in both its pagan and Christian incarnations.

Emperors and assassins – The dirty dealing that made Rome an Empire: 44 BCE

The most momentous period in the history of Rome was the shift from republic to empire, which took control of Europe out of the hands of the senate and put it into the hands of a single man, an emperor. The key events in this drama were not political debates on the floor of the senate or even bloody conflicts on the field of battle, but darker doings – the stroke of the assassin's blade and the conspirator's whisper, the clandestine meeting and the shady deal. These shadowy devices would change the way that Europe was governed for centuries to come.

The rise of Caesar

Probably the greatest Roman general of them all was Julius Caesar, and it was his rise to greatness that led to the eventual downfall of the republic. At the time that Caesar was coming to prominence (around 70 BCE), Rome had been convulsed by a divisive civil war and was beset with steadily worsening social and economic problems, despite its extravagant military successes and domination of much of the Mediterranean world. Although Roman provinces extended from Greece to Spain and from Africa to the Alps, it was essentially ruled by the elite of a small city-state. The patrician families who had controlled the Roman republic as it came to prominence in the Punic Wars of earlier centuries (see 'Espionage and the Rise of Rome', page 78) were still in control two hundred years later. They jealously guarded their wealth, power and status and resisted the reforms that were necessary to meet the changing needs of Rome. Masses of landless rural poor were flocking to the cities, facilities and food supplies were struggling to keep up and the iniquitous system of taxation and provincial governance was causing unrest in Italy and in the provinces.

Threatening the position of this selfish and greedy oligarchy, collectively known as the Optimates, was Caesar. Covered with glory from his campaigns, backed with the loyalty of legions of soldiers and popular with the citizens of Rome, upon whom he lavished money, feasts and games, Caesar threatened to break free of the constitutional safeguards intended to curb his powers. After his success at conquering Gaul, the Optimates were even more afraid of him and they allied with one of Caesar's main rivals, the general Pompey the Great. With their backing he passed a number of laws intended to strip Caesar of power upon his return from Gaul, triggering the Civil War.

Caesar's armies triumphed over Pompey's at the Battle of Pharsalus (48 BCE), but Pompey's eventual death did not come in battle; rather at the edge of an assassin's blade. He fled to Egypt, hoping to find sanctuary there, but advisors to the young Pharaoh, Ptolemy, decided that they could win favour with Caesar by dispatching him. They kept his boat waiting offshore and lured him into a small boat by putting two old comrades from a former campaign in it. As they pulled towards the shore the two supposed friends pulled out blades and stabbed him in the back before cutting off his head.

The Ides of March

With his greatest rival assassinated, Caesar proceeded to mop up the rest of his opponents and returned to Rome to be declared *dictator*, a constitutional position of great power but limited duration. Now that the civil war was over, the senate (which mainly represented the ruling aristocracy) wanted him to restore the republic and return to the old status quo, but Caesar probably realised that the old status quo wouldn't work and engaged in a programme of painful reform. He increased the size of the senate so that he could flood it with his own supporters, manipulated official appointments as he saw fit, undertook major civil and economic reforms at home and in the provinces and tried to re-establish law and order on the increasingly unstable streets of Rome.

Inevitably, however, these moves clashed with patrician self-interest and the antagonism of the Optimates grew. It was further inflamed by the fear that Caesar was planning to have himself declared king, a position regarded with loathing by the republican Romans for whom the tyrannies of the Roman kings of old (who had been overthrown in the 6th century BCE) were a legendary evil. Caesar's action did little to disabuse the senate of this notion. He accepted unprecedented honours from the senate itself, such as the title 'Imperator' as a family name, the erection of numerous temples and statues in his honour, and the issue of coins minted with his image, a tribute never before accorded to a living Roman (but associated with Greek kings). He allowed peoples in the eastern provinces to worship him as a god. He named his grandnephew Octavian as his successor, sparking fears that he was trying to establish some sort of hereditary principle. In February 44 BCE, Caesar's chief deputy Mark Anthony offered him a crown at a public feast and he rejected it, but this is widely believed to have been staged at Caesar's instigation to try and calm the rumours and had little effect.

His autocratic style, his assault on the powers and status of the oligarchy and his apparent designs on assuming the kingship combined to drive the Optimates to a conspiracy. The chief members of the conspiracy seemed to represent the two main strands of opposition to Caesar. Gaius Cassius Longinus, usually referred to as Cassius, was a general who had risen to prominence during a mainly disastrous campaign in Persia, where a Roman army under the general Crassus had been defeated by the Parthians at the Battle of Carrhae (53 BCE). Cassius had been accused of deliberately withholding his troops from the battle so that Crassus would be killed and he could take over, and even of taking a bribe from Caesar (a rival of Crassus) to do this. Back in Rome Cassius became part of the corrupt and self-serving republican faction, and, according to Roman historians, plotted Caesar's death through a combination of greed and jealousy. He represents the vested interests opposed to Caesar's reforms, and is often accused of having been leader of the plot. He was instrumental in convincing the most significant plotter, Marcus Junius Brutus, to join the conspiracy.

Brutus has been widely portrayed as, in Shakespeare's words, 'the noblest Roman of them all,' because his opposition to Caesar was honourable and just, while he himself was a paragon of noble virtues. In practice he was more complicated than this; his actions show that he could be amoral and vicious, but also thoughtful and principled. He was close to Caesar, having become a confidant and trusted colleague of the dictator, and was even rumoured to have been Caesar's natural son, as his mother and Caesar had once been lovers. Despite this he joined the conspiracy, and his motivation in doing so appears to have been his republican ideals – he represents the anti-monarchic opposition to Caesar.

The conspiracy may have started in 45 BCE while Caesar was away in Spain, defeating the last remnant of Pompey's forces left over from the civil war. Cassius, previously antagonistic to Brutus, cultivated his friendship assiduously, while Brutus also received anonymous appeals playing on his and Caesar's ancestral antecedents. Caesar was descended from the ancient kings of Rome, while an ancestor of Brutus had killed the last Roman monarch in 510 BCE. Brutus was now called upon to re-enact his ancestor's glorious tyrannicide. He was finally won over to the plot when Cassius claimed that Caesar would soon call a meeting of the senate to have himself declared king in the provinces outside of Italy. Reportedly Brutus said he would have to 'defend my country' and 'die for its liberty.'

With Brutus now on board the conspiracy grew rapidly, eventually including some 60 people, including many close colleagues of Caesar's. Brutus had to work closely with Caesar without giving anything away, and although he maintained a calm public face his wife, Portia, divined that all was not well and was made privy to the plot. When a meeting of the senate on the Ides of March – 15 March – was announced, the plotters decided it was time to strike. They gathered at the house of Cassius, each one concealing a dagger beneath his robes, and then went to Pompey's Theatre, part of a great civic complex constructed by Caesar's old rival. The senate was being redeveloped at the time, so senate meetings now took place in a temporary hall just outside the theatre. Here they waited. Many of them were convinced that the plot had been uncovered and were ready to flee, but Brutus stood impassive and calm. Nearby, in the theatre itself, a group of gladiators had been stationed to help control any crowd problems.

Caesar, meanwhile, had indeed received intelligence of the conspiracy. A list of the plotters had been thrust into his hands, but he failed to pay any heed to it. Even his wife seems to have got wind of the danger, pleading with him not to go to the senate meeting. One of the conspirators, stationed at Caesar's house, helped to calm her fears. When Caesar eventually arrived at the meeting, another of the conspirators distracted his deputy, Mark Anthony, by engaging him in a long conversation outside the senate. Caesar took up his seat and prepared to handle the business of the day. The conspirators pulled out their daggers and struck – Caesar was stabbed 23 times, slumping against the base of a statue of Pompey in a final irony.

Carving up the Empire

Unfortunately the conspirators had not thought beyond the murder of Caesar and had no plans for what to do next. In the confusion Caesar's heir, Octavian, and his deputy, Mark

Anthony, seized power and in 43 BCE formed a triumvirate with Lepidus, a former ally of Caesar's. The secret dealings of this group would determine both the immediate shape of the republic in the aftermath of the assassination, and later the demise of the republic.

In November 43 BCE, the three men met at Bologna and agreed on a policy of proscription – condemnation of prominent persons so that their estates could be confiscated and their wealth used to fill the treasury. In secret they drew up a list of names, sentencing hundreds of the most prominent people in Rome to death and disgrace. Although different sources give different figures, the scale of this vicious wealth-grab is clear – around 200 senators and more than 2,000 *equites* ('knights' or minor nobility) were proscribed, including many who were allied to or had helped the triumvirates. Octavian even proscribed members of his own family. Other names were added to the list out of spite or personal animosity, or to settle old scores.

Thus enriched the triumvirate proceeded to hunt down and destroy those who conspired against Caesar. In 40 BCE the triumvirs met up again, at the town of Brundisium – this time in order to carve up the republic. The west was given to Octavian, the east to Mark Anthony and Africa, in the south, to Lepidus. Absolute control over the lives of hundreds of thousands of people was thus apportioned in a discussion between three men.

The first Emperor

Over the next few years Octavian secured his position (for instance, in 36 BCE he expelled Lepidus from the triumvirate) and worked to undermine Anthony's. He made skilful use of propaganda to turn public opinion against Anthony, portraying him as having been seduced by the dark magic of Egypt, where Anthony lived openly with Cleopatra and had a number of children with her, despite being married to Octavian's sister. Octavian's masterstroke was to obtain a copy of Anthony's will, presumably via some form of Roman 'black bag job' (the term used in the intelligence community for a covert op such as a burglary). He read it aloud to the senate, revealing that Anthony wanted to recognise his children by Cleopatra and to be buried in Egypt. It was the last straw, and with the full backing of the senate Octavian embarked on the final act in the drama that would make him sole ruler of Rome. His armies defeated Anthony's at Actium in 31 BCE, and Anthony and Cleopatra subsequently committed suicide in Egypt.

Octavian was now master of Rome and was to remain so for 45 years. He changed his name to Augustus and accepted the title *princeps* – 'the first' – but in all respects except name he was emperor. The republic was gone; the empire stood in its place. His actions during the rest of his reign would define the rest of Roman history, but because of his achievements much of this history would be a secret one. By concentrating all power in the hands of one man and instituting an absolutist autocracy model of government, Augustus ensured that power politics would now centre on a constant round of conspiracies foiled or successful. From now on, the primary concern of the emperor would be to gain intelligence about threats to his person, while the primary concern of anyone who coveted power would be conspiring. Emperor Domitian (81–96 CE), whose paranoia led him to a reign of tyranny that in turn led to his assassination, famously said, 'the lot of all Emperors is necessarily wretched, since only their assassination can convince the public that the conspiracies against them are real.'

Augustus recognised this in his own lifetime, setting up two institutions that would play a big part in the subsequent secret history of Rome. One was the *cursus publicus* – the official postal service. Up to this point post had been carried by private messengers, but now postmen became official government agents whose person was inviolable and who travelled all over the empire. Perhaps inevitably emperors were soon using them as a secret service, gathering intelligence, carrying secret messages and even carrying out covert ops such as assassinations. For instance, the emperor Gordian (238 CE) sent cursus publicus messengers armed with a fake secret message to Vitalianus, the governor of Mauretania Caesariensis. When they arrived they asked to talk to him in a private room and promptly assassinated him.

Augustus also created the Praetorian Guard as a cadre of bodyguards drawn from outside the traditional spheres of Roman influence, specifically to protect him against plots and assassination attempts. However, over the centuries the Praetorian Guard grew powerful and themselves became the greatest threat to the security of emperors, proclaiming and deposing them at will.

It is possible, then, to draw a thread from the plot to assassinate Caesar right through to the endless cycle of clandestine power plays that would come to characterise Roman history. In seeking to save the republic from the tyranny of kingship and preserve the free and open conduct of government through constitutional forms – in other words to protect Rome from the forces of secrecy and subversion – the conspirators ensured the opposite.

The Assassins of Persia: 1090–1265 CE

The Assassins, also known as the Hashshashin (from their supposed use of the drug *hashish*), were a medieval Islamic sect, legendary for their murderous activities and quasi-mystical training methods. In 19th-century Europe tales of the Assassins, based on spurious medieval sources such as the travelogues of Marco Polo, became wildly fashionable and the popular myth of the sect was established.

According to this partly fictionalised account, the Assassins were a secret brotherhood based in the impenetrable mountain fortress of Alamut and led by a charismatic Svengali-figure, Sheikh Hasan-i Sabbah. They would capture the fiercest guards from the Silk Road caravans that passed by their mountain fastness and spirit them away to Alamut, where they would awaken to discover a paradise of lush gardens populated by harems of beautiful maidens. Their senses addled by powerful doses of hashish (a paste made from cannabis that is taken in doses hundreds of times stronger than modern spliffs, with intense psychedelic effects), the recruits would then meet the mysterious Sheikh, who told them that they were in paradise. Then they would once again be put to sleep, to awaken in ordinary surroundings. If they wished to return to paradise, they were told, they must swear absolute obedience to Hasan and carry out assassinations at his command. Under the influence of more hashish, the brainwashed acolytes became deadly killing machines, who could be directed at the sect's enemies.

The myth of the Assassins caught the public imagination at a time when Romantic culture was embracing all things oriental, including, for a few intrepid bohemians, hashish. The mysterious sect has since been woven into the rich tapestry of conspiracy myth (particularly *Manchurian Candidate*-style mind control conspiracies), while parallels have been drawn with the suicide bombers of modern Islamic fundamentalist terror. However, it is also common to discount the story of the Assassins as the fevered fancy of Romantic fantasists intoxicated with a heady mix of orientalism and drugs.

Neither of these modern viewpoints is accurate, although the truth is undeniably strange. The Assassins did exist, and they did play a major role in shaping the politics and power balance of the medieval world through terror and assassination. During their sinister reign they destabilised Persia, governed parts of Syria and performed contract killings for the crusaders.

The name 'Assassins', believed to derive either from the name of their leader Hasan-i Sabbah or from their alleged drug use, was a derogatory one given the sect by its enemies. They called themselves the *ad-dawa al-jadida*, 'the new doctrine'. Their origins lie in the turbulent and complex history of Islamic schisms, since they were a branch of the Isma'ili Shiite Fatimids. The Fatimids were a dynasty of Shiite Muslims who claimed descent from Fatima, daughter of the Prophet, and therefore considered themselves to be rightful rulers of the Islamic Empire, rather than the Sunni Abbasid caliphate. The Fatimids started off in Yemen, but were constituted as a kind of secret society themselves. Their modus operandi was to send missionaries to lands outside their rule, where they would practise their faith in secret and seek to convert leading citizens, such as generals and rulers, and so take control (although they also made free use of armies, invasion and other more usual forms of conquest). By the 11th century their influence had spread as far afield as Spain, Sicily and Sardinia, and a Fatimid dynasty ruled large parts of North Africa and the Near East from Cairo.

The Assassins were a particularly fervent group of Fatimid missionaries, formed in the 1070s in support of the Fatimid Caliph's son Nizar, in his dynastic struggle for the succession, and hence sometimes known as Nizaris. In 1090, under Hasan-i Sabbah, they captured the fortress of Alamut, in Kazvin, in the mountains of Northern Iran. From this impregnable base they developed their ideology and their power, becoming the Assassins of legend. For the Assassins, targeted murder of high-ranking members of inimical branches of Islam became a religious duty and a means of spreading their political and religious influence. There is no real evidence that they used drugs or brainwashing techniques, but they are believed to have gone about their sinister business with grim efficiency.

Individuals or small cells of Assassins would infiltrate the hometown of the target and live there quietly for some time, disguised as tradesmen or religious ascetics. Observing the target carefully over time they would build up a picture of his movements and choose the right moment to strike. Usually they would carry out the assassination in public, often in the mosque during Friday prayers. The Assassins preferred to use a dagger, at close range, to minimise the chances of escape for the target. As with today's suicide bombers they wanted maximum publicity, to enhance the impact of the murder and their reputation as fearsome enemies. However, unlike modern suicide bombers they took care not to injure anyone else and did not allow suicide, preferring to be killed by the victim's guards.

In 1092 the Assassins claimed their first victim, Nizam al-Mulk, vizier for one of the Abbasid caliphs in Baghdad. Soon afterwards they made alliance with Ridwan, the ruler of Aleppo, in Syria, and for two decades became de facto rulers of the area. After Ridwan's death, however, his successor Ibn al-Khashab drove them out of the area and thus made their list, meeting a sticky end at the point of an Assassin's dagger in 1123. The following year Hasan-i Sabbah died, but the sect continued to grow in strength through the early 12th century, eventually coming under the rule of Rashiduddin Sinan, known by his legendary title, 'the Old Man of the Mountains' (probably a mistranslation).

By the late 12th century the Assassins in Syria had established good relations with the Christian crusaders in the Levant, and in 1173 they briefly considered converting to Christianity, probably in order to benefit from favourable tax laws. However, Christians in the Kingdom of Jerusalem, jealous of their tax-exempt status, objected, and negotiators sent by the Assassins were murdered. Relations were nevertheless maintained, and in the Assassins the crusaders found a valuable ally against the Saracen king, Saladin. In 1175 two attempts were made on Saladin's life, the second assassin getting close enough to wound him.

In 1192 the Assassins became embroiled in the complex politics of the crusader kingdoms. Someone – historical speculation points to Richard I (the Lionheart) of England – hired them to polish off Conrad of Montferrat, king of Jerusalem. Conrad was a rival of Richard's vassal Guy of Lusignan for the throne of Jerusalem. With support from Philip II of France and Leopold of Austria, Conrad replaced Guy as king in April 1192. His reign was short. On 28 April he was returning from dinner at the house of a friend when he was set upon by two Assassins and stabbed to death.

The sect continued to exert its sinister influence over Middle and Near Eastern politics until the mid-13th century. Weakened in part by the depredations of the Assassins, the Abbasid caliphate was in no position to resist the marauding Mongol hordes. Hulagu Khan, grandson of Genghis and brother of Kublai, was dispatched to conquer Persia and crush the Assassins. In 1256 he arrived at the gates of Alamut with the largest Mongol army ever assembled, but was not called upon to test the fortress's supposedly impregnable defences because the Assassin sheikh promptly surrendered in the misguided hope of receiving mercy. Hulagu razed the fortress to the ground, and by 1265 the last remaining Assassin strongholds in Syria fell to another invading army under the Mameluke sultan, Baybars I.

After nearly 200 years of secret influence the Assassins were finished as a power in the region, but the Nizari Isma'ilis lived on, eventually breaking up into several groups, some of which still exist today. The most prominent of these are the Qäsim-Shâhîs, or Khojas, best known through their leader, the Aga Khan, last descendent of the fearsome Assassin sheikhs. The legend of the Assassins lives on, however, as an archetype of sinister orders that pull the strings of power from hidden strongholds, using mind control and murder to carry out their dark agenda.

*

Secret dealings of the papacy: 189–1503 CE

The Roman Catholic Church, and in particular the papal institutions at its head, have long been associated with secrecy, shady dealings and covert activities. It has been called the largest secret society in the world, described as having the best intelligence service on the planet, and accused of everything from bribery and money laundering to sexual abuse and murder. Many of these accusations have themselves been part of disinformation campaigns used to further anti-Catholic agendas (see page 124), but many others may have some basis in truth. Throughout its long history the Church has been heavily involved with the temporal world as well as the spiritual world, and very often this involvement has been via clandestine means.

Even in its earliest days the Church moved in a world of secrecy, espionage and danger. Persecuted by the imperial authorities, Christians had to practise their faith in secret and stay out of the grasp of the Roman secret police known as *frumentarii* (originally army supply sergeants, these officers were later used for a range of secret police-style activities). Early Church historians such as Eusebius record that the Christians established their own underground to help smuggle those at risk beyond the reach of the authorities, and their own espionage network to help forewarn them of approaching danger. St Cyprian, for instance, was saved from the frumentarii when he was forewarned of an arrest warrant and went into hiding. Pope Victor I (pope from 189–191 CE) had a mole at the very heart of the imperium – the emperor's mistress, Marcia, a secret convert who helped him to secure the release of condemned Christians.

In these early days the Church used espionage defensively: to protect itself against the threat of extinction. However, in the early 4th century CE, after the conversion of Constantine and the establishment of Christianity as the official religion of the Roman Empire, the tables were turned. Now the Church, through its influence with the emperor, had real temporal power. As the Western Empire declined and fell during the next few centuries, the Church moved to fill the resulting power vacuum, both locally by taking control of territory around Rome and further afield by trying to control secular rulers. Meanwhile the bishop of Rome sought to assert his authority within the Church itself, creating the papacy by claiming primacy for Rome over Constantinople, for Roman Catholicism over Eastern Orthodoxy, and for papal authority over that of the bishops. (The title of Pope was not formally reserved for the bishop of Rome until 1073, but it is used here throughout for convenience.)

Forging the rock of the Church

The tools of deception, double-dealing and secrecy were central to realising both the temporal and the spiritual ambitions of the papacy from the very beginning. Both the establishment of the Papal States as a territorial entity, and the assertion of papal authority over that of the bishops – the two central planks of papal power – depended on forgery and double-cross.

The Papal States were created in 756 CE when Pepin the Short, king of the Franks, presented the lands of Ravenna to Pope Stephen III (sometimes known as Stephen II owing to a dispute over the legitimacy of a previous pope). The impetus for this generous gift was the presentation by Stephen of an impressive document from the days of ancient Rome – the Donation of Constantine. Dating from 315 CE, the Donation recorded that Emperor Constantine, in gratitude for his miraculous recovery from leprosy, presented the territories surrounding Rome to Pope Sylvester I, and pronounced Rome to be supreme over the other main centres of the Church, including Constantinople, Alexandria and Jerusalem. It even claimed that Constantine had shifted the imperial capital from Rome to Constantinople so that the authority of the pope would not be diminished by the presence of a rival power, implicitly acknowledging that the pope was superior to the emperor.

The Donation had the desired effect on Pepin, who recognised it as genuine and ceded Ravenna to the Pope. The Papal States were to survive for over a thousand years, while Pepin's implicit recognition of the Pope's authority profoundly increased papal power for centuries to come. For instance, 44 years later, Pope Leo III conducted Charlemagne's coronation as Holy Roman Emperor. Papal influence on Holy Roman Emperors remained strong for centuries afterwards.

All this was achieved thanks to a forgery, for the Donation of Constantine was almost certainly a fake, probably cooked up to order by Stephen. As early as the 15th century the Italian scholar Lorenzo Valla showed that the document was riddled with inconsistencies, including mistakes in the dating, incorrect forms of Latin and improper use of the name Constantinople for what would then have been called Byzantium.

Shortly after the reign of Stephen III, Stephen IV (in office 768–772) sought to enlarge the Papal States through a gift from the king of the Lombards, 'barbarians' who had by then conquered much of Italy. Stephen IV had gained office thanks to the support of two important church officials, Christopher and his son Sergius. In helping him to the papacy, however, they had angered the Lombard king Desiderius, who offered Stephen more lands to add to his existing territories if he gave the two of them up. Stephen promptly agreed and handed over the two men to meet a grisly death, explaining his actions by claiming that they had been plotting against him. His double-crossing was justly rewarded, however, when Desiderius refused to hand over the promised land.

At this time there was still debate within the Church over the relative authority of the bishop of Rome and other bishops, many of who were wealthy and powerful in their own right. Once again, a pope called on the art of forgery to assert his authority. Nicholas I (858–867) was in dispute with Hincmar, the archbishop of Rheims. To back up his claims to papal supremacy, he pointed to a collection of documents called the Pseudo-Isidorian Decretals. These purportedly dated back to the very early days of the 1st-century Church, and seemed to show that Rome had the power to depose other bishops and make laws. In fact the Decretals were recent forgeries, but Nicholas was happy to insist that he had ancient copies proving the validity of his arguments.

The Borgias

Probably the most infamous of all papal families are the Borgias. To further their ends the Borgias used intrigue, secret deals, corruption, bribery, betrayal and murder. They gained notoriety as poisoners, assassins and incestuous sex fiends. But in doing so they helped to fuel the cultural Renaissance of Europe and establish the Papal States as a political and territorial entity of genuine power, which was to last for hundreds of years.

The first Borgia Pope was Callistus III (1455–1458), who managed to make himself deeply unpopular in his short reign but also successfully elevated his nephew Rodrigo to a cardinalship and to the important position Vice-Chancellor of the Holy See. Over the next 30 years Cardinal Rodrigo Borgia consolidated his position in the Church, amassed great wealth and lived a debauched life, fathering several illegitimate children including Cesare and Lucrezia. At one point Pope Pius II was forced to reprimand him for his 'unseemly' behaviour, which included notorious orgies.

In 1492 Pope Innocent VIII died and Rodrigo bribed his way onto the papal throne, using his spending power to purchase the votes of 17 cardinals including at least one who was probably too old to legitimately take part in the election. Once installed, as Alexander VI, he set about practising nepotism, corruption and self-enrichment on a scale unparalleled in the history of the papacy.

In fact Alexander's nepotism had begun while he was still a cardinal. He had manoeuvred Pope Sixtus IV into issuing a declaration circumventing the illegitimacy of his children, and then proceeded to obtain for them noble titles or church positions. His son Giovanni, for instance, was made Duke of Gandia, while Cesare was given lucrative church offices from the age of seven. When he became pope, Alexander made Cesare a cardinal at the age of 18. Other relatives were also made cardinals.

Alexander's plan was to enlarge and consolidate the Papal States, and, eventually, to help his son establish a new royal dynasty in Italy independent of the papacy. To this end he made alternating alliances with the two major European powers, France and Spain, favouring whichever would help him most at the time. But he also used his children – principally Lucrezia – to forge useful marriages with powerful Italian families. Initially she was married to Giovanni Sforza, a scion of the Sforza family who controlled Milan, but when the power of the Sforzas weakened Alexander schemed to arrange an annulment. He bullied the Sforzas into pressuring Giovanni to admit to a failure to consummate the marriage. With the marriage duly annulled, Alexander was free to marry Lucrezia into another, more useful family.

According to some sources, however, Lucrezia had managed to get herself pregnant by a young servant. Cesare and his father dealt with the matter in a typical fashion. A corrupt Vatican hearing declared her to be still a virgin, and the servant was imprisoned and murdered. The baby was born in secret but Alexander was keen to have him recognised (so that he could award him a strategically important property) and issued papal bulls that variously listed the paternity of the boy as either Cesare or Alexander himself. Inevitably, rumours of incest became rife and to this day Lucrezia is vilified as having slept with both her father and her brother.

The career of Cesare, meanwhile, was proceeding along similar lines. Apparently displeased with the choice of a career in the Church that his father had made for him, he decided to clear the way for his assumption of a more secular role as a politician and soldier. On 13 June 1498, Cesare's older brother, the duke of Gandia, rode off to a party accompanied by a masked man. The next day his body was recovered from the Tiber, his throat slashed. Suspicion soon fell on Cesare, who was known to be resentful of his older brother's influence with Alexander. With him gone, Cesare was now free to resign the dignity and begin his political and military career.

If Cesare was to be successful he would need a powerful backer, so Alexander made a deal with Louis XII of France, who wanted papal dispensation to leave his wife. Alexander issued a bull annulling the marriage, Cesare carried it to France as papal legate and Louis made him duke of Valentois and married him to a princess. With French backing Cesare was now able to invade and subjugate the territories of Romagna, nominally under papal control but in practice independent and troublesome. To help fund his campaigns Alexander engaged in unbridled corruption, selling indulgences and church offices and confiscating the estates of enemies or rivals.

Lucrezia had been married to a Neopolitan princeling, the duke of Bisceglie, but the fluctuating balance of power in Naples meant that this poor man had now lost his usefulness too. Cesare, possibly acting on Alexander's orders, murdered him. Alexander then encouraged both French and Spanish designs on Naples, taking advantage of the resulting confusion to subjugate two powerful families who were local rivals of the Borgias. At one point he went to oversee operations himself, leaving control of Rome and the Vatican, and thus the Roman Catholic Church, in the hands of his 20-year-old daughter,

Lucrezia. He also engaged in a programme of corrupt fundraising to build up an impressive dowry for her, creating new cardinals in return for huge sums. With this money in hand he was able to marry Lucrezia to Alfonso d'Este, heir to the duchy of Ferrara, an important principality. Despite her reputation as a poisoner and temptress, Lucrezia is remembered in Ferrara for being a pious and faithful wife, famous for her sensible administration and patronage of the arts.

Through more scheming and intrigue with France, Alexander secured a free hand for Cesare in central Italy, but the Borgias were threatened by a conspiracy from within their own ranks. In 1502, discontented minor noblemen sided with the Orsini, deposed former rulers of Romagna, and defeated Cesare's army. No one was better at double dealing than Cesare, however, and he disposed of his enemies through simple treachery. Summoning the ringleaders of the conspiracy to a truce meeting, he had them taken prisoner and executed. Alexander promptly employed a similar ruse to dispose of his rival Cardinal Orsini, luring him to a meeting and then having him thrown into prison where he subsequently died. In the following months Alexander used poison and assassins to get rid of several other rivals or former confederates who knew too much, confiscating their goods to enrich himself.

The Borgias were at the height of their power. They had subdued or destroyed most of their local rivals, carved out extensive territories in central Italy, allied themselves with the powerful d'Este family, and become fabulously wealthy. Thanks to yet more scheming on Alexander's part, Cesare had been promised Sicily by France and much of Tuscany by Spain. He was planning new military conquests that would help to establish the Borgias as a powerful dynasty in their own right. But in 1503, disaster struck. Both Alexander and Cesare were mysteriously taken ill after dining with Cardinal Corneto. Many sources claim that they were poisoned, and some even say that they had attended the dinner specifically to poison Corneto, only to suffer when he surreptitiously switched the glasses around. Less romantic historians maintain that they simply caught malaria.

Whatever the cause, the outcome was that Alexander died and Cesare was left weak and sick for a vital period (although he was still able to send a group of thugs to break into the Vatican and steal as much loot as they could find, while his father lay unburied). Although he recovered, the balance of power had swung away from him and an implacable enemy of his father soon became Pope Julian II. Julian schemed with the Spanish to have Cesare arrested, and although he escaped he never regained his Italian possessions. In 1507 he died fighting in the service of the king of France.

In the end, then, the ruthless scheming, corruption and duplicity of the Borgias failed to secure the dynasty they had dreamed of, but did leave an important legacy. Cesare's former dominions became part of the Papal States, helping to secure them as a political and territorial entity of genuine power, which was to last for hundreds of years and play an important role in subsequent European conflicts such as the Napoleonic Wars. The Borgias also left their mark on culture through their patronage of the arts. Not least, Cesare served as the model for Niccolò Machiavelli's most famous and influential work *The Prince*, which stressed the importance to statecraft of espionage, intelligence and the other tools of secrecy, inspiring legions of shadow warriors, secret diplomats and clandestine rulers in years to come.

The Gunpowder Plot – Conspiracies within conspiracies: 1605

One of the most famous conspiracies of all time, the Gunpowder Plot of 1605 is still commemorated in Britain every 5 November, with bonfires, fireworks and the burning of an effigy popularly known as a 'Guy', after Guy Fawkes, one of the main conspirators. Much of the official story of the plot is well known, especially in Britain where it is routinely taught to schoolchildren, but anyone who looks at the story in greater detail will soon find that it is not as straightforward as it seems. There is much evidence to suggest that the Houses of Parliament were never in serious danger of being blown up and that to some degree the plot was concocted as a ruse to inflame anti-Catholic sentiment and further the personal agenda of Robert Cecil, the earl of Salisbury, successor to Sir Francis Walsingham as the secretary of state and spymaster of late Tudor and early Stuart England.

The official version

After the Gunpowder Plot was foiled and the conspirators either killed or captured, interrogated and executed, the government took the unusual step of issuing a sort of official history of events, known as the 'King's Book'. It's basically this account that is taught to schoolchildren today. According to this version, the Gunpowder Plot was conceived in 1604 by a group of Catholic gentlemen led by Robert Catesby, dismayed at the failure of the new king, James I, to fulfil his early promises of tolerance towards Catholicism. They determined on a bold plan to destroy Parliament that would, at a stroke, remove the heads of state and most of the leading politicians of the land, including King James, his eldest son and his ministers. The plotters would seize the King's remaining offspring and raise a Catholic revolt throughout the land.

Guy Fawkes, who had served in a regiment of exiled English Catholics on the Continent and had experience with explosives, was recruited to help, and the group hired a house near to Parliament, intending to dig a tunnel underneath it. When this proved impractical, one of the plotters, Thomas Percy, rented a cellar directly under the House of Lords, in March 1605. Fawkes, posing as Percy's servant, managed to smuggle 36 barrels of gunpowder into the cellar and concealed them beneath a pile of wood and bits of iron. The conspirators awaited the sitting of Parliament.

After numerous delays, a new Parliament was scheduled to open on 5 November, but one of the conspirators, Francis Tresham, foolishly felt compelled to warn his brother-in-law Lord Monteagle, an MP. A vague but alarming letter was delivered to Monteagle on the night of 26 October, as he sat down for dinner, and he had it read aloud to him and his guests:

> *My lord, out of the love I bear to some of your friends I have a care of your preservation, therefore I would advise you as you tender your life to devise some excuse to shift of your attendance at this Parliament, for God and man hath concurred to punish the wickedness of this time; and think not slightly of this advertisement but retire yourself into your country, where you may expect the event in safety, for though there be no appearance of any stir yet I say they shall receive a terrible blow this Parliament and yet they shall not see who hurts them. This counsel is not to be condemned because it may do you good and can do you no harm, for the danger is passed as soon as you have burnt the letter; and I hope God will give you the grace to make good use of it, to whose holy protection I commend you.*

Monteagle immediately sent the letter to Cecil, the king's chief minister and the man responsible for protecting the king against plots, but Cecil and his advisors were apparently unsure of its import and waited until the king returned from a hunting trip before showing him the letter and considering action. The king quickly guessed what was afoot and the Privy Council ordered a search of the cellars under Parliament, although not immediately. In fact they waited until the day before the opening. The store of gunpowder was discovered and Guy Fawkes was captured. Under torture he subsequently revealed the names of the plotters and the details of the plot.

The plotters meanwhile had escaped to the Midlands, meeting up with a band of Catholic supporters and eventually holing up at Holbeche House on the Staffordshire border, on 7 November. Here they prepared to make a stand, but suffered another misfortune when some powder they were drying near a fire exploded, injuring several. The next day the law arrived and in the ensuing battle Catesby and three others were killed, while most of the rest were captured. Even some Jesuit priests, who were only peripherally involved with the group, were tracked down and brought to trial. All of the conspirators were gruesomely executed, except for Francis Tresham. He was locked up separately in the Tower of London, but died in December, supposedly of a urinary tract infection, although most sources agree that he was poisoned.

The Gunpowder Plot had been foiled, the nation rejoiced, Cecil had saved a grateful king and the Catholic cause in England was dealt another shattering blow, effectively removing any lingering hopes of putting a Catholic on the throne.

A government plot?

There are problems with many aspects of the official story. Many of the details derive from the confessions of two of the plotters – Fawkes and Thomas Wintour – but the authenticity of both of these is in doubt: for instance, the signature on Fawkes' confession seems to have been forged. It is not clear whether the plotters really did try to dig a tunnel under Parliament and the reasons given for its abandonment differ; water from the Thames was leaking in, the work was too hard for gentlemen, or the foundations of the Parliament building got in the way. How was a known Catholic agitator (Thomas Percy) able to hire a cellar directly under Parliament? In fact it was rented to him by a close friend of Robert Cecil.

Access to gunpowder in Stuart England was tightly controlled, and stores were kept under guard in the Tower of

London. Yet the plotters were apparently able to obtain 36 barrels of the stuff (possibly from Flanders) and smuggle it across London, literally under the noses of the government. Fawkes was even able to replace spoiled powder by getting more from the Continent.

The Monteagle letter provides some of the biggest problems with the official story. Did Tresham send it, and if it wasn't him (and he had no trouble convincing Catesby and Wintour that it wasn't), who did? If he did send it, he must have realised that it would probably undermine the whole plot. Monteagle received it while spending the evening at a residence where he had not stayed for months – how did the sender know he would be there on that particular night? The reception of the letter sounds like deliberate theatre. Why did Monteagle have it read aloud to his guests? To make sure there were witnesses? According to a reputed confidant of Monteagle, he was actually expecting the letter.

The official version records that Monteagle sent the letter directly to Cecil, despite the lateness of the hour. What it doesn't record was that much of the rest of the Privy Council were conveniently in attendance at Cecil's, including the Lord Admiral, the Lord Chamberlain and the Earls Northampton and Worcester. This group of august personages apparently failed to understand the fairly obvious meaning of the letter and 'had' to show it to the King. They then waited until the very night before the opening of Parliament to act – a ploy to maximise the apparent jeopardy and the impact of the discovery?

The fates of the plotters are also a matter of some controversy. Some writers have suggested that the explosion at Holbeche House was no accident (ie it was orchestrated by a traitor within the group), and there is mystery surrounding the deaths of two of the leading plotters, Robert Catesby and Thomas Percy. Although one would expect that the authorities would want to capture them alive for interrogation, the soldier that killed them was in fact awarded an unusually large pension. Even more strangely, they were apparently both killed by a single bullet! Finally there is the mysterious death of Francis Tresham. Why was Tresham treated differently to the other plotters, and never brought to trial? Why didn't Monteagle try to help him? Despite the care Tresham had taken to warn him, Monteagle made no effort to plead for his life, although he did manage to have another conspirator spared. Was he poisoned? Did he really die at all? Some leading scholars argue that Tresham's death was faked, and that he was allowed to escape to Spain under the alias Matthew Brunninge.

Plots within plots

Question marks surround the Gunpowder Plot, but what was the real story? It is now widely believed that Robert Cecil, the Earl of Salisbury, had some sort of hand in the plot, subverting it and eventually unveiling it at a time of his choosing, and then covering up his tracks. What was his motivation?

Cecil's father, Lord Burghley, was the man who had brought Francis Walsingham into Queen Elizabeth's service, and who had initially built up the spy network that Walsingham perfected. Cecil followed in his father's footsteps and became a major player in government affairs at a young age. By the 1590s, with Walsingham and his father gone, Cecil vied with Robert Devereux, the earl of Essex, for the Queen's ear and effective control of the court, and thus the country. He lured Essex into attempting the impossible task of subjugating Ireland, which ended in disgrace, and Essex sealed his fate in 1601 with an attempted coup known as the Essex Rebellion (in which some of the Gunpowder Plotters were also involved).

Cecil was now in complete control of court and helped to ensure the smooth succession of the crown to James VI of Scotland on Elizabeth's death. However, his position may not have been totally secure. It was widely known that Cecil had previously supported an alternative successor to Elizabeth. It would serve his purposes to prove his value to the new king. Like Walsingham, Cecil also pursued a vigorous anti-Catholic policy. He was constantly aware of the dangers posed by Catholics at home and abroad, and in 1604 had been angered by intelligence from his main agent on the Continent, Thomas Allyson, that English Jesuits were fomenting a plot against the English monarchy. Later that year Cecil's diplomacy secured a peace treaty with Spain, freeing his hands to deal harshly with domestic Catholics. One of the strongest pieces of evidence that Cecil, whether or not he had instigated it, certainly used the Gunpowder Plot to further his own agenda, is that he went to such lengths to frame Father Henry Garnet, head of the Jesuit order in England, and lay the blame for the plot at the door of the Jesuits.

If Cecil had much to gain from creating or subverting the Gunpowder Plot, how did he do it? Two of the most suspect players in the drama are Francis Tresham and Lord Monteagle, the author and the recipient of the letter that shattered the conspiracy. Tresham was a disgruntled Catholic gentleman with plenty of reason to resent the state and its treatment of him and his family. He had also been involved in the Essex Rebellion of 1601. In all respects he was a likely plotter. But he was also a dissolute gambler who had run up considerable debts, and thus needed money. He was known to have spied on Catholic relations for the court before the Gunpowder Plot. After the letter was sent, Tresham seemed to know that the Plot was definitely uncovered and made plans to leave the country, even while the other plotters were assuming that they were still undetected.

Equally murky is the role of Lord Monteagle. According to the official version Monteagle's only involvement was as the recipient of the letter. In practice, however, he seems to have known about, and possibly even encouraged the plot from an early stage. Monteagle was also a Catholic, and had also been involved in the Essex Rebellion. After it collapsed he was lucky to escape with his life and was fined an enormous sum of money, leading to speculation that this was when he became a government informer and one of Cecil's agents.

Since the accession of James I, Monteagle had gone to some pains to reassure Cecil and the King that he was a conformist – a Catholic who saw the error of his ways and who was loyal to the Protestant monarchy – and had benefited with honours and favour. But to his Catholic friends, including Catesby, Gresham et al, he showed another face, talking like a dangerous Catholic firebrand. At a meeting with Catesby, Tresham and Father Garnet, the Jesuit, in July 1605, Monteagle was asked if he and the others 'were able to make their part good by arms against the King.' According to Garnet, 'My Lord Monteagle answered, if ever they were, they were able now', and then added, quoting Monteagle directly, '"the king is so odious to all sorts"'. This testimony, supplied by the captured Garnet, was later suppressed by order of Cecil, and mentions of Monteagle in the confessions of others were actually struck from the official record.

Monteagle's attempts to gain the confidence of the plotters were not entirely successful, however, for Catesby seems to have had his suspicions and did not trust him enough to involve him in the Gunpowder Plot. His suspicions might have been confirmed by the extravagant rewards Monteagle enjoyed, which included an annuity and a land grant, and by the lengths to which Cecil went to preserve Monteagle's reputation. Cecil wrote to one of the officials involved in the trial of the captured plotters: 'Lastly, and this you must not omit, you must deliver, in commendation of my Lord Monteagle, words to show how sincerely he dealt, and how fortunately it proved that he was the instrument of so great a blessing ... because it is so lewdly given out that he was once of this plot of powder, and afterwards betrayed it all to me.'

In summary then, although there is little in the way of hard facts, there is plenty of suggestive evidence, allowing us to speculate about the truth behind the Gunpowder Plot. It seems unlikely that the whole thing was fabricated by Cecil – he did not net any big names from among the Catholic aristocracy, including rivals at court who would surely have been targets of his. Perhaps the most likely story is that Cecil, through his network of spies and informers, got wind of a real plot, and determined to subvert it for his own ends – in particular his campaign against the English Jesuits. Using Tresham and Monteagle (and possibly others), first as *agents provocateurs* and later as informants, Cecil orchestrated events so that he could 'discover' Fawkes and the gunpowder in dramatic circumstances, and later frame the Jesuit Father Garnet as a key conspirator. Finally, he covered up his tracks by suppressing the role of Monteagle and having Tresham either murdered or smuggled out of the country.

The consequences of this complicated saga of conspiracy and double-cross are still with us today in the form of Britain's annual bonfire celebrations. Less genially, the anti-Catholic fervour that was stoked by the Gunpowder Plot lingered for centuries, finding expression in periodic bloody sectarian riots. More directly, Cecil had succeeded in hammering another nail into the coffin of Catholic aspirations to the throne, and further secured Protestant control of England.

Freemasons, Rosicrucians and the Illuminati: 17th century to the present day

The essential ingredient of any grand conspiracy theory is a secret society that controls world events from behind the scenes. Even the most cursory search of the web or the conspiracy shelf at your local bookshop will turn up a number of favourite contenders for this role; among the top three will be the Freemasons, the Rosicrucians and the Illuminati. Conspiracy theorists claim that these secret orders are covertly responsible for everything from starting the American and

French Revolutions to controlling the global economy and plotting to enslave the world's population. Do these organisations really exist? What is their history? More importantly, what is the truth of the wild claims made about them?

In 17th and 18th-century Europe, amid the ferment of the Enlightenment and the transformation of the medieval world into the modern one, old certainties and institutions became increasingly inadequate for the developing intellectual elite. Many men of letters and science, groping for new philosophical, moral and spiritual truths to accompany the new learning, turned to an esoteric blend of occult and religious thought known as Hermetic philosophy. Supposedly based on ancient sources, Hermetic philosophy was a fusion of magic, alchemy, astrology and religion synthesised in the Renaissance. Although it had 'ancient' antecedents, some of its teachings were progressive and radical for the age. Ideas that were developed included the view that all religions were equal and to some extent simply different expressions of the same central truth; that spirituality should involve personal insight and development, rather than being mediated by established institutions; and that this spiritual equality should translate to earthly affairs, which tied in with developing notions of individual rights and liberty.

Many of the scholars and intellectuals who fell into this way of thinking were known to each other. They corresponded, or met at universities or new institutions like Britain's Royal Society. A common trope in conspiracy circles is the idea of an Invisible College of the intellectual elite, and it is quite possible that 17th and 18th-century intellectuals thought of themselves in this way, in a purely informal sense.

It was in this context that a number of today's usual suspects appeared, of which the oldest are the Freemasons. Freemasonry probably grew out of medieval stone masons' guilds. In the Middle Ages the craft of masonry combined elements of architecture, engineering and stone working, and like any craft of the time it jealously guarded its knowledge and privileges. When coming together to work on a major project such as a cathedral, the masons would gather in a lodge – something similar to a workman's hut. Over time the masons' guild developed traditions and rituals surrounding their craft and admittance to a lodge, with emphasis on their mastery of the then mysterious rules of geometry and tools of architecture (such as the compass). The 'free' in Freemasonry is thought to refer to masons who worked a particular type of building material called freestone. During the 16th and 17th centuries Freemasons' societies started to admit non-masons and further develop their unusual spiritual philosophy, which shared many elements with Hermetic philosophy, and it is from the 17th century that we have the first record of intellectuals joining a Masons' Lodge.

By 1717 there were enough Lodges in London alone for four of them to get together to form a Grand Lodge. By this time senior Masons already included noblemen, a tradition that was to continue in Britain where several royal princes have served as Grand Masters. Not surprisingly this lends weight to arguments that Freemasonry is a club for the elite, although one of its principals is that initiates start off equal, whatever their status in the 'outside' world. Today there are thought to be about 600,000 Masons in the UK, and maybe 3.5 million in North America. For them Freemasonry probably offers a combination of men's club, the chance to explore areas of spirituality outside of their normal purview, a bit of theatre, the thrill of being 'in' on a secret and the opportunity to do some networking.

Freemasonry is often associated with another secret society – the Rosicrucians, sometimes also called the Brotherhood of the Rosy Cross or variations on the same theme. Rosicrucianism effectively invented itself. Between 1614 and 1616 three mysterious tracts appeared, telling the allegorical story of Christian Rosenkreuz, a knight who undertakes a spiritual quest and achieves personal transformation. Of anonymous authorship, the works, collectively known as the Rosicrucian Manifestos, employed many of the concepts of Hermetic and related esoteric philosophies, and spoke of a secret brotherhood of magical adepts, working together for the good of mankind, and in opposition to corrupt institutions such as the papacy. In practice the brotherhood was fictional, but soon esoteric philosophers across Europe were clamouring to join up. Eventually small groups of them got together to form shortlived Rosicrucian societies, and some of these people also joined the Freemasons. Similar ideas influenced both groups, and they probably influenced each other.

The third in the triumvirate of supposed uber-secret societies are the Illuminati ('Enlightened Ones' or 'those who have seen the light'). In fact several unrelated groups in history have styled themselves in this fashion to indicate their belief that they possessed special information or insight, but conspiracy theorists are referring to the Bavarian Illuminati, a quasi-Masonic group of republican freethinkers formed by law professor Adam Weishaupt in Ingolstadt, Bavaria, in 1776. They actually called themselves Perfectibilists. Establishing branches around Europe they attracted around 2,000 members, including several progressive aristocrats, writers and philosophers, to discuss ideas that were considered dangerous at the time – eg that established governments and churches were corrupt and should be replaced. In 1785 the group was quashed by edict of the nervous Bavarian government and had entirely ceased to exist by 1790. Thanks to the writings of roughly contemporary conspiracy theorists, however, they acquired a legendary reputation and were accused of being behind the revolutions that were convulsing America and Europe at the time.

So what is the truth about the influence of these groups on history? Neither the Rosicrucians nor the Illuminati existed for long enough or in significant enough numbers to directly affect the events with which they are linked, although their cultural and intellectual impact may have been considerable. Perhaps these orders provided a talking shop where future revolutionaries developed their ideas and intentions, or perhaps they simply reflected the cultural and intellectual currents of the time. We can only speculate on the direction of causality. Certainly the ideas with which they were associated so frightened the reactionary forces of the establishment that they were demonised at the time. Today, by a strange transference, they are vilified *as* the establishment by reactionary forces who feel excluded or alienated from the mainstream.

The evidence surrounding the Masons is much more suggestive. By 1730 Freemasonry was established in America and became popular with the colony's elite, many of whom would play a prominent role in the Revolution. Benjamin Franklin, for instance, became grand master of the Pennsylvania Freemasons. Other Revolutionary American Masons included Paul Revere, Admiral John Paul Jones and General Andrew Jackson. According to one estimate, no less than 50 of the 56 signatories of the Declaration of Independence were Masons, although other sources disagree and put the figure at eight. Perhaps the most prominent American Mason was George Washington. A lodge master at the time of his inauguration, he chose to take the oath of presidential office on a Masonic Bible. Certainly the design for the Great Seal of the United States, now found on dollar bills, was heavily influenced by the esoteric ideas of the Masons, and features Masonic symbolism such as a pyramid with an eye above it. Masons were also associated with the French Revolution, though less specifically. For instance, Denis Diderot and Voltaire, two of the main French Encyclopaedists, were both Masons. The *Encyclopédie*, a grand project involving many writers, advanced freethinking republican concepts and was banned by the authorities soon after its publication during the 1750s. It is sometimes regarded as a kind of intellectual manifesto for the French Revolution. Also, several of the early revolutionaries were Masons.

Was all this merely a coincidence, or were the American and French revolutions Masonic plots? Again, untangling the lines of causality is difficult. Freemasonry was popular with the sort of intellectuals and activists who would provide the inspiration and impetus for the revolutions, so it is not surprising that so many revolutionaries should also have been Masons. As Masons, they would have met to discuss then radical notions of liberty, equality and fraternity, the founding precepts of both revolutions. They may have used the network of contacts built up through Masonry when it came to organising – for instance, Freemasons are believed to have been responsible for the Boston Tea Party of 1773. Even if Freemasonry did not specifically plan the revolutions, it certainly played an important role in fomenting them.

An instance where Masons were involved in an explicitly revolutionary secret society was the Carbonari, or 'Charcoal-Burners', of Italy. Taking their name from a common cottage industry practised in southern Italy, the Carbonari grew from Masonic groups who opposed foreign occupation of Italy and favoured unification of the diverse Italian kingdoms. Above all, however, they wanted to overthrow absolutism and effect a constitutional monarchy or republic. In other words, they wanted to take the high-minded principles of Masonry and translate them into action. The Carbonari organised themselves along Masonic lines, with grades and rituals and secret signs. Many of the founders were probably Masons, and Masons could automatically join as high grade 'Masters'. Between 1812 and 1830 the Carbonari organised and led uprisings in Naples, Piedmont, Parma, Modena and Romagna, while foreign offshoots helped to instigate the 1820 Spanish Revolution and French uprisings in 1821. After 1830 the movement petered out, its thunder stolen by more progressive Italian organisations, but it helped to prepare the intellectual and practical ground for Italian reunification over the next few decades.

The real Odessa Conspiracy – The CIA, the Gehlen Org and West German intelligence: 1945–1961

The Odessa Conspiracy is an enduring staple of conspiracy theories and notably fiction, thanks to books such as Frederick Forsyth's *The Odessa File*. The basic theme of these stories is that a secret organisation was founded to help Nazi war criminals escape justice by going into hiding, changing their identities or fleeing to new lives abroad (usually in South America), and to preserve their hold on the ill-gotten loot of the Third Reich, including stolen artworks and gold bullion and cash taken from Holocaust victims. The organisation was named 'the organisation of former SS members', or Odessa, from the German acronym.

While Odessa itself may be fanciful, there are many elements of truth to the fiction. There were well-established 'ratlines' for smuggling war criminals out of occupied Germany, set up with the collusion, and possibly at the behest, of American intelligence and the Catholic Church (see 'From P2 to Opus Dei', page 41). Operation Paperclip, which recruited Germany's leading scientists for the rocket programme and other, shadier, scientific pursuits, was a slightly more above-board, American version of Odessa (see page 231). Much of the Nazi loot is still missing to this day, while Swiss banks have openly admitted that they still hold millions of dollars of money taken from Jews and other victims of the Nazis. They may be holding far greater assets in secret. But the most shocking and significant true-life version of Odessa is the sorry tale of the Gehlen Org, a CIA-funded Nazi spy ring that became NATO's most important intelligence agency and fell victim to one of the most successful Soviet infiltrations of the Cold War.

By late 1944 it was clear to many on both sides that the war in Europe was coming to an end and that Nazi Germany was doomed to defeat. The Allies, and in particular the Americans, were turning their thoughts to the likely shape of post-war geopolitics and concluding that the communists might prove to be as great a danger as the Nazis. As early as 1944, William 'Wild Bill' Donovan, head of the Office of Strategic Services, soon to become the CIA, was pressing his government to establish a route whereby useful Nazis could come over to America. Some prominent Nazi intelligence officials were thinking along similar lines, planning to surrender to the Americans, believing accurately that they would offer the least hostile reception and might even welcome their aid against the communists.

The day after the surrender of Nazi Germany, on 1 May 1945, the joint chiefs of staff ordered Eisenhower to arrest all suspected war criminals, but 'to make such exceptions as you deem advisable for intelligence and other military reasons.' By then, the most significant of these 'exceptions' was already in American hands. Reinhard Gehlen was the Gestapo general in charge of *Fremde Heeres Ost*, Foreign Armies East, the military intelligence agency responsible for the Eastern Front. Gehlen had built a reputation as an impressively accurate analyst of Soviet forces, but also for brutal and evil methods, obtaining his intelligence by torturing and starving thousands of Russian POWs.

After falling out with Hitler, and clearly sensing which way the wind was blowing, Gehlen decided that he must turn himself over to the Americans, but not before providing himself with suitable bargaining chips. He and his senior officers microfilmed their vast archive of data on the Soviets and packed it in metal drums, which they buried in a remote meadow in the Austrian Alps. Gehlen then tipped off the Americans about his defection, and demanded an audience with top brass. Accordingly he was flow to Washington on 24 August 1945, disguised as an American general, for a briefing with top intelligence officials. Meanwhile his buried cache of intelligence treasure was unearthed and whisked away by the Americans.

Gehlen, who had astutely calculated that the Americans

knew virtually nothing about Soviet capabilities and would be desperate for information, offered them his knowledge, his data and even access to a ready-made network of anti-communist assets in occupied Eastern Europe. The Americans liked what they heard. They were also willing to be convinced that Gehlen was not so much an ardent Nazi as an ardent anti-communist, like themselves.

Gehlen spent ten months working with top US officials at Fort Hunt, in Virginia, where he impressed everyone with his professionalism, ability and knowledge. His biggest supporter was Allen Dulles, formerly Office of Strategic Services chief in Germany and later director of the CIA. So impressed were the CIA that they sent him back to Germany to set up his own intelligence agency, named the Gehlen Organisation, or sometimes simply the Org, bankrolled by the Americans on the basis that he would not recruit any former SS, Gestapo or SD members (the SD was the Nazi Party's own intelligence service). Gehlen established himself at a base in the Spessert Mountains of central Germany and promptly broke his promise, enrolling some of the most notorious Nazis, including former Gestapo chiefs and mass murderers. As well as providing a secure home and occupation for war criminals, the Org probably also helped to run the ratlines to South America. The CIA almost certainly knew about all this, but turned a blind eye because of the quality of intelligence the Org provided. Dulles's opinion on Gehlen was, 'He's on our side, and that's all that matters'.

Over the next decade the US spent an estimated $200 million on the Org, which grew to employ 4,000 people. In 1956, the Org became the official West German intelligence agency, the *Bundesnachrichtendiest* or BND. Through these agencies Gehlen was hugely influential, shaping US and NATO policy towards the Soviet Bloc. The Org supplied NATO with two-thirds of its raw intelligence data on Warsaw Pact countries. Unbeknown to the Americans, however, was that what they thought was amazingly high grade information was often very poor, distorted to serve Gehlen's own ends – exaggerating the communist threat and thus his own importance. Worse was to come.

Facing Gehlen across the Iron Curtain was his counterpart in the East German intelligence agency, the HVA; the spymaster Markus Wolf. Desperate to infiltrate the BND, Wolf targeted Gehlen's weak point – his assumption that the anti-communist credentials of his ex-Nazi recruits were beyond suspicion. What Gehlen hadn't counted on was that hatred for the Americans and their NATO allies, Germany's conquerors, sometimes outweighed all other considerations. Heinz Felfe, an ex-SD official whose home city of Dresden had been razed to the ground by Allied raids, was just such a man. Felfe was recruited by the KGB and then infiltrated into the BND. By feeding him intelligence material, and even allowing him to 'uncover' some minor agents, the KGB boosted Felfe's credentials until he had risen to be head of the BND's Soviet counterintelligence agency, a position that also gave him access to American and British intelligence. For three years he did enormous damage to Western interests, until exposed by a captured Polish agent in 1961. The furore forced Gehlen to resign. He was never brought to account for his war crimes or the damage he had inflicted on Western intelligence.

For many conspiracy theorists, the Org was just one link in a far greater post-war right-wing conspiracy, forging links with the underground Masonic lodge P2, Operation Gladio, the Vatican and right-wing dictatorships and undergrounds in South America, Spain, Italy and around the world (see 'From P2 to Opus Dei', page 41). Some even link its baleful influence to the resurgence of neo-Nazi movements in the present day. Whether or not there is a continuous thread running from the establishment of the Gehlen Org to modern fascists and the ongoing secret of the Nazis' missing loot, it is a fact that the CIA helped some of history's vilest criminals avoid justice, while paying them huge salaries. The predictable consequence of this deal with the devil was one of the worst intelligence disasters in Cold War history.

The CIA's refusal to come clean about this shady period in its early history continues to this day. Despite new freedom of information laws and congressional orders, the CIA still refuses to declassify any of the relevant documents.

From P2 to Opus Dei: Right-wing conspiracies at the heart of the Catholic Church? 1945 to the present day

Post-war Italian history has been turbulent and often violent; it is littered with corpses. Three of the most sensational post-war Italian deaths are those of Aldo Moro, prime minister of Italy, in 1978, apparently at the hands of left-wing terrorists; Pope John Paul I, also in 1978, apparently from natural causes; and Roberto Calvi, a banker with links to the Vatican and to organised crime, found hanging under Blackfriars Bridge in London in 1982 – an apparent suicide. Incredibly these three deaths, and many more, may be linked to a vast and sinister right-wing conspiracy that has cast a long shadow over global events since the end of World War II. According to conspiracy theorists, these events were orchestrated or influenced by: a secret Masonic lodge known as P2; corrupt Vatican officials, financiers who ran the Vatican Bank and others linked to it; the Mafia; and even the CIA. Heavily implicated are the current pope, John Paul II, the right-wing Catholic sect Opus Dei, and many major figures in contemporary world politics.

The ratlines and Operation Stay Behind

The story begins with Italian fascist Licio Gelli. During the Spanish Civil War Gelli volunteered to fight for the Fascist Black Shirt Battalion under Franco, and during World War II served as a liaison officer between Mussolini's Fascists and the Nazis, specifically Hermann Goering's SS Division. After the war he came to the attention of the Allied secret services and supposedly helped to organise the 'ratlines'. These were programmes to keep wanted Nazis and Fascists (as well as Soviet defectors and deserters) out of the hands of the authorities and smuggle them abroad to various destinations; mainly South America. Among the famous names believed to have escaped in this fashion were Klaus Barbie, Adolf Eichmann and Josef Mengele.

The ratlines were organised with the help of US intelligence agencies, and, according to many accusers, the Catholic Church. Priests with fascist sympathies sheltered and fed war criminals and used the extensive network of Church contacts in South America to help with the transfers. The motivation for covert Allied support of the ratlines was a widespread realisation, even before the war was over, that communism would be the next enemy, and the fear that a war with Soviet Russia might happen imminently. Combating communism became far more important than de-Nazification, and anyone who might help with the coming fight was considered valuable. The same principle and process lay behind both the Gehlen Org (described above), and Operation Paperclip, the secret programme to spirit Nazi scientists to the US (see page 37 and page 231 respectively). For fascists like Gelli, the ratlines were a way of preserving friends, getting rich and building up a network of influence in the shadowy world of the secret services.

The existence of the ratlines is widely accepted, but many writers also claim that groups of Nazis and Fascists were deliberately left behind in most countries of Western Europe, in an operation known as Stay Behind. Supposedly the plan was that cells of hardened anti-communist warriors planted throughout Europe could form the basis of an instant Underground force should the Soviets invade, and would also be available to help counter any home-grown communist insurrections. By the 1950s the domestic communists of Italy were achieving notable electoral successes and the anti-communist powers, led by the Americans, were becoming concerned. According to the conspiracy theorists, they authorised the formation of Operation Gladio, effectively the Italian branch of Operation Stay Behind, and a network of right-wing agents and agitators was recruited to be ready to resist a communist takeover. The key man in this operation, supposedly, was Gelli, whose extensive contacts in the intelligence and neo-fascist communities made him ideal.

Whether or not this is true is uncertain, and judicial investigations in Italy have offered little support for the Operation Gladio theory. If Gelli was coordinating it, he was doing it from Argentina, where he had moved in 1954. Here he allegedly became very cosy with Juan Perón and other right-wing leaders, although he is the main source for this claim. Meanwhile, behind the scenes, he was creating the secret Masonic lodge, P2.

P2

Gelli had joined the Italian Freemasons in 1963, but traditional mistrust of the Masons was enshrined in a law which meant that Italian Lodges had to register members with the government. Gelli set about creating a lodge within a lodge – a so-called 'covered' lodge, where the membership was secret and only he knew the complete list. Membership would be restricted to the elite of Italian/Catholic/Latin American society (in contrast to the Freemasons, where anyone can join and hierarchies from the outside world are meaningless). Gelli named it after a 19th-century Italian Lodge, so it became *Propaganda Due*, or P2 for short.

Members of P2 included financiers and businessmen, media people, senior civil servants and politicians, lawyers and judges, generals and admirals, Mafia dons and, crucially, much of the Italian secret services, including several intelligence chiefs. They also included many prominent clergy, including senior members of the Curia, the 'government' of the Vatican

City and thus the Church. This was despite a strict rule that Catholics were not allowed to be Masons on pain of excommunication. Supposedly the head of the Italian secret service, on joining, had presented Gelli with extensive files on prominent Italians, which he then used to blackmail them into joining his secret society.

Gelli alone knew all the members of P2. He was *Il Venerabile*, the Leader, but was also known as *Il Burattinaio*, the Puppet Master. Allegedly he had engineered the return to power in Argentina of General Perón, and some writers even claim that Perón acknowledged his debt by kneeling at Gelli's feet! Gelli also engineered the close relationship between the financial institutions of the Vatican and the dirty money of organised crime, which was to have such grave consequences for Pope John Paul I.

The murder of Aldo Moro

Although the threat of Soviet invasion had receded, the Italian communist party continued to be a source of anxiety to the anti-communist powers. In the early 1970s, Operation Gladio was allegedly authorised to start taking direct action to forestall communist influence in Italy and began a campaign of bombings designed to foment popular anti-communist sentiment. It didn't work, and by the late 70s Italian prime minister Aldo Moro was actively working to bring the communists into government in solidarity with his centre-left party. In March 1978, he was kidnapped by a radical leftist group called the Red Brigades, and after being held in captivity for 55 days was murdered.

Conspiracy theorists argue that the Red Brigades were created and run by an unholy coalition of Operation Gladio forces, the Italian secret services, the CIA and, of course, P2. Supposedly Moro, while on a trip to Washington, had been specifically warned by senior American officials not to get into bed with the communists if he valued his life. He is said to have cut short his trip and returned home a frightened man. When he failed to heed the warnings the Red Brigades were sent into action to murder him and smear left-wing politics into the bargain.

Certainly there were many strange elements in the saga. Letters written by Moro while in captivity allegedly contain coded warnings, and some of them were suppressed at the time. Senior politicians such as Romano Prodi gave cryptic hints that the police knew where Moro was being held captive even while they were engaged in a massive nationwide manhunt. Many aspects of his kidnap and murder remain mysterious, despite extensive investigations. But few serious commentators give much credence to the P2/CIA plot angle.

The death of John Paul I

Albino Luciani was elected pope on 26 August 1978, taking the name John Paul, and died just 33 days later after one of the shortest reigns in papal history. Immensely popular during his short office, the 'Smiling Pope', as he was known for his accessible approach and lack of airs and graces, might also have proved to be one of the most radical and influential figures of the 20th century, had he lived. In stark contrast to popes previous and subsequent, John Paul I was considering relaxing the Church's hard line on contraception and is widely believed to have favoured a programme of liberal reform within the Vatican. Given the potential influence of the Church on Catholics around the world, such a change of direction could have had profound consequences for social and religious issues on a global scale. His untimely death set history on a very different path. To understand why, it is necessary to examine the complex state of Vatican politics prior to his election.

During the 19th and 20th centuries there had been a considerable debate within the Church between liberal and conservative factions, and the forces of reactionary, right-wing Catholicism had gone to considerable lengths to crush their opponents. In the 19th century the Vatican had used its intelligence networks to spy on and discredit liberal thinkers, while the Vatican of the 1920s was accused of being excessively cosy with Mussolini and his Fascists. Some anti-Catholic writers accuse Pius XI of colluding with the Fascist takeover of Italy in return for huge sums of cash and the Lateran Treaty of 1929, which formally recognised the Vatican City as an independent state over which the pope and the Curia had sovereignty.

During the council known as Vatican II, which sat from 1962 to 1965, the clash between liberal and conservative factions came to a head. Thanks in large part to the efforts of John XXIII, Vatican II liberalised many aspects of Church practice and made it possible for progressive critics within the Church to speak out. The traditionalist old guard of the Curia were dismayed, and intense battles continued over issues such as birth control. John XXIII's successor, Paul VI, vacillated on the topic, eventually coming down on the conservative side. As it turned out, Cardinal Luciani had been one of the voices urging him to adopt a more liberal stance.

Apparently the traditionalists did not realise this, for when Paul VI died and the supporters and opponents of Vatican II locked horns in the papal election, they were happy to accept Luciani as a compromise candidate. He was almost unique in not having had a Curial or diplomatic career, and thus seemed to stand apart from the factional politics of the Vatican. He also seemed to have little ideological baggage, famously being only a 'simple' priest who considered himself unworthy for high office. Presumably the right-wing old guard expected him to be at least neutral, and possibly easily led. They were soon to discover their mistake.

Not long after his coronation the new pope met with UN representatives to discuss population issues and sparked a furore by giving a speech in which he admitted considering changes to the Vatican's hard line on contraception. Conservative elements in the Curia took the extraordinary step of censoring the pope's own comments in the pages of the official Vatican newspaper. There was also talk that John Paul I (Luciani) was considering reforms affecting the Church at every level, which must have been particularly disturbing to rightwing Catholics given that he was considered 'soft' on communism and that his father had been a committed socialist.

But what was most alarming to the entrenched traditionalists who ran the Curia, according to conspiracy theorists, was the new pontiff's investigation into the murky waters of Vatican finances. It was in this sphere that the unholy Italian alliance of P2, the Mafia and the Church had borne fruit with financial misdeeds on an epic scale.

One consequence of the Lateran Treaty was that the *Istituto per le Opere Religiose* or IOR, the Institute of Religious Works, commonly known as the Vatican Bank, was free from the usual oversight and regulation that affected other financial institutions. This naturally made it the perfect vehicle for money laundering, and it is widely believed that it became profoundly tangled up in a web of dirty money. The finger is particularly pointed at P2, which supposedly used its unique network of mafioso, bankers and financiers, and high-ranking Vatican officials to link the IOR with a flood of dirty money from drug dealing, racketeering etc via a number of suspect private banks. According to one theory, the Bank's major involvement in money laundering came when a change in the law in Italy meant that the Vatican's massive share portfolio would come under public scrutiny. Fearing embarrassment if the size of their holdings became public, the Vatican Bank decided to divest itself of the shares. Gelli introduced them to Italian banker Roberto Calvi, head of Mafia-linked Banco Ambrosiano, who offered to buy the portfolio in return for huge sums of dirty money thus laundering the ill-gotten funds.

Whether or not this scenario is true, it is certain that the Vatican Bank, and in particular its American branch under Archbishop Paul Marcinkus, was heavily involved with Mafia money laundering and sinister financiers such as Calvi and Sicilian banker Michele Sindona. Also implicated was the Vatican Secretary of State Cardinal Villot, the head of the Curia, an arch-conservative painted by many conspiracy theorists as the arch-villain of the papal murder mystery.

This then, was the cabal of right-wing interests ranged against the new pope. According to the conspiracy theory of his death, most clearly and convincingly articulated in David Yallop's book, *In God's Name*, John Paul I had quickly perceived the rot at the heart of the Vatican, analysed a complex mass of documents and identified the key culprits – in particular, he had become aware of the startling level of P2 membership among leading figures in the Vatican. These men would be relieved of their responsibilities and moved to harmless positions, and the work of cleaning house could begin. On the night of his murder he supposedly took to bed with him a sheaf of vital documents relating to the Vatican Bank and its financial shenanigans.

On the morning of 29 September 1978, the body of Pope John Paul I was discovered by the papal secretary, John Magee, sitting up in his bed. He had died of a heart attack. This, at least, was the official story. In fact it later came out that the body had been discovered much earlier than originally said, by a nun called Sister Vicenza who was a papal housekeeper. There were also discrepancies over the treatment of the body, which was immediately removed for embalming, making a post-mortem impossible. This was in violation of Italian law but not, the Curia argued, of Vatican law, which specifically prohibited a post-mortem. In fact this was not true either – a post-mortem had been carried out on the body of Pope Pius VIII in 1830. Even after the embalming process there should have been blood and organs available for testing, but these had mysteriously vanished. So too, according to conspiracy theorists, had the documents the pope had been reading, his glasses and even his will.

What would a post-mortem have discovered? According to conspiracy theorists, it would have shown that John Paul I was poisoned; that he had been murdered, by Villot acting in league with P2 and the crooked bankers, with the tacit support of all those who feared the pope's liberal agenda. There is, however, a different view, best encapsulated by John Cornwell's book, *A Thief in the Night*. According to this view Pope John Paul I was not the sharp witted detective hero of Yallop's scenario, but an intellectual lightweight who was not equal to the task of being pontiff and whose poor health, coupled with the notoriously poor medical care offered by the Vatican, meant that his sudden death was no mystery.

There is plenty of evidence to back up this alternative version. During his short tenure John Paul I repeatedly complained that he should not have been picked and visitors commented on his loneliness and isolation. On one occasion he caused consternation by dropping a file of top-secret documents over a wall onto Vatican rooftops. His health was known to be poor and he suffered from serious cardiovascular problems. He had previously suffered a minor embolism (where a blood clot blocks a blood vessel) and showed symptoms of a much more serious one on the night of his death, but had ignored suggestions that a doctor should be called in. Health care in the Vatican was notoriously bad: the previous pope, Paul VI, had practically been killed by a charlatan who later took photos of his corpse. The embalming of Paul VI had also been an embarrassing disaster – the body had rotted so fast that its nose fell off when it was lying in state. Perhaps the Vatican had rushed to embalm John Paul I to avoid a similarly distasteful disaster on one of the hottest days of the year. As for the 'stolen' documents from the papal bedroom – it later turned out that they were safely in the possession of his sister's family.

The Masonic murder of God's Banker

There is plenty to suggest, in other words, that the mysteries surrounding John Paul I's death owe more to cock-up than conspiracy, but the scandals surrounding the Vatican Bank were genuine enough. Over the next few years much would be revealed, but a rash of assassinations would also ensure that much would remain hidden. Many of the senior Catholic clerics were able to keep their powerful jobs, but investigations overseas were starting to unravel the web of deceit around the Vatican Bank. Eventually Mafia-linked Sicilian banker Michele Sindona and Archbishop Paul Marcinkus, who had presided over Vatican Bank misdeeds in America, would both be jailed.

The most dramatic development, however, would be the strange death of Roberto Calvi. Calvi's close association with the Vatican had earned him the sobriquet 'God's Banker', but he was engaged in a fraud of epic proportions, eventually stealing over a billion dollars from the bank he chaired, Banco Ambrosiano, by routeing the money through the Vatican Bank. According to P2 conspiracy theorists, Calvi was forced to steal the money by Gelli, who funnelled it into right-wing causes and personal bank vaults (Gelli supposedly once said, 'All bank doors open to the right'). When the holes in the accounts grew too large to cover, Calvi supposedly approached the Mafia, via his P2 connections, offering to use his position to help launder money for them. This he did, but he also skimmed off huge amounts to stay afloat.

By 1979, Italian authorities were closing in on Calvi but the assassination of a key investigator took the heat off him. This was followed by the brutal murder of a journalist who had allegedly sent John Paul I the list of P2 members that alerted him to their infiltration of the Vatican. Two investigators pursuing Sindona were arrested and slung in jail, amply illustrating the reach of P2's influence. More assassinations followed, but eventually both Sindona and Calvi were brought to trial. In 1980 Sindona got 25 years. In 1981 Calvi was sentenced to four years' imprisonment but was freed pending an appeal.

In June 1982, his body was found hanging from London's Blackfriars Bridge, his pockets stuffed with bricks. Incredibly the Metropolitan Police treated his death as suicide but subsequent investigations showed that Calvi had been strangled before being thrown off the bridge. The bricks were clear Masonic symbols, and his grisly death closely resembled punishments depicted in Masonic legends. Later investigations and confessions suggested that Calvi had been murdered by the Mafia, as retribution for his theft of Mafia funds. But the Masonic symbolism of his murder suggests that there may well have been a P2 connection.

By this time, however, P2's ring of infamy had been blown open. In 1981, Gelli's Tuscan villa was raided, yielding a list of P2 members that shocked the Italian nation, and which included Silvio Berlusconi, now prime minister of Italy and controller of most Italian mass media. Gelli vanished and an investigation by the government concluded that while P2 was probably a criminal secret society, there was no concrete proof of anything. He resurfaced briefly in 1982 to help the Argentinean government buy Exocet missiles from the French during the Falklands War and then went underground once more, presumably finding refuge in South America like the many Nazis he helped escape justice after the war.

Opus Dei

Detractors of the John Paul I murder theory point out that it implicates his successor, John Paul II, who would surely have become aware of the web of scandal and deceit and yet took no action. To proponents of the theory, however, this makes perfect sense. John Paul II is closely associated with reactionary right-wing elements in the Church today, and this association stretches back to his pre-papal career. To the conspiracy theorists, his election was deliberately intended to safeguard the hidden right-wing agenda of the Vatican, but may also have signalled a subterranean power struggle between the right-wing factions competing to pursue that agenda – namely P2 and the Catholic sect Opus Dei.

To mainstream observers these conspiracy theories seem far-fetched and few would seriously suggest that John Paul II knew about, approved of and covered up his predecessor's murder. But there is little doubt that the current pontiff has used his term in office to push a covert right-wing agenda, and that, partly thanks to his authority, Opus Dei has become a hidden power of enormous influence in the Church and wider society today.

So who are Opus Dei? Founded by José María Escrivá in 1928, Opus Dei (meaning 'God's work') is a 'personal prelature' of the Catholic Church. To Opus Dei apologists, a personal prelature is simply a type of Church institution that exists outside of any particular geographic administrative unit (ie the diocese of a bishop), and answers directly to the pope. To Opus Dei detractors, a personal prelature is a handy way of building a power base within the Church that is free from the supervision or interference of the normal regulatory structures – in other words, a charter for developing a secret society in plain view.

According to its own literature, Opus Dei recruits both clergy (numbering 1,800) and lay members (numbering 84,000) to do God's work. This includes funding and running charities, educational programmes, spiritual development courses and medical clinics, and simply living a Christian life. According to its detractors, Opus Dei is much more sinister and has similar aims and means to P2 – it indoctrinates members into its extremist right-wing agenda and infiltrates them into every sphere of modern life, enabling it to build up enormous wealth and influence which it uses to promote that agenda. To distinguish the truth behind these competing claims it is necessary to look more closely at Opus Dei's controversial founder and the network of influence Opus Dei has built up around the world.

José María Escrivá was a Spanish priest who witnessed first hand terrible anti-Catholic atrocities carried out by socialist forces during the civil war. His experiences strengthened his desire to set up a personal prelature with a licence from the pope himself to further the religious and political ends of Opus Dei, the movement he had founded in 1928. Doubtless they also strengthened his hatred of communism and his extremist right-wing beliefs, which led him to support General Franco's fascists and to openly express his admiration of Hitler. A notorious quote attributed to Escrivá is: 'Hitler against Jews, Hitler against Slavs ... this means Hitler against communism.'

Escrivá established a set of precepts and training disciplines for Opus Dei members, which controversially include scourging or self-flagellation. Although long used in the Church as a means of aiding spiritual meditation and achieving self-purification, it has also led to accusations of brainwashing and claims that Opus Dei tries to indoctrinate new members in the manner of a sinister cult. Escrivá has also attracted criticism for supposed misogyny, racism, homophobia and bitter intolerance of other religions. According to Robert Hutchison, author of *Their Kingdom Come: Inside the Secret World of Opus Dei*, one of the most thorough investigations of the organisation to date, Escrivá was motivated by an atavistic longing for the days when the Church was a significant temporal power and one of the pillars of the feudal social order. It could be argued that today's Opus Dei has a sort of neo-feudal agenda, aimed at maintaining a rigidly stratified social order where everyone knows their place and communism in any guise is the ultimate enemy.

According to critics, Opus Dei operates by recruiting lay members who retain their civil occupations and progress to positions of influence, from which they can work to combat communism and further the aims of the organisation. In this manner Opus Dei has supposedly infiltrated the media, academia, trade and industry and politics, as well as, of course, the Church. It has become fabulously wealthy and influential, and is particularly powerful in Spain, Latin America and the US.

In Spain, Opus Dei members occupied key seats in Franco's cabinet in the 1960s and in the recently defeated government of José María Aznar. In South America, Opus Dei-linked clergymen and statesmen have offered moral and political support to repressive right-wing regimes from Argentina to El Salvador. One of the best-known members is Peru's Cardinal Cipriani, who was a close ally of the Fujimori dictatorship. During the Japanese Embassy hostage crisis, when left-wing guerrillas took control of the building for several weeks, Cipriani is alleged to have smuggled microphones into the building, hidden in a crucifix, while posing as a neutral go-between. Supposedly these microphones were instrumental in helping the government to massacre the guerrillas after they had surrendered. In America, Opus Dei influence has spread to the highest levels. Members include former FBI Director Louis Freeh and two Supreme Court Justices, Antonin Scalia and Clarence Thomas, who are key to determining constitutional and judicial responses to moral and social issues such as gay rights.

Pope John Paul II and the Third Secret of Fatima

Opus Dei's most spectacular recruitment success must be Pope John Paul II. Escrivá had set up a Roman arm, known as the *Centro Romano di Incontri Sacerdotali*, which had the specific aim of communicating Opus Dei's agenda to leading members of the Church hierarchy. Among several bishops who were brought into Opus Dei's 'orbit' was Karol Wojtyla, archbishop of Cracow. His strong anti-communist sentiments, developed through his struggles against the anti-Catholic powers of communist Poland, made Wojtyla a natural ally. After he was elected pope in 1978 Opus Dei had a direct line to the summit of Catholic power.

As John Paul II, the new pontiff used his position to combat communism around the world. It is widely believed that he saw the fight against godless communism as a struggle of near-apocalyptic proportions. His convictions were almost certainly strengthened by his attempted assassination and the revelation of the Third Secret of Fatima.

On 13 May 1981, the pope narrowly escaped death from an assassin's bullet. As he greeted crowds in St Peter's Square in Rome, his eye was caught by an image of the Virgin Mary carried by a young girl. At the exact moment he bent down to hug the girl, Mehmet Ali Agca fired two shots at his head. They missed, and although a third shot struck the pope in the stomach, he survived. The official story was that Agca was a lone nut, but the Italian government's own investigations, together with evidence from former Soviet bloc countries and even the former head of the CIA, William Casey, revealed that Agca was recruited and manipulated by the Bulgarian secret service acting in cahoots with a Turkish terrorist organisation called the Grey Wolves, at the behest of the KGB. The Soviets, fearful of the new pope's anti-communist fervour, particularly in the light of events in Poland at the time, had decided that the pope must die.

Although the Bulgarian connection was covered up by all concerned (the investigating magistrate, Ferdinando Imposimato, claims that his superiors urged him to 'let it go'), probably because the Western powers did not want to undermine their rapprochement with the Soviets under Gorbachev, the pope most likely knew about it. For one thing, he had a very close relationship with the virulently anti-communist President Reagan and his devoutly Catholic CIA Director William Casey, which became even closer after Reagan too survived an assassination attempt. The Americans would regularly brief John

Paul II with secret documents and spy satellite data and he would pass back intelligence gleaned from priests in eastern bloc countries.

The pope's near-death experience led him to have a mystical experience similar to the Fatima vision of 1917. This was part of a series of visions of the Virgin Mary, who appeared to three children near the Portuguese village of Fatima and revealed three great secrets to them. Two of the secrets were subsequently made public but the third, and purportedly the most dramatic, was never revealed. Written down by the last surviving visionary, Sister Lucia Santos, the legendary Third Secret of Fatima was stored in the Secret Vatican Archives, the forbidden library where the Vatican stores thousands (and possibly millions) of books and documents considered too controversial or explosive to reveal. Suspected contents of the Secret Archives include alternative versions of the Bible that undermine Catholic doctrine, records of Vatican misdeeds over the centuries (such as relations with the Nazis during World War II) and incriminating evidence relating to contemporary Church scandals such as child abuse by priests and Vatican Bank dealings.

After his vision, John Paul II is believed to have read the Third Secret for himself. At the time, there was a frenzy of speculation about what earth-shattering revelations or prophecies it might contain, but it has since been made public and proved to be something of an anti-climax. It is basically an account of a vision of a pope, together with many other clergy, being shot by evil soldiers. John Paul II, together with Santos herself, seems to have interpreted this as a reference to his own battle with communism, an interpretation doubtless strengthened by his brush with a Soviet assassin's bullet. In a major Church event at the Fatima shrine, he consecrated the world, but especially Russia, to the Virgin Mary. An obvious reading of the situation is that events had conspired to give the pope a near-messianic conviction that his anti-communist crusade was truly God's work.

In this light, it seems reasonable to ask whether John Paul II's zeal to defeat communism meant that he was prepared to overlook the less savoury aspects of right-wing organisations like P2 and Opus Dei in return for their help. The evidence suggests that he was. For instance, not long after his election, P2 member and Opus Dei ally Archbishop Marcinkus brokered big loans to the Polish ship-workers' union, Solidarity, a favoured cause of John Paul II's. The efforts of Solidarity are largely credited with ending communism in Poland. Opus Dei is also suspected of having helped to shore up right-wing regimes against communist insurgency in countries around the world. Perhaps as a reward, John Paul II has fast-tracked the canonisation of Opus Dei's founder, José María Escrivá, making him a saint in almost record time.

What about the relationship between Opus Dei and P2? While the untimely death of John Paul I and the election of John Paul II may have given P2 some breathing space, the raid on Gelli's villa and subsequent investigations revealing P2's links to financial misdeeds and organised crime meant that the secret lodge was running out of time. In fact, according to one particularly involved conspiracy theory, Calvi's murder was engineered by Opus Dei as part of a scheme to displace P2 as the main right-wing power behind the Vatican throne.

In this scenario, Opus Dei lured Calvi to London with the promise of a loan to help him make good his thefts from the Mafia and keep Banco Ambrosiano afloat, staving off further investigation by the authorities. Once he was there they betrayed him to Mafia enforcers who were after his blood, ensuring that the murder had Masonic hallmarks to indicate P2 involvement. With Calvi dead his bank collapsed and more details of P2's perfidy leaked out. The way was clear for Opus Dei to assert their dominance in the murky demi-monde of covert right-wing Catholic politics.

A vast right-wing conspiracy?

In conclusion, the Vatican and Opus Dei both claim that the conspiracy theories against them are simply lunatic, and there are convincing alternatives to the conspiracy theory deaths of figures such as Aldo Moro and John Paul I. Calvi and his fellow victims of the Ambrosiano fallout may simply have been victims of the Mafia milieu in which they moved, while the Church may have been largely in the dark about what was done with its institutions and money. John Paul II could argue that reforms of the Curia have been made since then. In other words there may be no over-arching conspiracies, except for those concocted by anti-Catholic polemicists, and nothing for the Vatican to worry about.

Alternatively, John Paul II and Opus Dei may simply be the latest in a long series of shadowy right-wing conspirators dating back to the end of WWII, who operate above the law to oppose communism, further a self-serving right-wing agenda and cover up their tracks – murdering anyone who gets in their way – from bankers and judges to prime ministers and popes.

Even if the truth lies somewhere between the two, there are disturbing implications. It would be hard to avoid the conclusion that powerful para-political groups have influenced and continue to influence international finance and politics at the highest level, with the possible collusion of the CIA, the Italian secret services, Latin American dictatorships and major contemporary figures such as former FBI director Louis Freeh, US Supreme Court Justice Antonin Scalia, Italian premier and media magnate Silvio Berlusconi and even the pope.

Who shot JFK? 1963

The assassination of President John F Kennedy remains the most celebrated and debated suspected conspiracy of all time. Finding a definitive solution to the JFK murder will probably never be possible, but the murky tangle surrounding the assassination and the subsequent cover-up vividly illustrates the influence of the hidden hand in recent history.

It is beyond the scope of this book to look at the assassination in any depth or to review the full range of evidence and the reams of witness statements in detail. The bare facts are known to most people. On 22 November 1963, President Kennedy was travelling in a motorcade through Dallas. At 12.30 pm, as the car slowed and turned a corner in Dealey Plaza, a volley of shots rang out and the president was fatally injured in the head (among other wounds). He was rushed to a nearby hospital but died soon after. His body was then flown to US Navy Bethesda Hospital for an autopsy.

Later that day Lee Harvey Oswald, a worker at the Texas School Book Depository (a building on Dealey Plaza), was apparently seen gunning down a Dallas police officer and was subsequently apprehended in the Texas Theatre cinema by a group of policemen, including one who shouted the immortal line, 'Kill the president, will ya?!!' Oswald had been in the Marines and had subsequently defected to the Soviet Union, but had then returned to the States. After two days of questioning, during which he made the famous statement, 'I'm just a patsy!', Oswald was being moved to a nearby jail when he was shot dead by nightclub owner and Mafia gangster Jack Ruby.

Kennedy's successor as president, Lyndon Johnson, previously vice-president, appointed the Warren Commission to investigate the assassination. After a ten-month investigation the Commission published its report, which concluded that Oswald had shot Kennedy from his 'sniper's lair' on the sixth floor of the Texas School Book Depository, firing off three bullets. Oswald had acted alone, without the involvement of any other parties.

The 'lone gunman' theory is undermined by a huge mass of suggestive evidence, which raise doubts about most aspects of the official version. The most important areas of doubt are:

~ Technical aspects of the shooting. There are many inconsistencies with the official version of the actual shots – their trajectory, timing and number. Evidence about the shots and from many witness statements suggests that the fatal shot came from in front of Kennedy (the Depository was behind him), probably from the famous grassy knoll.

~ Problems with Oswald as the assassin. He almost certainly did not have the skill to achieve the assassination, and there are many question marks over the official version of his personal history; his movements before, during and after the shooting; his links to the Mafia, the CIA and anti-Castro Cubans; and the circumstances of his arrest.

~ Ruby's killing of Oswald. Ruby claimed not to have known Oswald and to have acted alone. Evidence suggests he did know Oswald, was involved with the same circle of CIA, Mafia and anti-Castro forces, and had official help getting into the garage where he shot Oswald.

~ The handling of the crime scene and the president's body. The crime scene was not secured, evidence was mishandled or went missing, the reasons for moving the president's body to Bethesda remain obscure and nearly caused a fight at the time, and the relatively inexperienced doctors mysteriously chosen to perform the autopsy botched it badly. Witnesses disagree about many crucial aspects of the autopsy and the wounds the president received – in particular, many claim that forensic evidence that the president was shot from in front was suppressed or disappeared.

~ Lax security around the president. Inadequate measures were taken to secure the route of the motorcade and the president's Secret Service protection was specially scaled down for reasons never explained.

~ People in and around Dealey Plaza. There is a mass of witness material relating to strange people behaving oddly around Dealey Plaza before, during and after the shooting, including reports of 'agents' (people who looked like or identified themselves as unspecified agents), people around the grassy knoll, people seen with weapons, people seen firing weapons etc.

~ Testimony about conspiratorial links. Many people have since claimed that they knew or heard about people linked to the assassination, including CIA agents, members of the Mafia, leading businessmen etc.

~ Dead witnesses. Many crucial witnesses or people claiming to have important knowledge or who might have threatened to uncover a conspiracy have died in mysterious circumstances, which strongly suggests that someone is willing to kill to perpetuate a cover-up. Probably the most famous of these 'people who knew too much' was Robert F Kennedy, gunned down in 1968.

What does it all add up to? Without doubt, the official version is riddled with holes; what we're left with is very strongly suggestive of a conspiracy followed by a cover-up. So who did kill JFK and then cover it up? The usual practice is to look at who had motive or stood to benefit from Kennedy's death. Unfortunately a wide range of groups and individuals had reason to want Kennedy dead. The prime suspects include:

~ The military-industrial complex. This unnamed group of powerful interests, presumably including businessmen, politicians, military leaders and operatives, resented Kennedy's plans to scale back involvement in Vietnam and possibly cut back on military expenditure.

~ The South Vietnamese leadership. Kennedy was preparing to withdraw US support from them, having adjudged them to be corrupt and despotic.

~ Extreme anti-communists. Many accused Kennedy of being practically a communist. They included ultra-right wing oil millionaire HL Hunt, who supposedly said that he wanted Kennedy dead shortly before the assassination.

~ Oil men. Kennedy was planning to raise their taxes.

~ The Soviets. Supposedly Oswald, or someone pretending to be Oswald, was a communist agent, possibly a brain-washed/mind-controlled agent, sent to strike at the heart of the capitalist enemy.

~ The CIA. After falling out over the Bay of Pigs debacle, where a CIA-supported coup against Castro had gone horribly wrong, Kennedy had vowed to smash the CIA into pieces. In general Kennedy's agenda did not match the violently anti-communist agenda of the Agency.

~ Anti-Castro Cuban militants. Angry with Kennedy for not supporting the Bay of Pigs invasion and not taking a hard enough line on Castro generally. Had close links with both the CIA and the Mafia.

~ The Mafia. Claimed to have helped get Kennedy elected through their union contacts. After his election, Kennedy and his brother went after the Mob, massively increasing the number of cases brought against them. The Mafia were also angry about Cuba, since Castro's takeover had deprived them of massive business interests in casinos, drug running, prostitution etc. They had forged close links with the CIA and anti-Castro Cubans.

~ The FBI. FBI boss J Edgar Hoover, who acted like the power behind the throne of the American state, hated the Kennedys – and the Kennedys wanted to get rid of him.

Many conspiracy theorists argue that the most likely scenario is that a group of CIA, anti-Castro and Mafia elements got together to assassinate JFK, and then used their contacts in the government and the law enforcement agencies to cover it up. In recent years, however, there has been an emerging consensus that the most likely culprit was Lyndon Johnson, who effectively staged a coup and got away with it. The evidence against him is compelling.

Firstly, there's the motive. Johnson was an ambitious and ruthless politician, who resented the way he'd been sidelined as vice-president when he might have expected to be part of Kennedy's inner circle. He was also up to his neck in scandal, having become embroiled in no less than four criminal investigations, all of which conveniently faded away when he became president. Johnson also had links with the military-industrial complex, through his years of serving on various congressional and senate military/defence committees, and with leaders of the Texan oil and business community – Texas was his home state and power base.

Secondly, there are the means. Johnson was associated with a convicted murderer, Texan Malcolm 'Mac' Wallace, whose fingerprints have supposedly been identified on a cardboard box from the 'sniper's nest' in the Texas School Book Depository. Wallace, who had briefly worked for Johnson in Washington, is suspected of involvement in a string of deaths linked to the scandals surrounding Johnson, and has been fingered by a variety of witnesses as having been involved in Kennedy's death. The accusation is that Wallace, together with a number of other 'operatives', assassinated the president at Johnson's behest.

Johnson, through his friendship with J Edgar Hoover, his assumption of the presidency and his contacts at every level of federal and state government, must also rank as one of the only people with the contacts and the clout to pull off such a massive conspiracy and cover-up. How many people could have arranged for reduced security around the president on that fateful day? How many people could have engineered the train of irregularities surrounding the subsequent investigation at every level? Who appointed the Warren Commission, which is generally agreed to have produced a whitewash? It may be significant that Johnson originally ordered that all details of the Commission's investigation should be sealed until the mid-21st century. Who removed Robert Kennedy from office and was still in power when Kennedy started to run for president, threatening to re-open the investigation into his brother's assassination, and was promptly gunned down by another 'lone gunman'? (The lack of motive and strange behaviour of Robert Kennedy's killer, Sirhan Sirhan, including apparent memory loss, has suggested to many conspiracy theorists that he was the victim of a CIA mind-control/brainwashing programme, as with Oswald.)

Admittedly, Johnson's record once in office does not seem to chime with the image of a right-wing conspirator. He pushed through pioneering civil rights and social welfare legislation, and only reluctantly agreed to a slow build-up of US forces in Vietnam (although this doesn't change the reality that Johnson reversed Kennedy's policy on Vietnam). Perhaps most crucially, Johnson declined to stand for re-election for a second term in 1968, citing a wish to work for world peace unencumbered by political considerations – surely not the act of a man so desperate for high office that he would murder to reach it?

Whoever is to blame for the Kennedy assassination – and one of the few points of consensus amongst researchers is that it wasn't Oswald alone – they protected their conspiracy with an ongoing cover-up that has seen a large number of suspicious deaths among JFK witnesses and potential informants (Mac Wallace, for instance, died in a single-car accident in 1971). So we'll probably never find a definitive solution to the mystery or identify the killer(s) from the wide range of suspects. In the end, Kennedy had simply made too many enemies. They weren't going to let him change the course of history, because they wanted to direct it in the way they always had – from the shadows.

The Bilderberg group: 1954 to the present day

Most serious conspiracy theories agree that a cabal of top politicians, financiers and businessmen meet behind closed doors to secretly run the planet for their own ends. The current favourite candidate for this clandestine gang is the Bilderberg group, which stands accused of all the worst crimes the conspiracy community can invent: it is said to be a capitalist–Zionist secret society that has inherited the mantle of the Illuminati and plots the subjugation of the peoples of Earth for its own enrichment and power-crazed glee. The group has achieved such legendary status in conspiracy circles that it seems hard to believe it genuinely exists, but it does. According to a less lurid definition, the Bilderberg group is an informal annual convocation of influential political and economic leaders from Western Europe and North America, which meets in strict secrecy (Bilderbergers describe it as 'privacy') to network and discuss current and future world issues.

The group was started in 1954 by Denis Healey (former British Foreign Minister), Joseph Retinger (a Polish diplomat and anti-communist), David Rockefeller (international banker) and Prince Bernhard of the Netherlands. The intention, which remains the same today, was to provide a forum in which influential opinion-formers and decision makers from either side of the Atlantic could get together and discuss world issues without having to censor what they said, because the meetings would be held behind closed doors and the proceedings kept in strictest confidence. The first meeting was held at the Bilderberg Hotel, in the Netherlands.

A steering committee of annually varying makeup decides on the guest list for each year, inviting about 100 movers and shakers, including established names and up and coming ones. Invitees arrive at a chosen hotel (in a different country each year), where they engage in three or four days of meetings in which they can discuss present and future issues affecting the world. No press is allowed (although senior media figures including newspaper editors are often invitees) and, not surprisingly, there is heavy security.

Virtually everyone who is anyone in Western Europe and North America has attended over the years. People are invited regardless of political affiliation, although the preponderance of business leaders, financiers, aristocrats, royalty etc means that an awful lot of attendees are very rich. For instance, the guest list for the 2004 meeting included BP chief John Browne, US Senator John Edwards, World Bank President James Wolfensohn and Mrs Bill Gates. The attendance of Edwards, who at the time of writing has just been selected as Democratic vice presidential nominee in the 2004 American presidential elections, illustrates a tendency to invite rising stars of the political firmament. Bill Clinton, for instance, was invited in 1991 and used the meeting as an opportunity to network. In 1975, Margaret Thatcher made such an impact on American attendees that she subsequently became a firm favourite across the Atlantic.

So does the Bilderberg group constitute a global conspiracy? Many think so, claiming that they decide, for instance, who will be the next president of America, or which country will be invaded next. Serbians claim that the NATO campaign against their country was orchestrated and initiated by Bilderberg, and it figures heavily in the rants of figures as diverse as Osama bin Laden, David Icke and Oklahoma City bomber Timothy McVeigh.

Bilderbergers dismiss these claims as ludicrous, but admit that Bilderberg discussions form the 'background' against which major policy decisions are often taken. More specific instances leak out – for instance, during the Falklands War the British government wanted to secure support for sanctions against Argentina. The international community was cool on the idea, but at a Bilderberg meeting British politician David Owen gave an impassioned speech on the subject and shortly afterwards sanctions were agreed. Bilderbergers also admit that attendance can help people's careers, and it is true that virtually every American president and British prime minister of the last fifty years attended a Bilderberg meeting early in their career. Conspiracy theorists would argue that this is not simply because the steering committee has an eye for talent.

Even the most charitable assessment of the Bilderberg meetings, which might view them as well-meaning attempts to further the cause of 'rational internationalism' (in the words of journalist Jon Ronson), must allow that Bilderberg meetings provide exclusive access to the world's most powerful politicians for an incredibly elitist group of rich capitalists, which excludes representatives from the vast majority of the world's population. Above all, Bilderberg represents a capitalist agenda, and capitalism could be said to emphasise selfishness, short-termism and self-enrichment. Whether the Bilderbergers like the characterisation or not, they closely approximate the description of a tiny elite who decide world affairs from behind closed doors; a secret force, shaping the course of history.

The Fellowship, the Christian Right and US politics: 1930s to the present day

Many of those who rant so vehemently about liberal–Zionist conspiracies to subvert the constitution of the United States, make and break presidents at will and direct the course of global history to achieve their own dark ends, are ultra-conservative fundamentalist American Christians. How ironic, then, that it should be a number of their own who actually fit this unlikely bill. Disturbing evidence suggests that a shadowy alliance of fundamental Christian groups have gained an increasingly strong hold on American politics, to the point where they have selected as president one of their candidates, raised millions to get him into the White House and are now directing him in a bid to realise their own alarming dreams of making America a theocracy and triggering Armageddon in the Middle East.

There are many groups and organisations in America dedicated to crossing or breaching the separation of church and state, and the Christian Right has become an increasingly powerful above-board political movement. There are also some organisations with similar or even more extreme agendas that strive to stay out of the public eye, and one in particular, known as the Fellowship, that almost exactly resembles the sort of clandestine Illuminati-style society of which conspiracy theorists warn.

The Fellowship, also known as the Family, and through a number of different sub-organisations such as the National Committee for Christian Leadership or the National Leadership Council, is basically the Protestant, American equivalent of Opus Dei (see page 51). It is an ostensibly humanitarian evangelical organisation devoted to furthering the teachings of Jesus (or at least its interpretation of those teachings) in governing circles. Like Opus Dei, it is a ministry that preaches almost exclusively to the rich and powerful. Investigative reporters who pierce the shield of silence that the Fellowship has built report that it is explicitly set up to infiltrate power structures around the world and bring business and political leaders into its orbit. One of its favoured tools is the 'prayer breakfast', and the annual National Prayer Breakfast held in Washington is its highest profile event. Exactly what else the Fellowship gets up to can be hard to say, because it serves as a kind of umbrella group to numerous smaller 'cells', which raise their own funds and pursue their own specific agendas (Al Qaeda, which loosely translates as 'the Fellowship', operates in a similar way).

Among other operations the Fellowship funds a boarding house in Washington where several senators and representatives affiliated with the organisation stay. It also has extensive links to many other senior politicians and their staffs, as well as leaders of the oil and aerospace industries and prominent world leaders. By bringing together such high-ranking people behind closed doors, preaching the message of Jesus at them and exerting the personal influence that friends in high places can bring, the leaders of the Fellowship have helped to engineer some major diplomatic successes, such as the 2001 Congo–Rwanda peace process. Over the years, however, the Fellowship's preferred confederates have belonged to much the same constituency as those targeted by Opus Dei – right-wing hardliners with anti-communist credentials. The Fellowship has helped to forge close links between leading Americans and such unsavoury characters as Brazilian dictator General Costa e Silva, Indonesian dictator General Suharto, Salvadoran general Carlos Eugenios Vides Casanova (a known torturer of hundreds) and Honduran general Gustavo Alvarez Martinez (one-time death squad leader). In America, the Fellowship also seeks to advance the careers of a few chosen politicians who may help to bring their evangelical, fundamentalist agenda into high office. 'We work with power where we can,' says the Family's leader, Doug Coe, '[and] build new power where we can't.'

President George W Bush is widely regarded as one such 'new power'. While he may not have direct links to the Fellowship, commentators have pointed to his close affiliation with some hardline Christian conservative groups, such as the influential Council for National Policy, founded by bestselling author Timothy LaHaye, who has sold millions of his novels about the 'End Times', in which the biblical Apocalypse takes place in our near future. The CNP and another LaHaye group, the ominously named Committee to Restore American Values, were both involved in setting in motion Bush Jr's bid for the White House, apparently selecting him in what have been called 'kingmaking' meetings and then raising a substantial portion of the record-breaking campaign war-chest that helped Bush to buy his way into the presidency.

Through such groups Bush has become identified as 'our man in the White House' by ultra-conservative Christians, including many like LaHaye who are strict 'biblical reconstructionists' – believers in the literal truth of the Bible and the need to actively prepare the world for the Second Coming, if necessary by triggering the Apocalypse. For instance, Christian Zionists believe the Bible makes it clear that all of Israel must belong to the Jews before the Second Coming can happen, and that all the Palestinians must therefore be ethnically cleansed from the Holy Land. The Christian Reconstructionists want to turn America into a theocracy, a kind of religious dictatorship where strict religious law applies (eg abortionists and homosexuals should be imprisoned or executed).

These may sound like fringe groups, but they or those close to them have the ear of the White House and other senior government figures, and in the light of the ultra-conservative Christian agenda it is illuminating to re-examine many of the policies pursued by the Bush administration since achieving office. Domestically, Bush is coming down hard on abortion and homosexual rights, and ramping up the role of religion in government with faith-based policy initiatives. On the international stage, he supports controversial Israeli treatment of the Palestinians and portrays himself almost as a holy warrior in the fight against terrorism, while the invasion of Iraq should perhaps be seen in the context of reconstructionist beliefs that Armageddon will be unleashed from Babylon – ie Iraq.

Increasingly it sounds as though ultra-conservative Christians are attempting to subvert constitutional separation of church and state in America and take control of US domestic and foreign policy. Some groups raise funds and mobilise support using methods fairly traditional to US politics; others have a long history of secretly building a covert coalition of ultra-right religious and political interests from around the globe and peddling this influence to further their repressive agenda. Lining up alongside the Gehlen Org, P2 and Opus Dei, American groups such as the Fellowship have played their part in the secret history of post-war anti-communism, and may now be setting the agenda for the War on Terror that has replaced that crusade.

Using the myth of secrecy and conspiracy: Ancient times to the present day

Reading, investigating and weaving conspiracy theories can be extremely entertaining, while keeping an open mind in relation to the true causes of some historical episodes can be illuminating. But any discussion of conspiracies, secret societies and the like is irresponsible if it does not acknowledge the pernicious use and abuse of conspiracy theories to further bigotry, sectarianism, race hatred and even genocide. Throughout history all sections of society have made use of myths, fictions and folk tales about secrecy and conspiracy in order to demonise ethnic or religious groups with terrible results; disturbingly the process continues to this day. Today there are hundreds of millions of people around the world who routinely and unquestioningly believe in absurd and demonstrably bogus conspiracies, and use them to justify acts of violence and persecution.

The most obvious and consistent targets of these slanders are the Jews. Jews have suffered persecution throughout their long history, but particularly after the Diaspora – the scattering of the Jewish peoples around the world after the destruction of the Jewish states by first the Babylonians and later the

Romans. Thereafter, Jewish communities in Europe in particular suffered waves of persecution, with riots, pogroms and expulsions. The sources of anti-Semitism are varied and complex, but major contributors were the myths and legends about Jewish practices and conspiracies that were propagated throughout Europe.

The most dangerous of the slanders was the Blood Libel – the myth that Jews performed human sacrifices, usually of Christians, for ritual purposes. The legend first appears in pre-Christian times, during the 2nd century BCE, when a Syrian gentile claimed to have escaped from a coven of Jews who had held him captive for a year, planning to ritually murder him. In medieval times the Blood Libel took on a life of its own, springing up around Europe, where it was used to justify murderous riots against Jews in which debts could be written off and property stolen. For instance, in Norwich, England in 1144, the gruesome murder of a young boy was blamed on Jews, who were said to have used his blood to make *matzoh* (unleavened bread). The historian Thomas of Monmouth, writing about the incident, linked the spurious murder to a global Jewish conspiracy, in which the Jews were said to plan the murder of a Christian every year, somewhere in the world, for their own dark religious purposes. Similar conspiracy theories about the Blood Libel sprang up many times, usually resulting in riots against local Jewish populations.

The Blood Libel later became part of anti-Semitic propaganda used in 19th-century Russia and 20th-century Germany, to justify pogroms and the Holocaust. Disturbingly, it lingers on to this day in the anti-Semitic teaching of some extremist Islamic groups. In 1983, for instance, the Syrian Minister of Defence, Mustafa Tlas, wrote *The Matzoh of Zion*; its cover depicts a typical Blood Libel scene, with grotesque Jewish caricatures ritually sacrificing a victim. Similar myths have also been used against other groups. In Kosovo, in 2004, for instance, ethnic tensions boiled over when ethnic Serbs accused Muslims of drowning a young Serbian boy in a river. This incident is eerily reminiscent of one in Blois, France, in 1171, where the town's Jews were accused of murdering a child and throwing his corpse into the river. The typical story in a Blood Libel incident – a local conspiracy of Jews is kidnapping children and hiding them away for ritual torture and kidnap – is also very similar to the Satanic Ritual Abuse scares of the 1980s and to anti-Masonic propaganda (see below).

Perhaps the most famous example of a fake conspiracy is *The Protocols of the Elders of Zion*, a crude late 19th-century forgery purporting to be the secret minutes of a series of meetings of Jewish conspirators (the Elders), in which they relate their plans for the takeover of the world and the subjugation of all other peoples. A typical extract, from Protocol 2, Article 2: 'The administrators ... from among the public ... will easily become pawns in our game, specially bred from childhood to rule the affairs of the whole world.'

The *Protocols* first surfaced in Russia, in 1905, where they were used to help justify continued repression of Russian Jews, even though they were almost immediately identified as forgeries. Their authorship has been traced to Mathieu Golovinski, a virulently anti-Semitic reactionary propagandist in league with the Tsarist secret police. In 1921 the London *Times* ran a series of articles exposing Golovinski's source. It seemed that he had simply copied a tract called *Dialogue In Hell*, written in 1864 by Frenchman Maurice Joly. Joly's book is a fictional account of the plans for world domination being cooked up by Emperor Napoleon III. Golovinski had adapted this anti-Napoleonic diatribe into an anti-Semitic one by copying it virtually word for word and replacing 'France' with 'Zion' and 'Napoleon' with 'Jews'.

Bizarrely, despite their initial and subsequent repeated unmasking as forgeries, the *Protocols* have acquired a life of their own, and continually surface as 'evidence' of Jewish perfidy and involvement in a global Illuminati-style conspiracy. The *Protocols* have been brandished by anti-Semitic writers from US industrialist Henry Ford and Hitler, to modern-day paranoiacs and conspiracy-peddlers such as David Icke and modern neo-Nazi groups. They are also commonly touted by anti-Jewish propagandists in the Muslim world. In 2004 a copy of the *Protocols* was displayed (as a real work) in the Museum of Manuscripts at the Alexandria Library in Egypt. Dr Youssef Ziedan, director of the collection, explains its inclusion on the basis that: 'it has become a holy book for the Jew, their primary law, their way of life'. The assumption that there genuinely is a global Jewish conspiracy is widespread in the Muslim world, finding recent expression in an outburst by outgoing Malaysian prime minister, Mahathir Mohamed. In a speech on 16 October 2003, Mahathir insisted that, 'Jews rule the world by proxy. They get others to fight and die for them'. The myth of Jewish conspiracy is alive and well and still being used to justify the killing of Jews, much as it was more than 2,000 years ago.

The affliction of bogus conspiracies is not restricted to the Jews. Another group who have been tarred with conspiratorial slanders are the Freemasons. Their promotion of freethinking and anti-institutionalism naturally made them enemies among the traditional forces of church and state, while public ire against them was stoked by perceived elitism and corruption. In America, where Masonry was wildly popular during the early 19th century, public and establishment resentment boiled over in 1826 with the strange murder of William Morgan. A disgruntled ex-Freemason, Morgan was planning to publish the secret rituals of the Masons when he vanished. A group of Freemasons were held responsible for the abduction and presumed murder, but when they got off extremely lightly thanks to a court and jury that included many Masons it triggered a wave of anti-Masonic feeling. Politicians and churchmen jumped on the bandwagon and the Anti-Masonic

Party was formed, gaining considerable popularity. Many wild accusations about Masonic conspiracies were made and Masonry in America was shattered.

Anti-Masonry was also common in Europe, finding its most powerful expression in a case similar to the *Protocols* incident. In the 1890s, Europe was scandalised by the shocking revelations of Diana Vaughan, an ex-'High Priestess' of the Masons, who confessed that they were involved in orgies, devil-worshipping and a global conspiracy to subvert Christianity. Led by the Roman Catholic Church, the anti-Masonic clamour was deafening, but in 1896 English scholar AE Waite revealed that the whole Vaughan affair was a hoax, created by a pornographer called Leo Taxil. Taxil later admitted that he had written the hoax as a satire on the credulity of the Catholic Church. Despite admirably proving his point, Taxil was to discover that, like the *Protocols*, his creation had taken on a life of its own. The 'revelations' of the fictional Vaughan have surfaced many times since – for instance in the anti-Masonic rantings of fundamentalist Protestant groups in America.

Ironically, given the role of the Catholic Church in propagating anti-Masonic fables, Catholics themselves have often been the victims of this sort of dangerous slander. False accusations about papist conspiracies have been used to justify cruel repression of Catholics in Britain from the time of the Gunpowder Plot (see page 23) to the lies of Titus Oates' Popish Plot (see page 124) to the Gordon Riots of 1780. Hundreds of innocent Catholics were murdered during these disturbances.

Conspiracy theories can obviously be dangerous. In societies under stress, portions of the population who feel aggrieved or alienated will always be ready to blame the 'other', and eager to accept that responsibility for their failings and sufferings lies not within their own group, but with a sinister cabal of subversive elements. At the same time, rulers and establishment figures find it convenient to divert the anger of their subjects towards vulnerable and expendable groups. The conspiracy theory is the perfect tool for achieving these aims. Since its currency is the clandestine, it is effectively impossible to disprove. Evidence to the contrary can be dismissed as being part of the conspiracy itself. As injustice, poverty and suffering on the one hand and despotism on the other increase in the world, we can expect to see more of the abuse of conspiracy theories.

2

The World of Espionage

In the public imagination, spies and secret agents are the quintessential actors in the secret drama of history, and while James Bond may belong to the realm of fiction there is little doubt that the unseen world of espionage, with its spooks, covert operatives and codebreakers, has profoundly influenced the more visible aspects of history. This chapter looks at key episodes, from ancient history to the recent past, where the world of espionage has had a particular impact, whether through turning the tide of a battle, safeguarding the life of a monarch or subverting the rule of a nation. In some cases, such as the interception of Hasdrubal's message to his brother Hannibal or Richard Sorge's discovery of Japanese plans to wage war in the Pacific, a single instance of brilliant intelligence work can change the course of a war. Other instances, such as Francis Walsingham's superintendence of Elizabethan intrigue or the WWII codebreaking work of the Ultra project, involve the work of the entire intelligence apparatus of a nation over an extended period.

*

Espionage and the Rise of Rome: 270–203 BCE

From humble beginnings as a minor Mediterranean city-state, Rome became the most powerful empire of ancient history, a vast and enduring entity with a long shadow that stretches over Europe and the Near East to the present day. Despite intense Roman propaganda to the contrary, subterfuge and secrecy played an important part in both the creation of the Roman hegemony and in the shifting power plays among the Roman elite.

Spies in the republic

The Romans were relatively backwards at using espionage and other intelligence apparatus, especially when compared to their neighbours and rivals for power in the ancient Mediterranean and Near Eastern world. They never instituted a formal intelligence service throughout the long history of the republic or the empire and never moved beyond a piecemeal approach to foreign intelligence gathering.

Roman intelligence expert Rose Mary Sheldon convincingly argues that the failure of the republic to create formal intelligence institutions reflected the uneasy balance of power between the families that ruled Rome. These families jealously competed for power, wealth and status, making and breaking alliances, and undermining their rivals through scandal. While one or other family might briefly gain ascendancy, none had sufficient power to create state intelligence institutions that might be used by the ruling party against its rivals. Instead, each of the ruling clans used private, informal intelligence networks to keep an eye on competitors and try to undermine them. This system helped to maintain the balance of power between the ruling clans, which in turn preserved the republican nature of Roman government for centuries. In turn, this republican system was one of the great strengths of Rome, helping her to grow from a local city-state to a multinational power.

Espionage in the Second Punic War

Ultimately, however, Rome's burgeoning hegemony depended on its successes on the battlefield, and while most of these can be traced to the power of the Roman military machine, two of the most decisive victories owed much to the forces of secrecy and subterfuge.

By 270 BCE Rome controlled most of Italy and her sphere of trading and political influence had grown large enough to come up against that of Carthage (known to the Romans as the Poeni, hence 'Punic'), a rival city-state on the other side of the Mediterranean, in modern-day Libya, which controlled territory in Sicily, Sardinia, Corsica, Southern Spain and huge swathes of North Africa. The two powers became rivals and the First Punic War (264–241 BCE) was triggered by a Carthaginian attempt to expand further in Sicily. Rome was victorious but defeat simply made the Carthaginians redirect their territorial ambitions towards Spain, where they gained control of most of the Iberian Peninsula together with its mineral wealth and plentiful manpower.

As Carthage's strength grew, so did her ambition and her desire to crush Rome. This ambition was personified by the pre-eminent Carthaginian family of Hamilcar Barca, the general who had conquered Spain and who had raised his four sons, he said, like 'lion whelps', inculcated from an early age with a vitriolic hatred of Rome. Hannibal, the most celebrated of Hamilcar's sons, triggered the Second Punic War in 219 by attacking a Spanish ally of Rome and his subsequent trans-Alpine march into Italy with his army of men and elephants remains one of the most famous military exploits of all time.

Hannibal's highly trained, highly disciplined army, aided by his effective use of spies and scouts and cunning battlefield ruses, won a series of crushing victories against more numerous Roman armies. This sequence culminated in the Battle of

Cannae (216 BCE), where 50,000 men, including the flower of the Roman aristocracy, were slaughtered in a single day – one of the highest death tolls ever recorded in a single day's fighting.

Rome seemed to be in desperate straits but Hannibal lacked the resources to attempt an attack on the city itself. It had recently been fortified and Hannibal, having come via the difficult overland route, had no siege engines and only a relatively small number of men. Hundreds of miles from home, deep in enemy territory, he could not deliver the killer blow that would end the war. His one hope was to receive reinforcements, and in 207 BCE, after nine years of inconclusive warfare, this finally became a possibility. His brother, Hasdrubal, having gathered an army in Spain, followed Hannibal's own route into Italy, picking up more recruits as he went. If the two brothers could link up, Hannibal could finally win the war, guaranteeing Carthaginian hegemony over the whole of the Western Mediterranean.

The news of Hasdrubal's advance caused panic and fear in Rome. Two consuls were elected and sent out at the head of new armies. Livius Salinator was sent north to meet Hasdrubal while Caius Claudius Nero was supposed to go south to meet Hannibal. At this juncture, however, there occurred one of history's most important instances of what is known as Sigint – signals intelligence.

In the world of modern intelligence Sigint lies at the cutting edge of science and technology, employing an array of ultra-advanced, ultra-expensive hardware from satellites and supercomputers to bugs and cameras, to intercept and analyse communications of all sorts, from radio messages and telephone calls to emails and whispered conversations. Sigint existed in the ancient world as well – politicians and power-brokers used slaves as agents to listen in to the conversations of rivals, and set watch on their villas to see who came and went. The architect of one Livius Drusus specifically offered to design his patron a villa constructed 'in such a way that he would be free from public gaze, safe from all espionage and that no one could look down on it' – an early example of counterintelligence precautions.

Sigint was also of crucial military importance – never more so than when the consul Nero intercepted secret messages sent by Hasdrubal to his brother, explaining his line of march and detailing a proposal to meet up in South Umbria and then swing around to march on Rome. The Carthaginian dispatch riders had successfully crossed most of Italy but fell into Nero's hands at the last, an intelligence coup that was to change the course of history in the ancient world. Armed with this knowledge, he quickly realised that he must prevent the union of forces at all costs. He led the greater part of his forces in a forced march to the north to meet up with the army of Salinator.

The combined Roman forces met with Hasdrubal's army at the Battle of Metaurus on the 22 June 207 BCE, and won an overwhelming victory. About 10–20,000 men were killed, including Hasdrubal himself. Nero quickly returned to the south and apprised Hannibal that his hopes had been dashed by throwing his brother's severed head into the Carthaginian encampment. Although he was to remain undefeated in Europe, Hannibal's Italian adventure was effectively over. The Romans, under a brilliant new general, Scipio Africanus, opened new fronts, first driving the Carthaginians out of Spain and Sicily and then landing an army in Africa to attack Carthage directly. Hannibal was recalled to Africa, leaving Italy in 203 BCE. Thanks to Nero's Sigint, Carthage could no longer win the war. Further skulduggery on the southern shores of the Mediterranean would help to ensure that they lost it.

Undercover agents and covert ops in ancient Africa

By 203 BCE the Second Punic War had shifted to a new theatre of conflict, and the Roman general Scipio Africanus was bogged down in North Africa and threatened by a large army allied to Carthage, under the Numidian king Syphax. Scipio knew that if he was to strike a decisive blow at Carthage and finally win the war, he would first have to deal with the Numidians. Subterfuge would be the key.

Scipio needed to discover the layout of the Numidian camp and the disposition of their forces, and he used his top men as intelligence agents. Dispatching a legation to hold talks with Syphax, he attached a number of centurions disguised as slaves to gather information. To protect the identity of one centurion who had previously visited the camp, Scipio had him publicly caned, a punishment that would never normally be meted out to a high-ranking person. Their cover intact, the spies were able to wander the camp unchallenged while the legation jawed. Each time the legation returned to see Syphax, different centurions accompanied them, until all of Scipio's top officers were familiarised with the layout of the enemy camp.

Using this information Scipio was able to plan a sort of covert operation. His intelligence showed that the camps were more vulnerable at night, so he launched an attack under cover of darkness, firing the tents and stationing his troops outside the camp's exits. In the confusion, the enemy soldiers were slaughtered as they fled the burning camps. Scipio had overcome a superior force and opened the route to Carthage itself.

The Second Punic War was a finely balanced struggle for hegemony of the Western Mediterranean between the two great powers of the day. Rome and Carthage were evenly matched and the conflicts on both sides of the Mediterranean could have turned either way. At key moments, however, the forces of subterfuge played crucial roles in tipping the balance towards Rome. She went on to cement her control of Italy, Gaul, Spain, Sicily and Africa, and later expanded her sphere of influence eastwards to become the dominant power in Europe and the Near East for centuries. Yet it is entirely possible that, but for these key instances of successful espionage, Carthage would have prevailed and classical history would have developed very differently. Today we still bear the marks of Roman influence in many aspects of our culture and society, from law, religion and morality to place names, national boundaries and languages. If it weren't for Nero's Sigint or Scipio's covert ops, how different might we be today?

Francis Walsingham, Elizabethan Spymaster: 1530–1590

After the fall of Rome, the dark arts of espionage endured centuries of relative stagnation in Europe. Renaissance Italy, with her closely packed city-states constantly jockeying for power and influence, was to prove the perfect environment for them to evolve once more. The embassy became the heart of the intelligence gathering operation, and ambassadors and ministers became skilled at developing networks of agents and informers, and at the art of sending encrypted messages (known as cryptography). Encryption is the translation of a message into a form that is unreadable to one who does not possess the code or cipher used to perform the encryption. As information gathered currency as a tool of power throughout Renaissance Europe, encryption became more widespread and more important, as did the counter-art of decryption.

England, in comparison to the city-states of Italy, was backwards in the arts of espionage, but this was to change with the accession to the throne of Elizabeth I and the rise to prominence of Francis Walsingham. Walsingham was to become the greatest spymaster in Europe and his mastery of the dark arts of espionage would preserve England and her queen from assassins, plots and invasion, shaping the destiny of a nation for centuries to come.

Building Europe's greatest intelligence network

Francis Walsingham was probably born in 1530, to a Protestant family in Kent. He attended Cambridge University (a traditional recruiting ground for spies from Elizabethan times to the present day) for two years, developing outspoken Protestant views, but then left to study on the Continent, returning to England in 1550. At this point Walsingham probably had his first brush with intrigue, becoming involved in a minor way with an anti-Catholic plot to put Lady Jane Grey on the throne. The plot failed and the Catholic queen Mary Tudor ascended to the throne and began to persecute Protestants. Walsingham went into exile once again, and spent the next six years studying law and politics in Italy and central Europe, the perfect training ground for a would-be spymaster. Here he honed his skills as a linguist and a student of human nature, in addition to learning about cryptography and other aspects of spycraft.

In 1558 the Protestant Elizabeth I ascended to the throne and Walsingham returned to England. He was elected to the House of Commons as an MP and came to the notice of Elizabeth's chief minister, William Cecil, who had already established a small network of agents. Cecil offered him a position and Walsingham began a long career of defending the Queen and promoting the interests of the Protestant cause. He already had a network of contacts on the Continent, which he used to keep Cecil apprised of goings on throughout Europe, and he worked hard to build support for the cause of the Protestant Huguenots in France. In 1570 he was selected to become ambassador to France with mixed success. He negotiated treaties for Elizabeth and provided refuge for persecuted Huguenots, but was simply an appalled bystander to the St Bartholomew's Day Massacre of the Huguenots in 1572.

Recalled to England he was knighted, made a member of the Privy Council and appointed secretary of state, a post generally described as the equivalent of foreign secretary and domestic and foreign intelligence chiefs rolled into one. Over the next few years Walsingham developed the greatest spy network in Europe. He chose talented young men from home, particularly favouring Cambridge as a recruiting ground. It was from here, for instance, that he recruited Christopher Marlowe, the playwright and poet. Other writers he employed as spies included William Fowler and Matthew Royston. His patronage of the arts extended to his support for a travelling group of players known as the Queen's Men, although they too were employed for intelligence ends, sending him reports from the grand stately homes where they entertained.

Walsingham also undertook more foreign missions which helped him to recruit foreign agents such as Giordano Bruno, better known as the philosopher who was later burnt at the stake for supporting Copernican scientific theories. He had over 50 spies throughout Europe, many of who set up their own subordinate networks, and paid for many of them out of his own pocket. He had agents as far afield as Constantinople, Algiers and Tripoli. He could also be ruthless in his pursuit of the Protestant cause and his persecution of the Catholics, and was happy to torture suspects or capture agents to get information.

Walsingham's carefully cultivated spy network was the tool that enabled him to foil the numerous plots against Elizabeth, safeguard the interests of Protestant England and eventually alter the balance of power in Europe.

The plots against Elizabeth

In the late 16th century, England was in a precarious position and her new queen in deadly peril. As a newly Protestant country England found itself in the vanguard of the Reformation and on the wrong side of the massed Catholic powers of Europe. Both France and Spain, the two most powerful nations in Europe, were desperate to see England return to the Catholic fold, while at home much of the wealth, land and power remained in the hands of Catholic families of the old aristocracy. At first Elizabeth was able to stall the enmity of Spain and

France by offering the hope that she might marry into one of their royal families, but as it became clear that her equivocation was just a delaying tactic their attentions turned to plotting to depose her and put a Catholic on the throne. In the persecuted Catholics of England the plotters found natural allies, and in the person of Mary, Queen of Scots, they found an obvious candidate to replace Elizabeth.

Mary had a prior claim to the throne through her grandmother, elder sister of Henry VIII, and Catholics (who did not recognise Henry's divorce and subsequent remarriage to Anne Boleyn, mother of Elizabeth) insisted that the English throne was hers by right. In addition she had previously been married to Lord Darnley, himself a claimant to the throne. More to the point, she was a devout Catholic and had also been married to the Dauphin, who would have been king of France. So although she had been chased out of Scotland by hostile Protestant nobility and had fled to England to seek shelter from her cousin Elizabeth, she posed a real and present danger to the English queen. Most of the Catholic plots against Elizabeth involved liberating Mary from the imprisonment to which she had quickly been committed and putting her on the throne. If they succeeded England would once again fall into the Catholic sphere of influence, ensuring that the Catholic hegemony of Europe and the New World would endure for generations to come.

Walsingham was determined not to let this happen, and used his network of spies at home and abroad to discover plots in the making. In 1571 Walsingham uncovered the Ridolfi Plot. Roberto di Ridolfi was a Florentine banker working in London who hatched a plan to link a Catholic uprising in England with an invasion of eastern England by troops from the Spanish Netherlands, while freeing Mary, Queen of Scots and marrying her to Thomas Howard, duke of Norfolk, the country's leading Catholic nobleman. Ridolfi travelled extensively to Rome and Madrid, canvassing support from Philip II of Spain and Pope

Pius V. Possibly Walsingham's agents in the foreign capitals got wind of the plot, but the killer blow was dealt to it when one of Ridolfi's messengers was intercepted at Dover and incriminating letters were seized. The conspiracy was uncovered and although Ridolfi was abroad at the time and thus avoided capture, the duke of Norfolk was arrested, found guilty of high treason and executed in 1572. Not for the last time, Walsingham probably exhorted Elizabeth to have Mary executed as well, but she was wary of setting an uncomfortable precedent and instead Mary was kept under tighter guard and subject to still closer scrutiny.

In 1583 Walsingham's spy ring uncovered another plot centred on Mary. Francis Throckmorton, son of one of Elizabeth's courtiers, had become an ardent Roman Catholic and was caught up in a Franco–Spanish plot that also involved Bernardino de Mendoza, the Spanish ambassador to London, and Cardinal James Beaton, Mary's own ambassador in Paris. The plan was for the Catholic duke of Guise to lead an invasion force of English Catholic exiles and troops from the Netherlands, with the aim of putting Mary on the throne. Walsingham had a double agent inside Mary's French embassy – Cardinal Beaton's secretary Charles Paget – and a mole inside the French Embassy in London – Henry Fagot, aka Giordano Bruno, the renegade priest and philosopher. Throckmorton was acting as a go-between for Mary and Beaton, but, exposed by the intelligence of Walsingham's agents, was arrested and tortured until he revealed the details of the plot. He was executed and Mendoza was deported.

The Babington plot

Once again Elizabeth's advisors and parliament united in urging Elizabeth to execute Mary, but once again she refused, on the grounds that it wasn't proven that Mary had been party to the plot. But she did sign into law acts that made it treasonable to even be associated with plots against her person. Walsingham, equipped with these new powers, was determined that Mary's next slip would be her last.

As we have seen, Walsingham already had double agents in Mary's camp, helping him to keep watch on her. In 1585, however, he acquired another: Gilbert Gifford, a Catholic exile who had been training at the English College in Rome, a hotbed of anti-Elizabethan sentiment. Predictably, Walsingham had eyes and ears there already. One of his best agents, Anthony Munday, had infiltrated the College, and it was possibly through him that Walsingham first got wind of Gifford. Despite his religion, Gifford was willing to take the queen's shilling and become a double agent for Walsingham, known by the code name No 4. In a letter to his spymaster, Gifford wrote, 'I have heard of the work you do and I want to serve you. I have no scruples and no fear of danger. Whatever you order me to do I will accomplish.'

Gifford was as true as his word, embarking on a double life as an agent for the Catholic cause, travelling between Catholic safe houses under a number of aliases, including Colerdin, Pietro and Cornelys, and offering his services to the French Embassy in London. Walsingham probably knew that the French ambassador Michel de Castelnau was holding correspondence for Mary, thanks to his secret agent in the embassy, Henry Fagot, aka Giordano Bruno. Gifford offered to ensure that the letters were smuggled in to Mary under the very noses of her jailers. He passed the letters to the local brewer who supplied Chartley Hall, Mary's place of imprisonment, who would then wrap them in leather and hide them inside a hollow bung inserted into a beer barrel. Mary's servants would retrieve the letters and pass back responses in the same way.

Now that Mary had a new way to communicate with her allies, new plots were hatched. In May 1586 she wrote to Mendoza, now Spanish Ambassador to Paris, and to Beaton, urging a Spanish invasion of England. They, meanwhile, were backing a bold plan conceived by a dashing young English Catholic nobleman, Anthony Babington. Charismatic and popular, Babington had attracted a coterie of zealous young Catholics, and together they hatched a scheme to liberate Mary and assassinate Elizabeth, followed by a general Catholic uprising assisted by invasion from abroad.

Walsingham soon had wind of the Babington plan, possibly thanks to his agent Christopher Marlowe, who had been sent to the Catholic Seminary in Rheims under the cover of being a possible convert to Catholicism. Like the English College in Rome, the Seminary in Rheims was a talking shop for anti-Elizabeth intrigues; it was also home to John Ballard, a Catholic priest from Cambridge, who was a co-conspirator of Babington's. Ballard made contact with Mendoza and Beaton, and Beaton's cipher clerk Thomas Morgan helped to introduce Ballard and Babington to Gifford, presumably under the watchful eye of Walsingham's double agent Paget. Walsingham had every move in the complex game covered, and very little happened without him knowing about it.

Gifford acted as a go-between for Mary and Babington, but actually routed their correspondence through Walsingham. But Babington was cautious and encrypted his letter to Mary according to a cipher of his own invention. This did not deter Walsingham, who was acquainted with ciphers and encryption from his time in Italy, and who had set up a cipher school of his own and employed leading linguists and scholars such as Dr John Dee as cryptanalysts (codebreakers). His most accomplished cryptanalyst was another Cambridge graduate, Thomas Phelippes, who soon broke Babington's code and revealed his plot. Walsingham had the original letter resealed and sent on to Mary in the hope that she would reply, incriminating herself fatally.

On 17 July 1586, Mary wrote back to Babington, acknowledging his plan and pointing out the necessity of liberating her before assassinating Elizabeth, lest her jailer turn on her on hearing the news. The letter was duly intercepted and deciphered, and this probably would have been enough to condemn Mary, but Walsingham was leaving nothing to chance. In addition to his skills as a cryptanalyst, Phelippes was also a forger of rare skill. Walsingham had him add a postscript to the letter, asking for more information. As well as being more incriminating still, Walsingham hoped that the postscript would help him to secure the names of all the plotters involved.

Babington may have smelled a rat, because he did not take this bait but he did proceed with the planning. When he started to make arrangements to go abroad, however, the trap was sprung. Although he initially evaded capture disguised as a commoner, Babington was eventually arrested on 15 August. By this time Ballard had already been arrested and tortured. Both men, together with five co-conspirators, were horribly executed in London. Mary was tried in October and convicted on the evidence of the letters; Walsingham personally helped to present the case against her. Still Elizabeth was reluctant to sign her death warrant but was eventually pressured into doing so. Walsingham quickly arranged for the execution and on the 8 February 1587, Mary was beheaded.

The threat to Elizabeth's person and crown posed by Mary was ended and the Catholic forces ranged against her were deprived of the most obvious focus for their plots. But the threat to England was, if anything, even greater now. Philip of Spain was furious and vowed to crush the Protestant upstarts. Walsingham turned his attention and his intelligence apparatus towards combating the Spanish invasion threat.

Foiling the Armada

Walsingham's spy network had already helped to foil one threatened invasion of England. In 1577, William of Orange, a Dutch prince engaged in a bitter war to free his country from Spanish occupation, intercepted an encrypted letter sent by

Philip of Spain to his half-brother Don John of Austria, describing a plan to invade England from the Netherlands. William passed the message to his master cryptanalyst Philip van Marnix, who decoded it and passed it on to one of Walsingham's agents, Daniel Rogers. Forewarned, the English reinforced their defences and the invasion plans were called off.

Now Philip was preparing a much larger invasion force, assembling a great armada of ships. To discover what was afoot in Spain, Walsingham turned to a contact in Italy codenamed 'AB'. William Standen was a restless English Catholic with an abiding loyalty to his country of origin. He had settled in Tuscany in the 1580s, using the pseudonym Pompeo Pellegrini, and befriended the Tuscan ambassador to Madrid, who kept him informed of goings on in the Spanish capital. Standen in turn passed some information on to Walsingham with whom he had corresponded since 1582. In the spring of 1587, having dealt with Mary, Walsingham wrote to Standen to offer him £100 a year in return for becoming a fully-fledged agent.

Standen passed on information about Genoese ships being sent to Spain, and sent a Flemish agent of his own to Madrid. The Fleming was to make contact with his brother, who worked as a secretary to the Marquis of Santa Cruz, the man Philip had put in charge of the Armada. Lists of men and materials made their way back to Walsingham, showing that the Armada would not be ready to sail in 1587. England had another vital year to prepare what defences she could.

Using Standen's intelligence, Sir Francis Drake was able to launch a stinging attack on the Spanish fleet at Cadiz, 'singeing the King of Spain's beard' – Drake 'fired thirty of great ships and sank two galleys' according to a letter from Walsingham to Standen. The next year Standen moved to Madrid himself to more closely supervise the intelligence gathering, and when the great Armada was finally ready to launch the forces of England were forewarned and prepared. In the event the weather played the greatest role in defeating the Armada, but Cecil, his former boss, recognised the import of Walsingham's efforts, telling him, 'you have fought more with your pen than many here in our English navy with their enemies.'

Helping to defeat the Armada was to be Walsingham's last great service for his queen. Mistrustful of his power and still resentful of the role he had played in forcing her hand over Mary, Elizabeth removed him from office and ignored his petitions for compensation for the personal funds he had laid out on her behalf. Walsingham died two years later, penniless, but his legacy was priceless. One of Philip's agents wrote to him, telling him the news: 'Secretary Walsingham has just expired, at which there is much sorrow.' In the margin of the letter, Philip's own hand comments, 'There, yes. But it is good news here.'

Philip perhaps was aware of the impact Walsingham's skilful use of subterfuge and secrecy had had on European power politics, and the extent to which his hidden hand had steered the ship of the English state safely through the dangerous shoals of 16th-century religious conflict. By foiling the plots against Elizabeth's life and helping to defeat the invasion threats of Spain and France, Walsingham had ensured the Protestant future of England and sown the seeds for her challenge to Spanish dominance in Europe and the subsequent emergence of Britain as a global imperial power. Without his shadowy machinations the history of Europe and the world would have developed very differently. The Counter-Reformation might have triumphed throughout Europe and the colonisation of the world would have been a largely Franco–Spanish affair. One man had genuinely changed the course of history.

Spies of Napoleon vs spies of Wellington: 1796–1812

The French revolutionary wars and the Napoleonic wars that followed them changed the nature of warfare. For the first time entire nations were mobilised for total war, and entire populations were put under arms. Great armies ranged across Europe, moving between diverse theatres of conflict and waging campaigns on multiple fronts. The command structures of these armies evolved into highly organised and professional staffs that controlled strategy, tactics and logistics, and were crucial to the outcome of battles and the success of armies. The natural corollary of this new era of warfare was a new era of espionage. Intelligence became a central concern for commanders and a common currency for the new style of command structure. For the two most successful generals of the era, Napoleon and Wellington, whose rivalry was destined to decide the fate of Europe, espionage was an indispensable tool. Their clever use of intelligence helped to make them legendary figures, and determined the outcome of crucial battles and campaigns.

Napoleon's secret weapons

Napoleon relied on spies from the beginning of his career as France's top general. The campaign that helped to make his name was Italy, 1796. In March of that year, Napoleon assumed command of a tired and demoralised French army, suffering the consequences of an extended and difficult occupation of the Piedmont region. He knew that a quick victory was needed to raise morale and prevent a complete collapse, but he faced superior numbers in the shape of both Austrian and Piedmontese forces. His plan was to isolate the Piedmontese and force them out of the war, allowing him to give his undivided attention to the Austrians. First, he needed to sever the link between the two armies by overcoming a force led by the Austrian general, Argenteau. It was to prove a great victory and the start of a long road to glory.

The usual account of the battle with Argenteau has it that the Austrian was delayed by muddled orders, but it seems that Napoleon's first major triumph may have owed more to underhand methods. Overseeing his spy network in northern Italy was Napoleon's adjutant-general, Landrieux. Using his spies as couriers, Landrieux was able to secretly channel 100,000 francs (about $1.6 million today) to Argenteau, who promptly threw the battle, and retired from command shortly afterwards. With Argenteau out of the way, Napoleon was able to round on the Piedmontese and secure the region. Further lavish spending on collaborators and bribes helped to smooth the passage of Napoleon's forces across northern Italy to Venice, but it is telling that when Landrieux was temporarily incapacitated by an old wound, the little Corsican had to resort to a lengthy siege and a series of four battles over eight months to capture the fortress of Mantua.

Three years later Napoleon was back in Italy, but this time he faced logistical problems, having been unable to get enough artillery over the difficult Alpine passes. To the astonishment of many, he opted for a bold march on Milan, which he knew to house a huge Austrian artillery depot. Why bother with your own guns when you can capture the enemy's? To undertake such a move seemed like madness for a force lacking artillery, but Napoleon was acting on intelligence. Earlier in the campaign he had renewed contact with a spy who he had employed in his previous sojourn in Italy. His tongue loosened by the promise of cash, this spy revealed that the main Austrian force was at Turin, and only 7,500 men with little working artillery were left to defend Milan. Knowing he would face only token resistance, Napoleon marched on Milan and captured it.

Napoleon often used such intelligence without passing it on to his subordinates. When it proved accurate, his reputation for brilliant martial instinct was enhanced, adding to his aura of infallibility and genius. His authority over his marshals was one of the elements that made him such an effective general. Sometimes Napoleon's intelligence was wrong, in which cases he tended to simply blame a subordinate for not carrying out an order properly.

One of Napoleon's greatest agents was a trader from Strasbourg, Charles Schulmeister. An experienced smuggler,

Schulmeister had used his contacts and knowledge to help the French cross the Rhine in 1799. Over the next few years Strasbourg became a centre for espionage activities by both the French and Austrians; a sort of Napoleonic West Berlin, complete with double agents, exiles and kidnaps. In 1804 Schulmeister was detailed to spy on an important royalist exile, the Duc d'Enghien. The Duc was considered to be a dangerous figure, plotting against Napoleon from his base in Ettenheim, across the Rhine. Schulmeister was able to tip off Napoleon's spymaster, Jean-Marie Savary, that the Duc had crossed the Rhine and was in Strasbourg. Quickly dispatching a troop of men, Savary was able to seize the royalist and cart him off to Paris for execution.

Having proved his credentials, Schulmeister was now employed for a far grand mission. Posing as a double agent (which he likely was, since he took steps to cover himself with both sides in the conflict), Schulmeister was to approach the Austrian general Karl Mack von Leiberich at his HQ in Ulm. Napoleon was keen to launch a campaign against the Austrians in Southern Germany, but if the Austrians and their allies could unite he would be outnumbered. He needed to immobilise Mack's force and then encircle and destroy it, but as soon as Mack got wind of French movements he could easily slip away. Schulmeister's job was to convince him not to.

Posing as a Hungarian nobleman with access to the French headquarters, Schulmeister managed to convince Mack to employ him to spy on the French! The wily smuggler fed back a stream of disinformation to the Austrian commander, and convinced him, despite the doubts of his senior commanders, that the Austrian army should stay put. Even after Napoleon had crossed the Rhine and begun to encircle Mack, Schulmeister was able to convince him that the French were, in fact, withdrawing. He also passed on false reports that the British had landed on France's Atlantic coast and that Napoleon faced a rebellion at home. Thus bamboozled, Mack fell straight into Napoleon's trap and was forced to surrender. Napoleon reportedly told his staff, 'All praise to Charles – he was worth 40,000 men to me'.

Schulmeister's reward was to be made chief of police in Vienna after Napoleon had captured the city, but this turned out badly. After concluding a peace treaty on his terms, Napoleon withdrew and Schulmeister was captured by the returning Austrians. However, he managed to escape their custody and returned to France, where he was amply rewarded for helping to add to the legend of Napoleon and lived out the rest of his days in luxury.

Wellington's gentlemen spies

Thanks in part to his clever use of espionage, by 1808 Napoleon was master of much of Western Europe. He had occupied both Portugal and Spain and placed his brother Joseph on the Spanish throne. But this was to be the beginning of the end for Napoleon, as his nemesis Arthur Wellesley, the duke of Wellington, entered the fray. Wellington was to lead a coalition of British, Portuguese and Spanish forces through a protracted and bloody series of battles between 1808 and 1814. Key to some of his most important victories was his use of intelligence – in particular, two kinds of intelligence: Sigint and covert reconnaissance.

In early 19th-century Europe, Sigint meant intercepting enemy dispatches and breaking their codes. The French used codes of varying degrees of security. In the field they initially used simple ciphers known as *petits chiffres*, but in 1811 they switched to a more complex cipher known as the Army of Portugal Code. Tackling these codes was a unit led by General George Scovell, Wellington's chief cryptographer. Scovell assembled a team of Spanish, Portuguese, Italian, Swiss and Irish soldiers, called the Army Guides. The Guides were recruited for their linguistic skills and local knowledge, and became adept at intercepting and deciphering enemy messages.

Scovell and his Guides had no trouble cracking the French army's *petits chiffres*, and took only two days to decipher the Army of Portugal Code. But at the end of 1811 the French adopted a new, supposedly impenetrable code – the Great Paris Cipher. Where the *petits chiffres* had used a 50-number code, and the Army of Portugal Code a 150-number code, the Great Paris Cipher used 1,400 numbers, and came complete with a guidebook instructing cipher clerks on how to avoid the telltale slips that often enabled the enemy to break a code. For instance, cryptanalysts often looked at the beginning and end of a message, searching for repeated patterns that they could match to the usual forms used to start and finish a letter (eg names, dates, 'yours sincerely' etc). Cipher clerks using the Paris Cipher were instructed to add meaningless sequences of numbers to the ends of letters to confuse cryptanalysts.

Scovell worked on the Great Paris Cipher for a year, chipping away at it using the smallest clues to pierce a chink in its cryptographic armour. Occasionally captured letters included uncoded words or phrases, while reports from his Army Guides and from Wellington's 'exploring officers' (see below) provided useful correlating information such as the names of regiments, commanders and locations to which the intercepts might be referring.

By July 1812, Scovell was able to decipher a message from Joseph Bonaparte to Marshal Marmont, commander of the Army of Portugal, which had fallen into Wellington's hands. Deciphered, the message told Wellington that Joseph was marching to join Marmont with 13,000 men, while a force of cavalry and guns under another French general, Cafferelli, was due to join him in the next few days. Wellington had already been caught off guard by Marmont and was on the back foot, but this intelligence allowed him to set a trap for the French. At the subsequent battle of Salamanca, Wellington secured a complete victory over the Army of Portugal.

A still greater victory was to come. In December 1812, the British intercepted a message from Joseph to his brother Napoleon. Again, Scovell was able to decipher it, revealing a complete account of the French order of battle and plans. Using this intelligence, Wellington planned and achieved a great victory at Vittoria, finally wresting control of Spain from the French. As an added bonus, Joseph's coaches were captured, along with his copy of the code tables for the Great Paris Cipher.

Complementing the work of Scovell's Army Guides was an elite class of covert operatives who carried out extremely dangerous reconnaissance missions behind enemy lines. Known as 'exploring officers', these men were sent to sketch and make notes on the lay of the land and the disposition of enemy troops and defences. The greatest of these exploring officers was Lieutenant-Colonel Colquhoun Grant, perhaps the Napoleonic era's closest equivalent to James Bond. Grant was a fearless, intelligent and honourable officer. He refused to work in disguise and insisted on wearing his highly conspicuous red uniform, even when deep in enemy territory. By doing so he clearly set himself apart from mere 'vulgar' spies. Apart from anything else, this meant that he would not be summarily executed if captured, but treated as an officer and a gentleman.

On 16 April 1812, Grant and a local guide were scouting behind enemy lines when they were surrounded and captured. The guide was promptly shot, but Grant was delivered to the French headquarters and entertained by Marshal Marmont himself. Trusting that his captors would adhere to the traditional rules of the 'gentlemanly' conduct of war, Grant agreed to sign his parole (this was a document wherein the captor agreed not to try to escape – it meant that he could be allowed a certain degree of liberty rather than being chained in a dungeon). Grant calculated that, as a parolee, he would find it much easier to pass messages back to Wellington.

The French, however, were duplicitous. They knew what a dangerous man Grant was and were determined to get rid of him. He was to be sent back to France, where, according to a letter written by General de la Martinière to the French minister of war, 'he should be watched and brought to the notice of the police.' The meaning of this would have been clear to anyone who read it – Grant was to be turned over to the police, who, unconstrained by military codes of conduct, would treat him like a common spy. Unfortunately for the French, Grant himself contrived to see a copy of the letter, which de la Martinière had failed to encode. Judging that it allowed him to abrogate his parole, Grant escaped, disguised himself as an American officer and made his way to Paris in the company of a French general. Once there he sent a stream of intelligence back to Wellington before finding his way back to England and rejoining his commander in Spain.

Thanks in part to the Sigint and tactical intelligence provided by his crack intelligence units, Wellington was able to drive the French out of Portugal and Spain and chase them into southern France. The Peninsula War sapped the strength of Napoleon's army and led to his downfall not long afterwards. Wellington's spies had triumphed over Napoleon's.

Sigint, the Battle of Tannenberg and the Russian Revolution: 1914

Perhaps the single most important instance of signals intelligence turning the course of a battle, a war and history itself, is the World War I Battle of Tannenberg. This extraordinarily disastrous defeat for the Russians effectively determined the course of the war on the Eastern Front, though not before helping to ensure the long, agonising continuation of the Western Front, and playing a role in triggering the Russian Revolution.

On the Western Front the Germans were enjoying great success, forcing the French and British back almost to the gates of Paris. The French exhorted their Russian allies in the east to enter the war quickly, and the Tsar, ignoring warnings that his troops were not ready, ordered his armies in the north to move on Eastern Prussia. Although the Russian forces outnumbered the German forces facing them, they were poorly equipped, poorly trained, poorly supported and poorly led. The Germans, by contrast, were mobile, fast and effective.

Despite this, the initial Russian advance into German territory seemed to meet with some success. On the 19 August the First Army under General Rennenkampf advanced on the town of Gumbinnen, in East Prussia, and forced the outnumbered German Eighth Army under General von Prittwitz to fall back. During the Russian advance, however, two crucial events had occurred to set the wheels of history in motion. The first event was the capture by the Germans, during an initial skirmish, of 3,000 Russian prisoners, including a staff officer. Interrogation of this man produced the priceless intelligence that radio communications between the First and Second Armies and their command centre, North-West Army HQ, was all done *en clair* – i.e. without being encoded or encrypted in any way. By turning their antennae in the direction of the Russian HQ, the Germans could eavesdrop on their entire signals traffic.

The second event was that the First and Second armies became separated. Rennenkampf had pressed westwards without waiting for the Second Army under General Samsonov, which struggled to get underway and found the going hard, suffering in particular from a lack of supplies. In fact, after a few days marching, Samsonov was forced to divert south to try to secure his supplies, increasing the gap between the two Russian forces. The original Russian plan had called for Rennenkampf and Samsonov to use their troops to surround the massively outnumbered German Eighth Army. But instead of a united front the Russians now found themselves advancing separately through difficult country. The Second Army, in particular, was moving through treacherous marshland, and was thus forced to concentrate into a narrow column, unable to bring their full strength to bear on any Germans they might meet.

While Rennenkampf settled in to new HQ at Gumbinnen, apparently satisfied that he had dealt a stunning blow to the German army, North West Army HQ fired off an increasingly exasperated series of messages to Samsonov, urging him to close the gap. To the listening Germans this intelligence suggested a bold manoeuvre. Instead of dodging encirclement by the Russians, the Eighth Army could concentrate its entire strength in the south and assault the struggling Russian Second Army. In a brilliant plan conceived by Staff Officer Max Hoffman, a thin screen of cavalry would be left to deceive Rennenkampf in the north, while the rest of the German forces would encircle Samsonov in the south.

Hoffman's superior, von Prittwitz, had panicked in the face of Rennenkampf's initial advance, and had since been replaced by von Hindenburg and his chief of staff, the popular Erich von Ludendorff, who soon approved Hoffman's plan. To put it into effect, however, the Germans needed reserves to cover their rear, and in a fateful decision the commander-in-chief, von Moltke, agreed to release four reserve divisions from the Western Front for service in the east. Von Moltke believed that the battle in the west was nearly won, and that Paris would soon be his, but in fact the German advance was halted just 30 miles (100 km) short of Paris, and without the precious reserve divisions the Germans were unable to force the issue and prevent the Western Front from degenerating into a stalemate. If the reserves had not been diverted to the east, might the Germans have forced the French and British to make terms and closed the Western Front before the Americans ever entered the war? How many lives would have been saved?

Radio intercepts by the Germans provided them with a clear picture of the disposition of Russian forces, and by the 25 August their own units were in place and battle commenced.

German artillery rained down on the trapped Russian forces, and although they fought bravely there was nowhere for them to turn. The Second Army disintegrated as troops tried to escape through the marshes, where they drowned or were cut down by the encircling Germans. Over five days of fighting the Germans inflicted 50,000 casualties and took over 90,000 prisoners, as well as huge quantities of guns and ammunition. Samsonov committed suicide. After celebrating the victory at the nearby village of Tannenberg, scene of a legendary early medieval German defeat now to be commemorated as a shrine to German military brilliance, the Eighth Army then turned north to deal with Rennenkampf.

The crushing defeat at Tannenberg was to have dire consequences for the future in both Russia and Germany. As Russian casualties and bedraggled troops straggled back from the front, they brought with them reports of the incompetence of the aristocratic officer class and their contempt for the peasant cannon fodder they commanded. The disastrous defeat fuelled popular discontent and touched off the process that would lead to revolution three years later. Germany acquired two new heroes in the shape of von Hindenburg and von Ludendorff, who eventually became the country's de fact rulers. The German victory, achieved against overwhelming odds, attained legendary status, and was used as a potent rallying symbol by the fascists campaigning to restore German pride amidst the post-war depression. Rarely has battlefield Sigint had such widespread and far-reaching consequences.

Richard Sorge – Russia's master spy in World War II: 1930–1944

The spies whose stories are told in this section are among the very few who can genuinely claim to have changed the course of history. Perhaps uniquely among them, the unparalleled espionage work of Richard Sorge could have achieved this no less than three times. As it was, only one of his momentous discoveries was acted upon, but that was enough to turn the course of World War II.

Sorge was the son of a German oil engineer working in Russia, and returned to Germany as a child and fought in the German army during World War I. His family had strong links to communism – his grandfather had served as private secretary to Karl Marx – and the young Sorge immersed himself in communist theory. In 1920 he became one of the first members of the German Communist Party. His talent and revolutionary zeal brought him to the attention of the Comintern (Communist International) – an organisation dedicated to spreading the Revolution around the world, which also served as a fertile recruiting ground for the Soviet secret services. Sorge was selected to go to Moscow for training and in 1928 was sent to California to organise communist cells in the film industry, working undercover as a teacher. Here he proved his organisational skills, and on his return to Russia he was tapped by Jan Berzin, head of the GRU, the Soviet military intelligence agency. Berzin had spotted the potential of this bright, organised, charming and dedicated German, who spoke several languages and had little trouble picking up more – he would make the perfect spy.

In 1930 Sorge was sent to Shanghai, where he posed as a German (or occasionally American) journalist and succeeded brilliantly in developing a network of agents, assets and informants throughout China. As well as sending back useful information about the developing politics of Mao Tse-tung and Chiang Kai-shek, Sorge also picked up priceless information about German relations in the Far East. In particular, he discovered that Germany and Japan were to sign the Anti-Comintern Pact, bringing to life the Soviet nightmare of hostile neighbours encircling the still fragile communist state.

In 1938 Sorge was relocated to Japan. As well as information on the intentions of the increasingly militaristic regime, Japan also offered a way to spy on Germany, which would have to consult with its new ally on important plans and decisions. Spying in Germany itself had become almost impossible now that it had become a police state, but the Nazis would prove more vulnerable on the other side of the world.

To perfect his cover and help make contacts once in Tokyo, Sorge returned to Germany and posed as an ardently Nazi journalist. He used his considerable charm to make friends with leading Nazis in the Propaganda Ministry, and with their backing was soon able to secure a post as Japanese correspondent for the newspaper *Frankfurter Zeitung*. Once in Tokyo, he cultivated contacts in the German Embassy, especially with the military attaché, Colonel Eugene Ott, who later became the German ambassador. Sorge also set up a network of Japanese contacts, using clandestine communists, some of who were well placed in government or society.

Over the next few years Sorge discovered an enormous mass of information, which was passed on by radio to Russia. In 1940 he alerted his controllers to the signing of the German–Japanese Pact (which further strengthened the ties between the two powers), and in early 1941 he got wind of news of the utmost importance. His German military contacts let slip word of Operation Barbarossa – the German invasion of the Soviet Union. On 5 March he sent Moscow microfilm of German Foreign Office documents indicating an attack in mid-June, and on 15 June he was able to radio the exact date of the planned invasion. One of his sources, Colonel Kretschmer, the new military attaché at the embassy, actually told him that 'Germany had completed her preparation on a very large scale'. Incredibly, despite this and a flood of intelligence from other sources, Stalin chose to ignore the threat and dismiss warnings as disinformation. The Germans duly invaded and destroyed the unprepared Russian forces.

Sorge was furious but laboured on. His next intelligence bombshell would not go unheeded, perhaps due to his accuracy over Operation Barbarossa. In October 1941, Sorge discovered that the vacillating Japanese government had finally made up its mind about where to go to war. The Germans had been pressing their oriental allies to attack Russia and open an eastern front for the Soviets, and a number of divisions, desperately needed to stem the relentless German juggernaut in the west, had been pinned down on the Pacific coast waiting for such an assault. But influential voices in the Japanese cabinet had been pressing for the conquest of Malaysia and other Far Eastern regions, so as to provide Japan with vital raw materials. This faction had won out, and Sorge was able to report that the Japanese had decided against an attack on Russia.

Pinning all their hopes on the trustworthiness of their master spy, the Soviet leadership removed virtually all its forces from the east and hurled them into the fray in the west. The fresh Siberian divisions, unphased by the brutal winter weather, halted the German advance just miles from Moscow, turning the tide of war. The unprecedented defeats led Hitler to sack his senior field commanders and take personal charge of the campaign, with disastrous results. The course of the war on the eastern front, and possibly as a whole, was decided by Sorge's intelligence.

By now the net of Japanese counter-intelligence was closing in on Sorge. A leading Japanese communist had been arrested in 1939, and his interrogation had eventually led the *Kempai Tai*, the Japanese secret police, to Sorge's top Japanese assets. They in turn would lead to Sorge. In late October 1941, the *Kempai Tai* were finally on his tail, but by then Sorge had discovered one last, earth-shattering revelation. The Japanese would launch their Pacific campaign with a pre-emptive strike on American forces at Pearl Harbour in December. Sorge passed this information on to his radio operator for transmission, but before it could be sent the operator was arrested, and shortly afterwards Sorge himself was picked up. He was kept alive in prison for three years, but Stalin refused to trade a

Japanese agent for him (possibly because Sorge was one of those who knew of Stalin's culpability for failing to pre-empt the Nazi invasion), and in 1944 he was hanged.

Sorge's espionage had saved the Soviet Union, despite the obstruction of his masters. Could it have done the same for the Americans at Pearl Harbour? It's possible that Stalin, eager to have more allies join the war, would never have passed on the information to the US. What is not in doubt, however, is Sorge's status as one of the greatest spies in history.

Enigma and the Ultra secret: 1939–1945

Operation Ultra was the super-secret programme to decrypt the German Enigma codes, used to encrypt almost all of their radio traffic. It was the key to Allied victory against Germany and became the most heavily guarded British secret of the war. Careers and lives, perhaps even whole cities, would be sacrificed in the operation to keep the Ultra secret safe. Many would argue that Ultra is the single best piece of evidence for the argument that the key battles of the war were fought, and won, in secret.

The German Enigma system was based around the Enigma machine, regarded at the time as the ultimate cryptographic device. Invented in 1918 by the German Arthur Scherbius, the Enigma machine employed several of the most up-to-date technologies available to mechanise the process of encryption, whereby a message is converted into code.

An Enigma machine looked like a portable typewriter with a typical set of keys and a set of lettered lights that mimicked the keyboard (called a lampboard). Typing one of the keys sent an electrical signal through a complex pattern of wires until it arrived at one of the lights on the lampboard, which would be illuminated. The exact pattern of wiring was determined by a series of wheel-like scramblers, which revolved slightly with every keystroke. This meant that typing the same letter several times would light up a series of different letters on the lamp-board – each one encrypted according to a different cipher. If you knew the initial setting of the machine you could set up your machine in the same way, type in the encrypted message, and the decrypted letters would flash on the lampboard. If you didn't have the initial settings (which were determined by top-secret, heavily guarded code books), you would have to work through more than ten thousand trillion possible combina-tions of the scrambling system to decrypt the message, even assuming you knew the exact structure of the machine. You would then have to repeat this effort for each new message you wanted to decipher.

After World War I it emerged that the Allies had enjoyed considerable success in breaking German codes and reading their radio traffic. The German military were horrified and in 1925 held an enquiry into how to avoid the mistakes of the past and improve their cryptography. Scherbius' device was selected as the best option, and over the next few years his company, Scherbius and Ritter, supplied over 30,000 Enigma machines to the German government. Allied cryptanalysts, listening in to German diplomatic and military radio traffic, noticed the difference almost immediately. In 1926 they began to intercept radio messages that could not be deciphered, and soon they were forced to admit defeat. The Germans had the best system of cryptography in the world. German radio secu-rity was complete, their codes unbreakable. As war loomed, the Allies realised they were in trouble.

Fortunately both the French and Polish intelligence services were able to make important breakthroughs in the pre-war years. The first chink in Enigma's armour was provided by a German informant, Hans-Thilo Schmidt, in 1931. A disaffected clerk at cryptography headquarters in Berlin, Schmidt was cul-tivated by a French secret service agent who paid him a hefty sum in return for a look at documents explaining the con-struction of the Enigma machine. Using the agent's microfilm of the documents, it should have been possible for the French to construct their own Enigma, but this was only a first step. Somehow a cryptanalyst would need to work out the initial settings used to encrypt any Enigma message, and the French cryptanalysis service declared this to be impossible.

The Polish intelligence service refused to admit defeat. Under a post-war agreement they and the French shared intelligence, and the French were happy to turn over their findings on Enigma, which the Poles used to build an Enigma replica. Using the replica machine as a starting point, a brilliant young mathematician named Marian Rejewski pulled off the intellectual tour de force necessary to break the Enigma codes. The main weakness in any system of cryptography is repetition – some elements of messages are invariably repeated. The Enigma machine was supposed to account for this flaw, but Rejewski, through a combination of genius and hard work, was able to discover a way of spotting repetitions in an encoded message, and use these to work out the initial settings of the machine that had sent it. From there he could decrypt the messages it generated. Rejewski and his team constructed modified versions of the Enigma machines that they called *bombes*, possibly because of the clicking noise generated by the internal switches. These functioned as primitive computers and speeded up the process of decryption.

By 1934 the Poles were reading all German radio traffic, but over the years the machines received upgrades, such as extra scrambler wheels that exponentially increased the number of possible settings a cryptanalyst had to work through, and the Germans began to use a new cipher every day. Rejewski didn't have the resources necessary to crack the new, tougher codes, and just when they needed it most the Poles lost the ability to read German signals. Given the increasing anti-Polish rhetoric coming from the Nazis, it was just a matter of time before they invaded. Desperate to preserve the fruits of their labours, Polish intelligence presented two replica Enigmas and the plans for the bombes to British intelligence, who managed to smuggle them out of Poland just two weeks before the Germans marched in.

Now the baton passed to British intelligence, who were in the process of revamping their codebreaking apparatus. A new organisation was formed, and based at a Victorian manor house called Bletchley Park. It was to be called the Government Code and Cypher School (GC&CS, often referred to as 'the Golf, Cheese and Chess Society'), or, according to its official designation, Station X. The motley crew recruited to work at Bletchley Park have since become legendary figures in the secret history of World War II. They included some of the brightest and most eccentric men and women in Britain, such as Alan Turing, the genius considered the father of the modern computer, and Ian Fleming, creator of James Bond. Others were chosen for their skill as chess masters, linguists or by running a crossword competition in the *Daily Telegraph* (the prize was to be pressed into service by the GC&CS).

Equipped with the Polish replicas and bombes (which Turing improved), the Bletchley Park boffins developed a host of their own methods for cracking the Enigma codes. Many of these were based on the poor practice of the German cipher clerks operating the machine, who could be followed around the battlefields of Europe by listening out for their distinctive radio signatures, known as 'fists' – idiosyncrasies in the way they operated the Morse code keys. Many of these clerks were lazy or pressed for time, and so would use shortcuts when setting up their machines at the start of the day. For instance, clerks had to set their own 'message keys' – sequences of letters, supposedly chosen at random, that were used to set the day's codes. Some clerks would simply pick three letters that were next to each other on the keyboard; another would use the initials of his girlfriend. These shortcuts became known as 'cillies'. A variant on the cillies were 'kisses', where hard-pressed operators used the same message keys two days in a row. Later in the war Bletchley Park would develop the first electronic computer, Colossus, to speed up decryption still further.

By the time the Germans launched their blitzkrieg on France, the Bletchley Park cryptanalysts were able to routinely read the Enigma codes used by the Luftwaffe, which made use of a less sophisticated version of the machine, and whose operators seemed more casual about secure procedures. The overall codename for the Enigma codebreaking operation was Ultra. Almost immediately, Ultra proved its worth. As German forces stormed across the Low Countries and France, the British knew many of the details of their operations and plans. Although the beleaguered Expeditionary Force was not able to do much about them, British High Command at least had advance warning that a mass evacuation was likely to be necessary, helping them to pull off the implausible heroics of Dunkirk.

As German eyes turned towards Britain, Ultra would prove to be even more valuable. For instance, on 12 June 1940 Bletchley Park decrypted a Luftwaffe message referring to a 'bent-leg beam' directed at Britain. This chimed ominously with intelligence picked up from captured German airmen, who had been heard discussing a new radio guidance technology used by the Luftwaffe. The experts scoffed, but Churchill, who placed great reliance on Ultra decrypts, insisted that the matter be looked into. The RAF sent up a plane equipped with radio sensors and discovered that there was indeed a radio beam directed over the Rolls-Royce factory in Derby, where RAF fighter plane engines were made. German bombers were planning to simply follow the beam to this vital target. A basic jamming technology was developed and the Luftwaffe plans were thwarted. Later in the war the Germans would develop more sophisticated versions of this radio beam guidance technology, and the British, alerted by Ultra intercepts, would devise ever more ingenious ways of jamming them, in what became known as 'the Battle of the Beams'. The result was a dramatic fall in the accuracy of German bombing.

Through the summer of 1940 the Germans developed their plans for Operation Sealion, the invasion of Britain. The Luftwaffe was to play a key role, for no invasion would be possible without control of the air. Ultra picked up a series of messages that revealed every detail of the Luftwaffe plans and the disposition of their forces. When the air assault was launched on 15 August, codenamed *Alder Tag* (Eagle Day) by the Germans, Ultra intercepts in conjunction with radar technology (see page 222) were able to alert RAF command to the timing and location of the Luftwaffe raids. Air Chief Marshal Dowding was able to direct his thin resources to meet the German threat and the onslaught was beaten back. As the Battle of Britain continued, the Germans were shocked to find that the RAF seemed able to anticipate their every move. Luftwaffe losses mounted alarmingly, and on 17 September Bletchley Park intercepted a message ordering the cancellation of Operation Sealion.

While Bletchley Park achieved great success against the Luftwaffe Enigma codes, the Kriegsmarine (German Navy) codes proved much harder to crack. Kriegsmarine Enigma machines had extra scrambler wheels, and naval operators had much better security discipline. Able to operate in total security, the U-boat fleet wreaked havoc on Allied shipping throughout 1940 and the start of 1941. The loss of shipping came close to bringing Britain to her knees, demonstrating the desperate importance of codebreaking ability. A series of daring and ingenious Navy operations, such as the capture of German weather-observation trawlers, complete with their code books; the capture of a U-boat and its Enigma machine; and a clever practice called 'gardening', where the Navy seeded mines and listened out for German radio signals warning of their locations, in the process giving away their system of encoded grid coordinates; helped to crack the Kriegsmarine codes.

The benefits were dramatic. Ultra intercepts were able to guide the British Navy to U-boat supply ships in the South

Atlantic, and helped locate the *Bismarck* during the epic hunt for the dangerous German battleship. In combination with other technologies, such as aerial photography, sonar and radio intelligence (which involved tracking the sources of radio transmissions and analysing the pattern of radio traffic), Ultra helped to win the Battle of the North Atlantic in 1943, overcoming the U-boat menace and maintaining Britain's vital supply lines.

The key to Ultra's success was secrecy. If the Germans discovered that their radio transmissions were not secure, they would change their systems and Britain would lose its ability to eavesdrop. The military went to extraordinary lengths to ensure the secret was kept, but that vital intelligence could still be passed on to those who needed it. A protocol was instituted to achieve this, based around Special Liaison Units (SLUs). These were small teams of junior officers briefed on the Ultra secret, who were then attached to other units. Bletchley Park could pass information to them in strictest confidence, and they would then deliver the message to their liaison commander in person, destroying it afterwards, and, if necessary, telling the commander how he could or could not use the info. To communicate with the SLUs, GC&CS eventually developed its own brand of super-secure Enigma machine, a device called the Type X Coding machine, so secret that its design remains a mystery to this day.

A key element of the SLU secrecy protocol was that a cover story for the intelligence must be created. For instance, a spotter plane would have to be sent up to 'identify' targets, even when their exact location was known, so that the Germans would not become suspicious. In one notable incident this plan nearly went awry, but Ultra saved its own skin. In 1942 the Navy, guided by Ultra intercepts that revealed their course and timing, was regularly intercepting supply ships and tankers heading for North Africa to resupply Rommel's Afrika Corps. Care was always taken to send up a spotter plane first to provide a plausible source for the British intelligence, but on one occasion the Navy showed up despite a fog so thick that no spotter plane could possibly have been in operation. The Germans were suspicious, but thanks to further Ultra intercepts, the British were alerted that German military intelligence in Italy was calling for an investigation of a possible security breach. They quickly sent a message in a code they knew the Germans could read, congratulating a non-existent Italian spy on his helpful information regarding the supply convoy. The Germans were reassured that their codes were safe and instead blamed their Italian allies for the breach.

Quick thinking wasn't always enough. Sometimes keeping the Ultra secret required sacrifices. Partly thanks to Ultra, Air Chief Marshal Dowding had won the Battle of Britain despite being heavily outnumbered. But Dowding had rivals in the RAF who, not being privy to the Ultra secret, could not understand his tactics, which made little sense without the vital intelligence. When air chiefs held a post-Battle meeting to thrash over the lessons of the past few months, Dowding's chief rival, Trafford Leigh-Mallory, sent his squadron leader, Douglas Bader, to fight his corner. When Bader challenged Dowding, the senior man felt unable to reveal the Ultra secret to a junior officer and could not justify his position. His reward was to be sacked and replaced by Leigh-Mallory.

According to one version of the Ultra story, an even greater sacrifice was made by the citizens of Coventry. When a German Enigma operator sending a message about a bombing raid mistakenly sent the name of the target *en clair* (unencrypted), the British discovered that the Luftwaffe was headed for Coventry. To evacuate the city would have given the game away, so the citizens of Coventry were left to suffer the attack. However, other versions of the story refute this and claim that the event never happened.

Magic and the War in the Pacific

While Ultra helped to win the war in Europe, guiding the Allies in their development of the Overlord plan for the D-Day invasions, and ensuring the success of the deception operation surrounding Overlord (see 'The D-Day Deception', page 166), the Americans enjoyed their own cryptanalysis successes in the Pacific theatre. The American equivalent to Ultra was Operation Magic, which centred on the successful attempt to crack the Japanese coding machine that the Americans called 'Purple'. Although Magic had failed to forewarn the Americans of the Pearl Harbour attack, it achieved some pivotal successes, most notably the Battle of Midway in June 1942. Magic intercepts revealed a Japanese plan to fake an attack on the Aleutian Islands while securing their true objective, Midway Island. The US Navy pretended to be taken in, but lingered nearby. When alerted by further Magic intercepts that the attack was underway, they fell on the surprised Japanese and crushed them in a battle that turned the tide of war in the Pacific. Admiral Nimitz described Midway as 'essentially a victory of intelligence'.

Another coup for Magic was the killing of Admiral Yamamoto in 1943. Cryptanalysis revealed the Admiral's itinerary during a visit to the Solomon Islands. Yamamoto was renowned for his punctuality, so the Americans dispatched a squadron of fighters to meet his plane and shoot it down, thus removing one of Japan's most effective commanders.

The end of Ultra

From the beginning of the war until its end, the cryptanalysis effort was a vital cog in the Allied war machine. Some claim that Ultra was the decisive factor in the Allied victory in Europe. It almost certainly helped to shorten the war. According to some estimates, without Ultra's help in the Battle of the Atlantic the U-boats would have continued to cripple Allied shipping, with the effect of delaying the D-Day invasion attempt for months or even years. The Ultra secret was kept for decades after the war, partly because Britain had distributed captured Enigma machines to its former colonies, without mentioning that British intelligence would now be able to read all their radio traffic. GC&CS was disbanded and the entire Ultra project was dismantled, with every scrap of evidence relating to it destroyed (including the Colossus computer). British boffins were not even allowed to claim credit for having invented the first computer, and had to watch their American counterparts stealing all the glory with their post-war ENIAC machine, invented a full two years after Colossus. Not until the 1970s, when Commonwealth countries had moved on to more sophisticated ciphers, was the truth allowed to come out.

The Iran–Contra affair: 1985–1986

America's CIA has only been in existence for around fifty years, but in that time it has acquired a reputation for covert interference in the affairs of nations around the globe, resorting to troop-training, arms smuggling, torture, drug trafficking, assassination and terrorism to further the perceived interests of the United States. Most of these activities have remained wholly or partially secret, but occasionally the agency's dark dealings are exposed to the harsh glare of public scrutiny – most famously, during the scandal over the Iran–Contra affair. Newspaper articles and official investigations revealed a tangled saga of illegal arms trading, money laundering and subversion against a democratically elected government, in a CIA operation that spiralled out of control to include drug smuggling, terrorism and murder.

The Iran–Contra affair happened in part because Ronald Reagan's ultra-conservative administration did not have control of Congress. The Democratic majority in Congress opposed many of the Reagan administration's more hardline foreign policy moves, in particular its desire to fund right-wing opposition groups in Latin America in their struggle against perceived communist or communist-friendly groups. Senior administration officials, in cahoots with the CIA, decided to do it anyway.

Anti-communism was the guiding concern of the Reagan administration's foreign policy, and nowhere was this truer than in Latin America. The US has a long tradition of meddling in the politics of Latin America, forcing regime change and even assassinating disliked leaders without much regard for international law, on the basis that it is 'America's back yard'. In 1954, for instance, the CIA forced the democratically elected president of Guatemala to stand down after he dared to challenge the activities of US-multinational United Fruits. A campaign of death threats, propaganda and other 'psych-ops' destabilised the country until a right-wing coup could be launched with the help of CIA operatives, American mercenaries and US money and guns. The result was the installation of an oppressive right-wing regime that spent decades terrorising its people. In 1961 the CIA set up the assassination of Rafael Trujillo, dictator of the Dominican Republic, after he began to make life difficult for American business interests there. In 1973 the CIA carried out terrorist acts, trained and armed fascist paramilitary groups and carried out extensive 'psych-ops' to help bring down the government of Salvador Allende. General Pinochet became dictator, and the CIA helped him to liquidate thousands of perceived 'radicals'. The right-wing dictatorship lasted for 17 years.

During the 1980s the US became embroiled in a drawn out civil war in El Salvador, where leftist rebels were in conflict with the US-backed right-wing government. Across the border in Nicaragua, elections returned to power the socialist Sandinista party, threatening to create a new communist power base in the region. Soon the Sandinistas were accused by the US of funding the Salvadorian rebels, and the Americans started to look towards the *contrarevolucionario*, or Contras, a right-wing paramilitary group engaged in insurrection against the elected government. From 1982 the CIA started to train the Contras for their role as US-surrogates in the country, but the group, mainly composed of holdovers from Nicaragua's former Somoza dictatorship, proved to be unsavoury at best, robbing, terrorising and murdering the people who they were supposed to be protecting against communism. Amidst a wave of bad publicity for the Contras, the Democratically-controlled Congress passed the 1982–1983 Boland Amendments, which specifically made it illegal to fund or supply arms to them.

Meanwhile, in the Middle East, America was faced with another set of problems. Iranian-backed militants in Lebanon had kidnapped a number of Americans, and it seemed likely that the Iranians could help to get them back. Unfortunately relations between America and Iran were terrible. The US was helping to fund Saddam Hussein in his bitter war with Iran, while the Americans were still smarting from their humiliation over the American Embassy hostage crisis (when the Iranians had taken the staff of the American Embassy in Tehran hostage and an attempted rescue mission by Special Forces had gone disastrously wrong). There were, however, 'moderates' within the Iranian government who could be convinced to soften their anti-American stance and bring their influence to bear on the Lebanese hostage-takers, if they could only be 'appeased' in some fashion. An ideal solution for the Reagan administration would be some arrangement that could take care of both the Central American and Middle Eastern problems at the same time.

This solution first came into view in August 1985, when the Israelis acted as intermediaries for a proposal to secure the release of the American hostage Reverend Benjamin Weir in return for the delivery of 508 American TOW anti-tank missiles to Iran. The missiles themselves would come from Israel, and then the

US would replenish Israeli stocks. Orchestrated by Robert McFarlane, the president's national security advisor, the transfer went ahead.

In November there was a more ambitious proposal. Iran would arrange for all the American hostages in Lebanon to be freed in return for 500 American anti-aircraft missiles. The transfer began as before, but there were problems and the deal ran into trouble. At this point the Reagan administration had already violated UN resolutions and their own Arms Export Control Act. In January, they stepped deeper into illegal territory, with a new plan whereby the Americans would sell hundreds of missiles directly to Iran in return for help freeing the hostages, and the profits from the operation would be funnelled to the Contras. Overseeing this new operation would be the new national security advisor, Admiral John Poindexter, and his aide Colonel Oliver North. How much further the operation went is hard to say, despite being the subject of much subsequent congressional investigation. It seems very likely that both Reagan and his vice-president, George Bush, knew about the operation (for instance, the 1 January 1986, entry in Reagan's personal diary states 'I agreed to sell TOWs to Iran'), but investigators eventually accepted their claims of ignorance.

With CIA help, North oversaw the channelling of money to the Contras to pay for arms, in contravention of the Boland Amendments. But it seems that even more disturbing practices became a central part of the Contra operation. Perhaps inevitably, the Contras, an armed semi-criminal militia, became involved in drug smuggling. The considerable profits from this trade helped to fund their anti-communist insurrection, while the same planes that delivered the drugs to their American markets were often used to smuggle arms back into Nicaragua. Since all this chimed with their 'higher' ideological aims, North and the CIA not only turned a blind eye to the drug smuggling, but may have begun to help, if only by protecting the drug runners and ensuring that no one interfered with their landing strips and flights. Now the Iran–Contra operation involved not just illegal arms trading to suspect customers in violation of at least two laws, but also drug-production and smuggling and the money-laundering and other aspects of organised crime that go with it.

Soon the covert operation started to become all too public. In November 1986 a Lebanese newspaper printed allegations about the hostage-for-arms deal, shortly after a plane loaded with illegal arms came down over Nicaragua. Even as North and his staff started to shred the paper trail, the clamour in Washington was becoming deafening. Reagan was forced to appoint a Commission under Senator Tower to look into the matter, and in the subsequent investigation North and Poindexter took the fall (CIA director William Casey was also forced to resign; he died of cancer shortly afterwards).

The Iran–Contra affair raised uncomfortable issues about the relationship between the executive and legislative branches of American government. Should an administration be able to finance/conduct wars as it desires? How much congressional oversight should exist? These questions are more important than ever given the current 'War on Terror', in which the 'anti-terrorist' imperative has replaced the 'anti-communist' imperative that drove the foreign policy of earlier administrations. The CIA and the military are once again engaged in a very wide range of covert operations that probably transgress US and international laws, not to mention ethics. Has Iran–Contra taught subsequent administrations that they can't get away with this, or simply shown them how to avoid getting caught?

Iran–Contra should have had more serious consequences for the Reagan administration, but in practice the key players seem not to have suffered any real damage. Reagan was merely rebuked, served out his term, and was remembered on his recent death as one of the best loved and most respected presidents of all time. In all the plaudits heaped on his name for his role in the defeat of communism, little mention was made of the tactics that he sometimes championed. Reagan's vice-president, Bush, went on to become president himself. North and Poindexter were convicted of various charges but these convictions were overturned because of immunity agreements they had made. North is now a successful radio talkshow host and journalist, and has even run for Senate. In 2002 Poindexter was able to shrug off his shady past to the extent that he was appointed head of the Information Awareness Office, a controversial programme to monitor every communication of every person in America, decried by activists as one of the greatest ever threats to civil liberties.

What about the intended aims of the Iran–Contra operation? The American hostages in the Lebanon were freed, and the Iranians doubtless used their American weapons to help them combat Saddam's American weapons. The Iran–Iraq war ground to a halt in 1988, after costing tens of thousands of lives and destabilising the entire region. The Sandinista government was finally toppled in 1990, partly thanks to the cumulative weight of American economic and military pressure. The region still suffers from chronic instability, poverty and violence and many of the drug-smuggling operations set up or sanctioned by the CIA are probably still in operation in one form or another.

3

❧

Secret Diplomacy

❧

Treaties, pacts and all the other apparatus of diplomacy feature heavily in conventional history, and generations of school-children have bemoaned the need to rote learn lists of important treaties. But not all diplomacy is conventional, and some of the most important treaties on those schoolchildren's lists were the result of shady double-dealing that contemporary kids would never have known about. This chapter looks at examples that illustrate the central role that clandestine diplomacy has played in history, from the secret treaty that helped to seal the fate of the Stuart dynasty in Britain, to the tangled web of backroom bargaining that characterised European statesmanship in the late 19th century, and which ultimately led to the destructive madness of World War I.

The Treaty of Dover – Doom of the Stuarts: 1670

The 17th century was a time of bitter religious wars in Europe as Catholic and Protestant princes clashed over territorial, political and spiritual issues. In England this blend of issues found expression in the conflict between Parliament and king.

Although ostensibly centred on the relative rights of the monarchy and the people, there was also a strong religious element – Parliament was mainly Puritan while Charles I, with a Catholic wife and High Church leanings, was perceived to have Catholic sympathies. After the fall of Cromwell's Protectorate, in 1659, and the restoration to the throne of a Stuart monarch, Charles II, these politico-religious tensions resurfaced. Charles' response, involving covert diplomacy, a secret treaty and a clandestine pledge to allow foreign troops to invade his own country, was to have dire consequences for his line and for the eventual fate of the monarchy in Britain.

Charles' relations with Parliament were sour almost from the beginning of his reign: hardly surprising, given the manifold grounds for antipathy between them. Charles never forgot that Parliament had executed his father, and shared with his predecessor a belief in the divine right of kings. Also like his father, he was constantly in need of money and resented having to go to Parliament cap in hand to get it; he resented even more their constant cavils over granting his requests. On the Parliamentary side, there was deep suspicion of the suspected Catholic sympathies of Charles and his whole family.

These suspicions were grounded in fact. Charles's mother was a devout Catholic and he had spent eight years in exile on the mainly Catholic Continent. He was married to a Catholic princess and married his sister into the French royal family. His brother James presented even more of a goad to Parliament's predominantly Puritan sensibilities. During the Interregnum, James had actually fought in the service of both France and Spain, the pre-eminent Catholic powers, and in 1669 he converted to Catholicism and was forced to resign his position as lord high admiral.

By 1670, then, Charles and Parliament disliked and distrusted one another. Disastrous wars with the Netherlands (which were, in themselves, unpopular with Parliament) had left

Charles in desperate need of money. Unwilling to make the compromises necessary to get it from his own countrymen, Charles embarked on a dangerous course and approached Louis XIV, the king of France, for help.

Under Louis, the Sun King, Catholic France had become the dominant power in Europe and a natural enemy of Protestant England. Louis was keen to better the lot of oppressed Catholics in England, and also to secure English help for his military adventures against the Netherlands. At the very least he wanted to break up the new Triple Alliance of 1668, between England, Sweden and the Netherlands, which had thwarted his earlier attack on the Dutch during the War of Devolution.

Using his sister as a secret ambassador, Charles negotiated with Louis for a considerable financial subsidy that would help to free him from dependence on Parliament. In return he would ally England to France, improve conditions for Catholics in England, and, most contentiously, secretly convert to Catholicism. The deal was struck and in 1670 Charles signed the Treaty of Dover, complete with its secret protocol. He would receive a lump sum and an annual subsidy, and Louis promised to back him up with military assistance to the tune of 6,000 French troops should Parliament rebel.

Rumours about the treaty inflamed public opinion and made Parliament nervous, and Charles was forced to offer reassurances. In a speech to MPs he told them:

> *I know you have heard much of my alliance with France; and I believe it hath been strangely represented to you, as if there were certain secret Articles of dangerous consequence; but I will make no difficulty of letting the Treaties and all the Articles of them, without any the least reserve, to be seen by a small Committee of both Houses, who may report to you the true scope of them; and I assure you, there is no other Treaty with France, either before or since, not already printed, which shall not be made known.*

Not surprisingly, observers remarked that the king seemed uneasy and fumbled with his notes. He was walking a tightrope and must have feared meeting the same fate as his father if the truth about the Dover Treaty became known.

The treaty soon had consequences, as France invaded the Netherlands in 1672 and England was forced to join in, triggering the Third Anglo–Dutch War. At home, Charles tried to fulfil his responsibilities under the treaty with his Declaration of Indulgence (1672), which annulled the penal laws against Catholics. Neither move went down well. Parliament reacted by passing the Test Act of 1673, which prevented Catholics from holding office, and the unpopularity of the Dutch War meant that Charles was forced to sack all of his leading ministers.

Instead of alleviating Catholic persecution, Charles had encouraged it, and worse was to come. Anti-Catholic hysteria boiled over in the fake Popish Plot of 1678. Two ne'er-do-well bigots, Titus Oates and Israel Tonge, falsely alleged that there was a Catholic plot to assassinate the king and place his brother on the throne. By the time the deception was revealed and the hysteria had calmed, 35 innocent Catholics had been executed and Parliament had passed further repressive measures.

In the years to come Parliament would repeatedly attempt to force the king to remove his brother from the succession, and eventually Charles dissolved Parliament and ruled on his own for the final four years of his life, dying in 1685. When James ascended the throne the country was primed against him and the Glorious Revolution eventually followed. James was deposed and William of Orange, the very prince the Treaty of Dover had forced Charles to make war on, ascended in his stead. James' Catholic son was barred from the succession and the Stuart line ended with his daughter Anne. Once in control of England, William was able to defeat Louis XIV in the War of the Grand Alliance, marking the beginning of the end of French hegemony in Europe. Charles and Louis' secret treaty had not paid off for either of them.

Secret treaties and the Louisiana Purchase: 1682–1803

In 1803 the young United States of America acquired a vast tract of land from France. The Louisiana Purchase covered an area of 828,000 square miles (2,144,520 square kilometres), stretching from the Mississippi River in the east to the Rocky Mountains in the west and from the Gulf of Mexico in the south to the future Canadian border in the north. The new territory would make up all or part of the central 15 states of the Union, doubling the size of the US and establishing it as the dominant power on the North American continent.

Every American schoolchild learns about the Louisiana Purchase in History 101. What few know is that the true story of the largest land grab in American history is one of secret treaties and desperate diplomacy, capped by the skilful skulduggery of Founding Father Thomas Jefferson.

The story begins in 1682, when French explorer Robert Cavelier, Sieur de La Salle, claimed the Mississippi basin for France and named it after his king, Louis. At this point the British colonies on the east coast were small and insignificant, and the two superpowers of Europe, Spain and France, vied for control of the new continent as they did of the old. The lands of central North America offered vast potential wealth to whichever power could control them. The Spanish already controlled much of the southwest and the west coast; now the French could claim exclusive access to a swathe of land from the Gulf to what would become Canada.

Over the next century the French developed their hold on the Louisiana territory, enlarging their base at New Orleans, which controlled the vital transport artery of the Mississippi. Their aim was to place a check on British expansionism and prevent Britain from becoming dominant in North America. Meanwhile the British colonies on the east coast were also developing, and American colonists were eager to settle land further west. The competing claims of the colonial powers came to a head in the French and Indian War (1754–63), which eventually escalated into a global conflict known as the Seven Years War.

The war went disastrously for the French and they were forced to cede the land east of the Mississippi to Britain. They were determined, however, not to let New Orleans and the western Louisiana territory fall into British hands, and negotiated a secret treaty to transfer sovereignty to Spain. The Treaty of Fontainebleau was duly signed in 1762. The French writer Voltaire lamented the loss of the territory, asking how his country could abandon 'the most beautiful climate of the earth, from which one may have tobacco, silk, indigo, a thousand useful products.'

The territory flourished under Spanish rule, with extensive plantations and the further growth of New Orleans. Meanwhile the American colonies of Britain, emboldened by their effectiveness in the French and Indian War, decided to cast off the yoke of British rule and declare independence. Spain and her colony offered help during the War of Independence, and by the end of the 18th century the geopolitical map of North America had once again been redrawn.

By 1800, the United States was firmly established and beginning to feel her strength; her citizens were casting covetous eyes westwards. But there had been changes in the Old World as well. France had once again grown powerful under Napoleon, and he was developing his own ambitions for the Louisiana territory. He envisaged an empire for France in the New World, where French control of New Orleans would secure a flood of wealth from the inland colonies and the French sphere of influence would expand across the globe, overwhelming the British Empire. Possession of the Louisiana territory was key.

Napoleon engaged in secret diplomacy with Spain, bullying her rulers into signing sovereignty of Louisiana over to France in return for creating a new kingdom in Italy for the duke of Parma, son-in-law of Charles IV of Spain. In 1800, Charles agreed to sign the Treaty of San Ildefonso, or, to give its full name: A Preliminary and Secret Treaty between the French Republic and His Catholic Majesty the King of Spain, Concerning the Aggrandizement of His Royal Highness the Infant Duke of Parma in Italy and the Retrocession of Louisiana. One of Napoleon's obligations under the treaty was that he would under no circumstances sell or cede the land to any other power.

The Americans soon discovered the secret treaty, which caused anxiety in Washington – a strong France was a less preferable neighbour to a weak Spain. In 1801, President Jefferson ordered Robert Livingston, minister to France, to explore the possibility of buying the territory. Napoleon refused, but conditions on the ground in the New World soon changed his attitude. In order to secure the new French territory he had dispatched troops via the French colony of Saint-Domingue, but a successful revolt by slaves and ex-slaves forced the soldiers to return to France. Napoleon's dream of a New World empire was over before it had begun.

Meanwhile Jefferson employed a classic intelligence ruse to convince Napoleon to sell. Supposedly confidential letters between Jefferson and Livingston were deliberately allowed to fall into the hands of French agents. When deciphered, they fuelled Napoleon's worst fears. 'The day that France takes possession of New Orleans … we must marry ourselves to the British fleet and nation,' read one of the letters. The nightmare scenario for the French was that the Americans would ally with Britain, and together they would clear France from the New World. Far better to offload an expensive and difficult to defend colony, most of which was only nominally under French control anyway, to a country that posed no threat to France, and which would counteract British interests in the region. In return Napoleon could acquire some desperately needed cash for his war with Britain.

In March 1803, after the failure of Livingston's first offer Jefferson had dispatched James Monroe as a special envoy to

Paris, but by the time he arrived in April Napoleon had already decided on the obvious course and was willing to do a deal (completely ignoring the terms of the Treaty of San Ildefonso). Monroe's instructions were to offer $10 million in return for New Orleans and some land on the Gulf of Mexico; he and Livingston were startled to find that the entire Louisiana territory was on the table.

Jefferson himself, however, may have been expecting this outcome. In January 1803, before Monroe had even been sent to France, Jefferson had asked Congress for an appropriation for what would become the Lewis and Clark Expedition – a voyage of discovery up the Mississippi and across the continent, which would lay the groundwork for American exploitation of the region. By the end of April the Louisiana Purchase had been agreed. The United States would acquire the whole territory in exchange for 80 million francs – $15 million: $11.25 million for the land and the rest as a write off of outstanding claims made by American citizens on France and Spain.

Decades of secret diplomacy and clandestine land trading had come to an end. The United States was beginning its unstoppable westward march as a new doctrine of Manifest Destiny began to take shape. Thanks to Jefferson's acumen for underhand bargaining ruses, the US had become, at a stroke, a player on the world stage. In the words of Robert Livingston, on signing the Purchase: 'From this day the United States will take their place among the powers of the first rank.' The consequences are still being felt today.

Bismarck and the secret history of German Unification: 1862–1871

Germany is one of the world's economic superpowers and played a key role in 20th-century European and world history, yet is has only existed as a country for just over 130 years.

German unification was among the most important developments in 19th-century world history, with far-reaching economic, cultural and political consequences. This seismic shift
in world geopolitics was masterminded by one man, the Iron
Chancellor, Prince Otto von Bismarck, Duke of Lauenburg. As
prime minister of Prussia his mastery of secret diplomacy and
ability to manipulate public opinion through skilful ruses
enabled him to forge a new Great Power in the space of just
eight years.

When Bismarck was appointed prime minister in 1862,
Prussia was just one of a number of German principalities and
city-states, albeit the most powerful and economically developed. At this time Bismarck was already convinced of the need
to overturn the old status quo of German geopolitics and forge
a united Germany, but to do this he would need to overcome
obstacles external and internal.

The most obvious barrier to German unification was that
several Germanic territories were under the control of other
powers, most notably Denmark, which controlled Schleswig-
Holstein, and the Austro-Hungarian Empire, which controlled
many parts of northern Germany. A broader foreign threat to
Bismarck's ambitions was the continental system of the balance of power, whereby the Great Powers kept a close eye on
one another and would form alliances to prevent any one
power getting an edge on the others (eg through conquering
more territory). The Great Powers of the time (Britain, France,
Russia, Austro-Hungary and the Ottoman Empire) preferred
to remain an exclusive club and, already troubled by the rise of
Prussian power, had no desire to see a unified Germany threat-
en the status quo.

Bismarck knew that if he wanted to attack a neighbour he
would have to take great care to first isolate the target and
make sure that no other power intervened to protect them. To
achieve this, he would need all his guile and skill in conducting
clandestine diplomacy and securing secret treaties.

He started by securing the cooperation of Austria for an attack on Denmark. The Second War of Schleswig was concluded by a peace treaty signed in Vienna in 1864, which transferred control of Schleswig and Holstein to Germany. Bismarck then turned his attention to Austria, but before an attack could be launched he first needed to make sure that none of the other Great Powers would be tempted to intervene in her favour. Britain was of peripheral concern, since she mostly followed an isolationist course, but Russia, France or Italy might cause problems.

Bismarck had already secured a valuable alliance with Russia in 1863, by helping to broker the Alvensleben Convention, an agreement to settle the revolt of the Poles against their Russian overlords. At the time, Russia was isolated in Europe as general sentiment favoured the cause of the Poles. The Russians were grateful for Prussian support and could be counted on not to oppose an attack on Austria.

In 1865, Bismarck paid a secret visit to Napoleon III, emperor of France, to sound out his likely reaction to an attack on Austria. Although he concluded no official treaty or agreement, he left with an understanding that France would not intervene so long as Italy could be allowed to absorb the Austro-Hungarian province of Venetia. Bismarck's shuttle diplomacy ended with Italy, to whom he promised Venetia in return for a mutual assistance treaty. The way was now clear for the attack on Austria, and in 1866 the Prussian army gained a swift, crushing victory over its neighbour, annexing the territories of Hanover, Hesse-Kassel, Nassau and Frankfurt to form the North German Confederation.

In fact France did object to Prussia's thrashing of Austria, and French diplomat Count Benedetti was instructed to press demands for 'compensation' from Prussia. Bismarck skilfully deflected these demands with an agreement to offer support for a French attempt to annex territory from Belgium. Benedetti drew up a draft treaty but it was never concluded and the French shelved their designs on Belgium. Bismarck, however, had secured a valuable weapon that would reappear to haunt France later.

As well as external obstacles to German unification, there were also serious barriers nearer to home. Many of the Germanic states were historically conservative and therefore protective of their sovereignty; they feared Prussianification – ie they feared that entering into a confederacy with a state as dominant as Prussia was effectively the same as being annexed. They were also serious sectarian and socio-cultural issues. The Catholic south and Protestant north distrusted each other, and rapid economic and social advances in the north served to widen the cultural gap between the two.

With most of the northern states now in confederation with Prussia, it was this southern group of states that posed the main obstacle to German unification. How could Bismarck overcome their reluctance to join the German Empire? What better than a war against a powerful common enemy? Nothing overcomes internal divisions like an external threat. German nationalism was a growing cultural movement; its ugly side was xenophobia, and Germans already felt considerable hostility towards the French, at whose hands they had suffered humiliating defeats in the Napoleonic wars at the start of the century. If Bismarck could provide a war where, crucially, France would be seen as the aggressor, the southern states might forget their suspicion of Prussia and unite with her in a surge of nationalistic fervour.

The Hohenzollern Candidature

The opportunity to do just this arose when one of Bismarck's geopolitical intrigues went awry. Following a revolution and the abdication of Queen Isabella in 1868, the Spanish throne had been vacant for two years. Among the candidates dynastically 'suitable' was Prince Leopold of the Hohenzollern family, a relative of King Wilhelm of Prussia. Behind the scenes,

Bismarck had been pushing hard to place Leopold on the vacant Spanish throne, hoping to establish a German–Spanish axis that would help to neutralise the threat from France in any future confrontations over the balance of power in Europe. Bismarck was keenly aware of Germany's vulnerable position in the heart of Europe, surrounded on all sides by potentially hostile nations. If France had to worry about her southern border it might make her think twice about military adventures in the north.

Not surprisingly the French were up in arms at the prospect of a German prince on the Spanish throne, and bitterly opposed the Hohenzollern candidature. On 6 July 1870, the French foreign minister, the Duc de Gramont, a virulent anti-Prussian, gave a rousing speech to the cabinet in which he warned that unless the matter was resolved to French satisfaction, '... we shall know and do our duty without weakness or hesitation.' Inflammatory headlines in the French newspapers whipped up public sentiment further.

On 7 July, Gramont ordered the French ambassador to Prussia Count Benedetti to go to the resort town of Bad Ems, then in Prussia, where King Wilhelm was holidaying. Benedetti was instructed to present a French demand that Wilhelm promise to secure the withdrawal of Leopold's candidature. The king's position was that, since the candidature had nothing to do with him, he could not offer any such assurance. Benedetti was sent to talk to the king a second time, on 11 July, but in the meantime Leopold, anxious to avoid being the cause of an international incident, had already withdrawn his name. The French had won a diplomatic victory. In private, Bismarck fumed – it was a slap in the face for his secret plans.

But the French now made a fatal error, in the process furnishing Bismarck with the perfect opportunity to trigger the war he needed in the fashion he needed. Benedetti was told to approach the Prussian king for a third time, this time to secure a promise that Wilhelm would never in the future support a

Hohenzollern candidate for the Spanish throne. This was over-stepping the mark, and the terse but polite encounter that ensued on 13 July was described by King Wilhelm to Heinrich Abeken, the Prussian foreign office official who accompanied him. Abeken in turn telegraphed the report to Bismarck. The fateful Ems Telegram, in its unexpurgated version, read:

> *His Majesty the King has written to me [Heinrich Abeken]: 'Count Benedetti intercepted me on the promenade and ended by demanding of me in a very importunate manner that I should authorize him to telegraph at once that I bound myself in perpetuity never again to give my consent if the Hohenzollerns renewed their candidature. I rejected this demand somewhat severely as it is neither right nor possible to undertake engagements of this kind [ie in perpe-tuity]. Naturally I told him that I had not yet received any news and since he had been better informed via Paris and Madrid than I was, he must surely see that my government was not concerned in the matter.' [The king on the advice of one of his ministers] 'decided in view of the above-men-tioned demands not to receive Count Benedetti any more, but to have him informed by an adjutant that His Majesty had now received from [Leopold] confirmation of the news which Benedetti had already had from Paris and had noth-ing further to say to the ambassador. His Majesty suggests to Your Excellency that Benedetti's new demand and its rejection might well be communicated both to our ambas-sadors and to the Press.'*

The last line of the telegraph suggests that the king authorised Bismarck to publicise the telegram, but says nothing about editing it first. This did not deter the Chancellor, who knew exactly what he was doing. On 14 July Bismarck released the following, edited version of the Ems Telegram, to the media and to foreign embassies simultaneously:

After the news of the renunciation of the Prince von Hohenzollern had been communicated to the Imperial French government by the Royal Spanish government, the French Ambassador in Ems made a further demand on His Majesty the King that he should authorize him to telegraph to Paris that His Majesty the King undertook for all time never again to give his assent should the Hohenzollerns once more take up their candidature. His Majesty the King thereupon refused to receive the Ambassador again and had the latter informed by the adjutant of the day that His Majesty had no further communication to make to the Ambassador.

The changes are subtle but all important, for the telegram now makes it seem that King Wilhelm has acted insultingly towards the French ambassador. 'The Ems Telegram should have the desired effect of waving a red cape in front of the face of the Gallic Bull,' commented Bismarck. He was right. The French Assembly and the people were thrown into a rage over this supposed slight on their honour. General Leboeuf assured the government that the French army was ready 'down to the last gaiter button'. France declared war on Germany.

A few days later, Bismarck released to the newspapers Benedetti's 1866 draft of a secret treaty spelling out French designs on Belgium, further confirming German public opinion that France was an aggressive threat. Here was the external menace that Bismarck needed to overcome internal resistance to union. Bound to Prussia through a series of secret treaties and alarmed at what they saw as unprovoked French aggression, the southern German states joined the North German Confederation. To their shock, the French found themselves fighting a united Germany, rather than a Prussia that would have to worry about its neighbours. Defeat was swift and total.

The consequences of the Franco–Prussian war were profound and far-reaching. The German Empire was unified and

Wilhelm was crowned Kaiser (Emperor) at Versailles, head-quarters of the Prussian army, on 18 January 1871. Humiliation and crushing defeat caused massive political upheaval in France. The Second Empire fell and the Republic was established in its place. Revolution broke out in the capital and the Paris Commune was declared. In the ensuing civil war between reactionary and revolutionary forces, the seeds were sown for a long conflict between left and right in France. French power in the Continental system of the balance of power was seriously undermined. An immediate consequence was that the Papal States, no longer under French protection, were subsumed by Italy, completing the process of Italian unification.

The geopolitical map of Europe was redrawn, and Germany now became the greatest power on the Continent. Her rivalry with Britain would accelerate as she became an economic superpower. A direct consequence would be the massive naval arms race that preceded World War I. Also contributing to the build up to World War I were the harsh conditions imposed on the French. Part of the peace settlement was the acquisition by Germany of the territories of Alsace and Lorraine. The response in France was the evolution of revanchism, a policy of seeking revenge (*revanche*) for the insults and territorial losses of the Franco–Prussian War. Not only did it spur the tensions that led to the Great War of 1914–18, revanchism also set the French agenda for the Treaty of Versailles that concluded that war. The harsh conditions imposed on Germany, largely at the insistence of the French, would in turn help to trigger World War II.

Thus the Ems Telegram, Bismarck's ruse to trigger war, would echo down through history as the ultimate underhand manoeuvre by one of the great masters of the art of secret diplomacy. His reward was to be appointed as the first Reichskanzler (Chancellor) of the new Empire. Having proved so adept at orchestrating wars, he was to spend the next 19 years exercising all his diplomatic skill to maintain the balance of power in Europe and prevent the outbreak of a war that would, he believed, devastate Germany.

House of Cards – Secret treaties and the Great War: 1872–1915

Secret diplomacy reached its apotheosis during the build-up to the Great War of 1914–18. From the unification of Germany until 1915 the Great Powers tangled themselves up in an inextricable net of secret treaties and undisclosed alliances, building an invisible house of cards that would come crashing down amid the terrible carnage of a world war. The people of Europe were largely ignorant of the machinations of their leaders, kept in the dark by governments that traded territories and even whole nations under the table of international diplomacy. Even as the battle lines were drawn and the troops went over the top, few realised to what extent the history of the preceding 40 years was a secret one.

By 1872, Bismarck had secured the unification of Germany and a seat for the new nation at the top table of international politics, as one of the Great Powers of the world. Having established the status quo, he was content to maintain it, and for the rest of his career his diplomacy was aimed at maintaining peace and isolating France (in diplomatic terms). Aware of the strength of anti-German feeling in France and the growing appeal of revanchism, Bismarck wanted to make sure that France did not form a power bloc with other Great Powers – crucially with Great Powers bordering Germany, which might result in the encirclement of Germany. If this was to happen and a war was to follow, Germany would find herself in the near-impossible position of fighting on two fronts.

In fact, Bismarck was keen to prevent the development of opposing power blocs in Europe altogether. Perhaps he realised that such a situation was a recipe for war. As long as the Great

Powers maintained a balance of power that involved multiple counterweights rather than a simple opposition of two camps, a major war could be averted. Achieving this would mean attempting the difficult task of remaining friends with countries opposed to each other, but one of the benefits of secret diplomacy was that it allowed a government to conclude alliances with mutually distrustful partners.

The first expression of Bismarck's new, peace-seeking foreign policy was the *Dreikaiserbund*, or Three Emperors' League, of 1873. This was an agreement between the emperors of Germany, Austria-Hungary and Russia, to maintain 'benevolent neutrality' in the event of an attack by another power (ie they would not join in with the attack and would maintain normal relations with the victim) Bismarck's goal was to prevent a Franco–Russian accord that would sandwich Germany (at this time, Russia controlled Poland and her western border was Germany).

But opposing interests in the Balkans meant that Austria and Russia were not natural allies. Both powers coveted control over Balkan territories and nations, while Russia espoused a Pan-Slavic movement that threatened the very existence of Austria-Hungary. The Three Emperor's League broke down in 1878 when Russia went to war with Turkey in the Balkans and attempted to create a large Bulgarian state from the spoils. Some of the other Great Powers, including Germany and Austria-Hungary, objected, and at the subsequent Congress of Berlin forced Russia to back down. Relations between the three emperors soured and the *Dreikaiserbund* fell apart.

Still keen to keep the Russians from getting into bed with the French, Bismarck made periodic attempts to revive the Three Emperor's League. It was renewed in secret in 1881, but with a clause precluding 'benevolent neutrality' in the event of another Russo–Turkish war. In 1885, differences between Austria and Russia over Bulgaria once again led to its breakdown. But Bismarck didn't give up. In 1887 he concluded another secret treaty with Russia, but this time without the knowledge of the Austrians. The Reinsurance Treaty once again promised 'benevolent neutrality' on either side in the event of attacks by other Great Powers. But it also contained a clause stating that benevolent neutrality did not apply in the event of war between Russia and Austria, underlining to the Russians that they should not attempt to attack Austria.

Support for Austria was the central plank of German foreign policy. Austria-Hungary was probably the most vulnerable of the Great Powers. An ageing, reactionary holdover from medieval times, the Austro-Hungarian Empire was an anachronism in an era of nation states mainly predicated on ethnic or nationalist identities. Its government was weak and inflexible and its military even more hidebound and ineffectual. Germany was well aware that if Austria-Hungary fell apart it might find unfriendly, unstable nations or even antagonistic Great Powers on its very doorstep.

Recognising this, Bismarck concluded a new alliance with Austria-Hungary as soon as the Three Emperor's League fell apart. The Dual Alliance, started in secret in 1879, committed each power to benevolent neutrality in the event of attack by a single Great Power, but to mutual aid if Russia and France joined forces against either. The Dual Alliance provided the kernel of one of the power blocs that would eventually cause and fight World War I.

In 1882 the secret Dual Alliance became the secret Triple Alliance, with the inclusion of Italy. Again, Italy was not a natural ally of Austria, and coveted the ethnically Italian Austrian territories of Trentino and Istria, which it considered to be *Italia irredenta* – 'unredeemed Italy'; territories that should have become part of Italy at unification. Yet Italy was forced into the Austro–German camp because of a row with France over Tunisia. At this time, Africa was the stage on which the imperialist ambitions of the Great Powers were being played out, as they frantically carved up the Dark

Continent into colonies and spheres of influence. Italy's burgeoning imperial ambitions were focused on North Africa,
and Tunisia in particular, but the French had occupied it first.

A furious Italy signed up to the Triple Alliance, under which
the three Powers pledged to support each other militarily in
the event of an attack against any of them by two or more great
powers, and Germany and Italy additionally undertook to support one another in the event of attack by France. However, the
Italians included a proviso that let them opt out of any war
with Britain, with whom they had no quarrel. In 1883, Romania
secretly joined the Triple Alliance, creating a solid Central
European power bloc.

In 1890 Bismarck was forced from power in Germany, usher-
ing in a new era for European power politics. Where Bismarck
had tried hard to stay friends with everyone, German policy now
became more aggressive and confrontational. The first casualty
was the alliance with Russia. The Reinsurance Treaty was
allowed to lapse and Russia was left diplomatically isolated. Into
the vacuum moved France, herself isolated for so long by
Bismarck's clever manoeuvring. French capital flowed into
Russia, helping to build, for instance, the Trans-Siberian
Railway, French military advisors helped to modernise the Tsar's
armies and diplomatic overtures led to the establishment of
friendly relations. A military alliance was concluded in 1882 and
officially, but clandestinely, ratified in 1894. The terms of the
Franco–Russian Alliance stated that each country would come
to the other's aid if a member of the Triple Alliance attacked.

For both France and Russia the attractions of this alliance
were apparent. Both had been left isolated by German diplomacy; both felt threatened by the power bloc created by the
Triple Alliance (although this was secret, their intelligence
services probably knew all about it). The result was that
Europe was now divided into two opposing camps, with dangerous implications for the likelihood of war.

Crucially, however, Britain was still in 'splendid isolation' from the Continental system of power politics, partly because she had conflicts of interest with both of the Continental power blocs. She was hostile to Germany over conflicting spheres of interest in the Middle East and Germany's plans to build the Baghdad Railway, and later over the relative sizes of their navies. But she was also hostile to Russia over interests in Central Asia and France over interests in Africa. With the turn of the century, however, things would begin to change.

In 1902 Britain and Japan concluded a secret treaty – the Anglo–Japanese Alliance – that recognised their mutual interest in containing Russian expansionism. Although this treaty was incidental to European politics, it showed that the British were now engaged in the Great Power system. She became fully engaged in 1904 with the signing of the Entente Cordiale between Britain and France. Although this was a public agreement, there were secret articles relating to Morocco, which they agreed to carve up as they deemed fit.

In 1907 the anti-Triple Alliance power bloc was completed with the conclusion of the Anglo–Russian agreement. Although this was also public and did not appear to include any military clauses, it marked the establishment of a Triple Entente that appeared to encircle Germany and her allies. The battle lines for war had effectively been drawn up. Events now accelerated towards a European conflict centred on the Balkans.

In August 1914, Germany and Turkey concluded a secret treaty, bringing together two powers who were natural enemies of Russia over interests in the Balkans and of Britain over interests in the Middle East. Germany also struck up an alliance with Bulgaria. The German-led power bloc was complete. Russia had already concluded alliances with Serbia. Most of Europe was now tied into a complex network of secret treaties and alliances, which meant that when war did come, all of the European powers were dragged in.

Unrest in the Balkans had conjured the spectre of a European war since 1908, when Austria attempted to annex

Bosnia-Hercegovina. The subsequent Italo–Turkish War and the Balkan Wars of 1912–13 had destabilised the area still further. Any one of the nations could have been the flashpoint for a wider conflict. In the event, the assassination of Archduke Franz Ferdinand triggered Austria to declare war on Serbia, and, by extension, Russia. The other members of the opposing power blocs were drawn in via their alliances, and the first global war was begun.

Even after the outbreak of war the secret diplomacy continued. Italy had only ever been a half-hearted member of the Triple Alliance. In 1902 her commitment to it had been still further watered down by a secret Franco–Italian accord on North Africa. When war came Italy backed out of her obligations under the Triple Alliance treaty on the grounds that Austria had violated it by being the aggressor against Serbia. In 1914 Italy formally issued a declaration of neutrality, but behind the scenes she was engaged in secret negotiations with both sides. The side that could offer her more won out, and in 1915 Italy signed the secret Treaty of London with the Entente Powers, which guaranteed Italy a significant chunk of Austria in any post-war settlement. Later that year she declared war on Austria-Hungary and Germany. Similar manoeuvring saw Romania swap sides as well.

Contrary to the expectations of Britain and her allies, the intervention of Italy did not significantly hasten the war and it ground on until 1918 and the intervention of the Americans. By this time it had accounted for four empires (the German, Russian, Austro-Hungarian and Ottoman Empires) and fatally hamstrung those of Britain and France. The treaties and alliances that were intended to keep the Great Powers safe eventually plunged them into a gigantic and destructive war that effectively ended European domination of the globe.

This irony was not lost on the two countries that considered themselves to be above the now discredited European system of secret deals and treacherous treaties: the United States and the new Soviet Union. In 1918 the Soviets caused a stir when they published many secret treaties from the Tsarist archives, hoping to embarrass the 'evil imperialists'. The world was presented with stark evidence of the duplicity, disregard for democratic process and cynical pursuit of imperialistic self-interest evinced by the undercover diplomacy of the Great Powers. America, and in particular her idealistic president Woodrow Wilson, was shocked at the secret wheeling and dealing.

Wilson reserved particular contempt for the cynical horse-trading of the 1915 Treaty of London – effectively the highest bid in an auction for Italy's support during the war. As it was, Britain and France refused to honour the terms of the treaty at the Versailles Conference and Italy was left resentful and hostile; hostility that would help push Italy into the Axis camp in the run up to the next war. Wilson may have hoped that the post-war settlement he brokered, based on an ethos of ethical foreign policy, would help to change the way that international diplomacy was conducted. The build-up to World War II was to prove that little had changed.

The Nazi–Soviet Non-Aggression Pact: 1939

On 17 September 1939, Nazi and Soviet forces met in central Poland. Separating the armies was an unbridgeable ideological gulf, fuelled by indoctrination to a fever pitch of hatred and bigotry. Yet the two sides met as allies, not as foes, thanks to one of history's most significant secret treaties, the Nazi–Soviet Non-Aggression Pact. Conceived in secret and hammered out behind the backs of the other European powers, the pact's secret protocol allowed for the carving up of Eastern Europe between Germany and the Soviet Union with terrible consequences that would echo around the world.

The story of this unlikely but deadly alliance begins in 1926, with the signing of the Treaty of Berlin between Germany and the young Soviet Union. Both countries felt aggrieved by the terms of the Versailles settlement that followed World War I, and both felt themselves to be pariahs of the international community – Germany as a nation blamed for starting a war in which it was disastrously defeated; the Soviet Union as a lone island of communism amid imperialist states dedicated to its destruction. It was natural for them to come together to offer a degree of mutual support.

The Treaty of Berlin built on earlier trade agreements, extending economic and trade ties to a commitment to benevolent neutrality. Although it was not secret, a number of clandestine activities were authorised under its auspices. In return for technological aid, the Soviets provided secret training facilities for the German military, allowing them to train their forces and test new weapons in contravention of the Versailles Treaty. Out of sight of watchful Allied powers still suspicious of Germany, the Reichswehr experimented with new tank designs, poison gas and new airplane designs at secret locations in Russia. The German Army helped to train the Red Army in tactics, training and technology.

The rise to power of National Socialism, with its violent anti-Bolshevik creed, was an obvious blow to this 'special relationship', but the Soviet Union went to extreme lengths to ignore Nazi provocation and maintain German–Soviet links. As late as 1934 the Chairman of the Council of Commissars, Vyacheslav Molotov, insisted that the Soviet Union wanted 'to continue good relations with Germany ... one of the great nations of the modern epoch'. Soviet efforts were to no avail and the contacts between the states were broken off in 1934.

Over the next few years, as fascist aggression destabilised Europe and raised the spectre of another war, while at the same time Japanese militarism threatened the eastern border, the Soviet Union grew increasingly fearful on all sides. Stalin had little doubt that a new European war would come, warning of it as early as 1934; the issue for the Soviets was not which side to take but how to survive. As communists, they were indifferent to the fate of the imperialist powers or the details of how they would carve up the world. All that mattered was protecting the Soviet Union against isolation and encirclement, and staving off involvement in a war long enough for the industrialisation and strengthening of the Soviet state. The Soviet Union would take an entirely pragmatic course in pursuing foreign policy, ignoring contradictions or inconsistencies. This was the logic that would underlie the bizarre incongruity of the Nazi–Soviet Pact.

The first evidence of this logic was the adoption of a foreign policy of collective security, where the threat of collective intervention by other powers would deter any single state from aggression. This meant taking a seat in the League of Nations, previously dismissed by Lenin as 'the robbers' league'. Maxim Litvinov, an old-school diplomat with whom the West could do business, was appointed as the new Commissar for Foreign Relations. He quickly signed a series of non-aggression pacts with countries from Finland to France, and worked to strengthen US–Soviet relations as a foil to the growing threat from Japan.

As the events of the 1930s unfolded, however, the idea of collective security was exposed as a sham. Failure to intervene in the Spanish Civil War, to prevent a Fascist victory, was compounded by the policy of appeasement pursued by Britain and France towards the increasingly belligerent Germany and Italy. It seemed clear to Stalin that he could not rely on Western help to combat the Nazi or Japanese menace, and that the Soviet Union would be left to her fate by imperialist powers eager to see her destroyed. The Soviet position became even more precarious when the Axis powers concluded the Anti-Comintern Pact.

Within this context it made sense to attempt rapprochement with Germany, and during 1936 and 1937 the Soviets explored ways to improve relations with the Nazis; Litvinov insisted, to a French reporter, that cooperation with the

Germans was 'perfectly possible'. Soviet fears of isolation were further stoked by her exclusion from the Munich Conference in 1938, which provided the strongest evidence yet that the Western powers would do nothing to stop the Nazis.

But in 1938 the position changed abruptly and the Soviet Union found herself courted on all sides. Britain and France were floating the idea of reviving the old Triple Alliance that had encircled Germany in 1914, and made approaches to the Soviet Union accordingly. The German intelligence services brought word of this to Hitler, who was anxious to prevent the encirclement and drive a wedge between the potential allies. Overtures and negotiations from both sides went on into 1939; for the Soviets, it was a question of who could offer the most.

Britain and France, while not, perhaps, as ideologically repugnant as the Nazis, had little or nothing to offer. In practice a new triple alliance seemed likely to drag the Soviet Union into a war with Germany while the Allies looked on. Germany, on the other hand, could offer the economic benefits of the old Berlin Treaty, a guarantee to keep the Soviets out of an imperialist war and an accommodation over Poland, Russia's hated neighbour.

During April and May of 1939 Britain dithered over whether to try to pursue an alliance with the Soviets. When they finally decided to do so they sent only a low level mission to negotiate. Meanwhile Stalin had replaced Litvinov as Commissar for Foreign Relations with Molotov, more of a hard-nosed pragmatist, and the Nazis had started to change their tune with regards to the Soviet Union. Hitler's speeches no longer included attacks on the Bolshevik menace and German newspapers were instructed to tone down their anti-Soviet rhetoric. Goering confided to the Italian Foreign Minister that the Nazis were going to try a *'petit jeu'* with the Soviets.

In mid-May secret talks between Nazi and Soviet officials began, but they were limited to trade. Hitler, however, was impatient to procure an agreement with the Soviets in time to allow his carefully timed plans for the invasion of Poland to proceed. In public, the Soviets continued to talk to the British and French legations in Leningrad, but the talks finally broke down in August when the Western powers revealed their military weakness and their refusal to commit to full military involvement with the Soviets. The British and French and their allies even refused to agree to concede right of passage to Soviet forces in the event of a war. The Soviet generals were exasperated. 'Are we supposed to beg for the right to fight our common enemy?' complained Voroshilov, the leader of the Soviet delegates.

By the time the talks with the British and French ended in failure on 21 August, secret discussions with the Germans were far advanced. On 2 August, the German foreign minister von Ribbentrop made a pointed comment to a Soviet trade delegate, saying that German and Soviet interests could be harmonised 'from the Black Sea to the Baltic'. On 5 August, the Nazis first suggested that a secret protocol could be arranged. Germany and the Soviet Union would carve up Eastern Europe, with the Soviets to get eastern Poland, parts of Romania, the Baltic States and Finland.

Hitler was increasingly desperate to come to an accommodation. A draft treaty was exchanged on 17 August and on the 19th a trade agreement was concluded. Further discussions were scheduled for near the end of August, but Hitler took the unusual step of writing directly to Stalin to urge him to accept high-level talks in Moscow as soon as possible. According to Albert Speer he even considered going to Moscow himself. On the 23 August Ribbentrop arrived in Moscow and met Stalin. Following a phone call to Hitler, he agreed to virtually all the Soviet demands, and the next morning the Nazi–Soviet Non-Aggression Pact was signed, complete with its secret protocol giving the Soviets a sphere of influence in Eastern Europe from the Arctic to the Caspian. From the Soviet point of view the advantages of the pact were obvious. They had secured non-involvement in an imperialist war and gained territory and technological and economic assistance.

The impact of the pact was almost immediate. Hitler was now confident that he could invade Poland without fearing the consequences. Not only could he now be sure that the Soviets would not interfere, he also calculated that Britain and France, having got wind of the Pact, would back down as they had at Munich. On 1 September 1939, the Germans invaded Poland. The Soviets followed suit on 17 September, occupying the east and meeting Nazi forces in central Poland. The partition of Poland was formally ratified by the two conquering nations on the 28 September.

But the uneasy marriage of convenience could not last. Hitler had underestimated British resolve; the invasion of Poland had triggered a second world war. As that war reached an edgy stalemate in the west, Hitler turned his eyes eastwards. The secret pact that had allowed him to trigger World War II would prove to be no barrier to the most destructive campaign of all time – Operation Barbarossa and the invasion of Russia.

4

Ruses and Deception

War is one of the key determinants of history. War is the crux point of conflict between nations or the clash of civilisations. The victor shapes history. In a traditional view, war is one of the most straightforward, least devious endeavours; the epitome of honest virtues like courage, toil and determination. Soldiers and generals face one another and fight it out until one side is defeated. What could be more candid, less murky? In fact secrecy, deception and ruse are central to the art of war. More than two thousand years ago the Chinese sage Sun Tzu, the first and possibly greatest philosopher of war, stated that 'all warfare is based on deception'. The key elements in a conflict often revolve around clandestine or underhand practice, and instances of the use of ruse or deception have helped to decide some of the most important conflicts in history. Cunning practitioners have used deception to settle a conflict without having to draw a sword or fire a bullet. Even more cunning ones have practiced deception to start conflicts.

This chapter looks at ruses great and small, showing how the art of deception has shaped history in all its guises. A small deception, like that used in the conquest of Monaco, has

helped to shape the destiny of a small nation. Great deceptions, like those used to deceive Hitler in the build-up to D-
Day, and copied 40 years later in the first Gulf War, have
shaped the outcome of great endeavours. And deception is
very much at work in the modern world, as suggested by
recent controversies over the role of Iranian intelligence in the
decision to invade Iraq.

The Trojan Horse: c1200 BCE

The wooden horse of Troy has entered the popular imagination as one of the best known and most recognisable of classical symbols. It can also be seen as the *locus classicus* of the military ruse – the cunning stratagem used to deceive the enemy
and turn the course of a battle or war. While the tale of Troy
and the wooden horse may be entirely mythical, the story illustrates the important role played by ruse and deception in
ancient Greek warfare, particularly when set alongside other
incidents from Greek myth and literature, such as the tricks of
Odysseus, or the cross-dressing of Achilles (who posed as a
woman in order to avoid being recruited for the raid on Troy).
It is also instructive to look at the details of the tale of the
wooden horse, in particular the important role played by
Sinon, a classic example of a plant – an agent employed to
spread false or misdirecting information.

Most readers will know the basic outline of the story of the
wooden horse, and many may wonder how the Trojans could
have been so foolish as to fall for the ploy. But the details of the
tale show that the Greeks used a series of ploys that built up
into an elaborate ruse convincing enough to overcome the natural caution of the Trojans.

According to the story of the wooden horse, known from
many classical sources (though not from Homer's *Iliad*, which
does not cover the fall of Troy), the siege of Troy lasted for ten
long years. The Greeks had been mostly victorious in battle,

but could not breach the high walls of Troy and finally reduce the city. Exasperated, they decided that they would need a ruse to break the deadlock. Credit for the wooden horse scheme is variously attributed to either Odysseus, the king of Ithaca, a man noted for his cunning and guile, or a Trojan seer named Helenus, said to have been a deserter or captive. It was decided that they would pretend to sail home leaving behind a great wooden effigy, within which would be hidden their finest warriors – the ancient equivalent of an elite special forces unit.

Epeius the architect was instructed to build the giant structure, while a cover story was devised to explain its presence and fool the Trojans to bring it into the city. Earlier in the conflict the Greeks had raided a Trojan temple and carried off the Palladium, a giant statue sacred to the goddess Athena, said to have fallen directly from heaven and to have been given to the Trojans as a protective talisman. The rationale for the horse, the Greeks decided, was as an offering to Athena to placate her anger at the profanation of the Palladium and allow the weary warriors safe passage on their voyage home. Not only would this explain its construction, but it would encourage the Trojans to think about taking it into Troy, as a sort of replacement for the Palladium. According to Apollodorus, an inscription was duly engraved on the side of the horse: 'For their return home, the Greeks dedicate this thank-offering to Athena.'

To back up the story still further, it was decided to leave a man behind; a plant, who could feed disinformation to the Trojans and pass on the story that the Greeks wanted. Such a task would be extremely dangerous, as the Trojans were bound to suspect the man of being a spy. The man that was chosen was Sinon, said to be a cousin of Odysseus in some versions of the story.

For three days the Trojans witnessed strange goings on from their vantage on the high walls. There was much activity in the Greek camp, with hammering and sawing. Something strange was taking shape. Then, one morning, the Trojans awoke to discover that the Greeks had burned their tents, boarded their ships and left. The Greek camp was empty, their beachhead deserted. All that was left was a great wooden horse. It was as large as a ship, fashioned in timber from the slopes of Mount Ida. It had a mane spangled with gold and fringed with purple, blood-red amethysts ringed with green beryls for eyes, rows of white teeth in its jaws, pricked ears, a flowing tail that reached down to its heels, hooves of bronze, straps decorated with purple flowers, a bridle of ivory and bronze and a wheel under each hoof. Unbeknown to the Trojans, it also had a hollow belly, an opening in one side and air-passages concealed within the mouth. Lurking within, with all their armour and weapons, were the flower of Greek manhood, led by Odysseus himself.

When the Trojans rode out to view this marvel they also discovered Sinon. According to some sources he was tied to a stake by the horse; others say he was captured lurking nearby. Accounts of his interrogation by the Trojans also differ. In some versions he is horribly tortured but sticks to his story. In others he spins a web of lies that snares gullible King Priam of Troy into buying his tale. Much like a modern agent, Sinon was equipped with a cover story to give him credibility – he was said either to have been left as a sacrifice alongside the horse or to have escaped from the Greek camp after a falling out with Odysseus. In some versions he even bears self-inflicted wounds attesting to his veracity.

Sinon's lies were so effective at misdirecting the Trojans that they even discounted warnings from their own 'counterintelligence services' – the priest Laocoon and the prophetess Cassandra – although this was mainly down to divine intervention. Laocoon denounced Sinon as a fraud and the horse as a trick, famously declaring '*timeo Danaos et dona ferentes*' (literally, 'I fear the Greeks even when they are bringing gifts'). He even threw a spear against it to back up his words. In return, the gods caused two huge serpents to emerge from the sea and devour the unfortunate whistleblower and his sons. Suitably impressed, the Trojans decided that such an unlucky man could not have been right. Cassandra, meanwhile, warned the Trojans exactly what was afoot, telling them that Greek warriors lurked within. Unfortunately a divine curse meant that while her prophecies were inevitably accurate, no one would heed them.

Believing that the wooden horse would bring them luck and act as a substitute guardian for their city, the Trojans dragged the giant construction through their mighty gates and set it next to the shrine of Athena and the palace of Priam. In some versions, Helen, the cause of the Trojan War, then tried a ruse of her own. Circling the horse, she called out the names of the leading Greek commanders, but imitating the voices of their wives. She was such a good mimic that one commander nearly answered, but was stifled by Odysseus with such vigour that he suffocated!

Still all unawares, the Trojans set about celebrating their apparent good fortune. They feasted and drank and had orgies until most were insensible. When the revelry had died down and the city was quiet, Sinon initiated the Greek covert operation. He let the 'special forces' warriors out of the horse and proceeded to the battlements to wave a lighted brand, the prearranged signal to the Greek fleet, which was hiding off shore behind the Isle of Tenedos. While the infiltrated Greek special forces opened the gates of Troy and set about murdering the guards, the fleet sailed back to the beach and discharged the armies, who quickly joined in the brutal sack of the city. The ruse had succeeded and resulted in widespread murder, rape and pillage. The great city was burned to the ground and few survived.

According to related mythology, one consequence of the wooden horse deception was to be the founding of Rome. One of the founding myths of Rome held that the young Trojan prince Aeneas escaped the sack of Troy and, with the remnants of his shattered people, found sanctuary in Central Italy. There he founded the state that would become a mighty empire and one day conquer Greece. Rome is not the only city that traces its antecedents to Troy – according to Geoffrey of Monmouth's 12th century *History of the Kings of Britain* London was founded by a Trojan refugee named Brutus, from whose name comes 'Britain'. London's original name, supposedly, was *Troia Newydd* or New Troy.

Putting mythology aside, might there have been historical consequences to the wooden horse ruse? Despite Heinrich Schliemann's well known 19th-century 'discovery' of Troy at a site in the Dardanelles, most scholars doubt that a single city analogous to Homer's Troy ever really existed. It is more likely that the *Iliad* is a conflation of various stories from Bronze Age Greece and represents a combination of memories of historical war raids by the Myceneans, the dominant Greek civilisation of the time. If the *Iliad* and the related tales are based on historical fact, however, the Trojan Horse ruse can be seen as a potential turning point in a conflict of civilisations. This masterstroke of deception could represent the moment when Bronze Age Greece became the pre-eminent culture in the Eastern Mediterranean, and not the Asiatic power of Troy. Would the later history of Greece, with all its consequences for subsequent history, have been the same if Troy had never fallen?

The conquest of Monaco: 1297

Today Monaco is a byword for luxury and the cosmopolitan rich; a millionaire's playground of gambling, super-yachts and Formula One. It owes much of its current success to the foresight and astute leadership of the ruling Grimaldi family. Nowadays the Grimaldis are better known for the extended royal soap opera they seem to enact, from the fairytale marriage of Prince Rainier III and Grace Kelly, to the tragic death of Princess Grace, to the tabloid-friendly antics of Princess Stephanie. But they owe their hegemony of this tiny Mediterranean kingdom to the wiliness of a 13th-century ancestor, who stormed the impenetrable fortress of medieval

Monaco with a handful of men, thanks to a ruse that would not look out of place in a Robin Hood film.

In the 13th century the Côte d'Azur was the stage for an epic conflict between warring clans of Genoese noblemen. Genoa, a northern Italian city-state, was at the height of its power as a mercantile and naval empire. Genoan merchants, bankers and sailors controlled the fortunes of kings and queens, emperors and crusaders. Their mercantile empire stretched from Britain to the Black Sea and their dominion over the waves was such that the Mediterranean was known as 'the Genoese Lake'. Within the city-state, however, a power struggle raged between powerful clans which split into two parties – the Guelphs and the Ghibellines – whose rivalry reflected wider geo-political struggles between the papacy and the Holy Roman Empire. In the Guelph camp was the Grimaldi family, once rulers of Genoa but by the 1270s forced into exile.

The Grimaldis, with their fleet and small army, sought refuge on the coast of Provence, from where they plotted their revenge and harassed the sea lanes. Their security rested on gaining access to and control over strategic fortified ports such as the rock of Monaco. Monaco was an ancient port town, first settled in prehistoric times and later renowned for its Roman temple to Hercules. In 1215 the Genoese Ghibellines, supporters of the Holy Roman Emperor and enemies of the Grimaldis, constructed a sturdy fortress to control the harbour from atop a mighty crag of rock. Situated on the border between Provence and Genoa, Monaco attained great strategic importance.

Eager to gain a fortified foothold on the Provencal coast and a secure base for their operations, the Grimaldis cast covetous eyes at Monaco. The strong fortifications and elevated position of the fortress meant that a frontal assault would be difficult if not impossible, particularly with the small forces under Grimaldi command. A senior scion of the family, Francois Grimaldi, known as *Il Malizia*, The Cunning, hatched a daring plan. On the night of 8 January 1297, Francois and a troop of soldiers approached the gates of the fortress disguised as Franciscan monks, their swords concealed beneath their heavy robes.

Assuming that the callers were innocent itinerant monks, the guards opened the doors and let them in. As soon as he was within the gates Francois threw off his robes and brandished his sword; his men followed suit, forcing the defenders back from the doors. At this, the main party of Guelph troops who had been hiding in the shadows leapt forth and stormed through the open gates, overpowering the guards and taking the fortress with minimal casualties. Grimaldi was master of Monaco, a position that his family has continued to occupy, with brief interludes, ever since. Subsequent Grimaldis increased the size of Monaco, though it remains the second smallest country in the world, after the Vatican City, and safeguarded its independence (under their rule) through careful dealings with the surrounding states. By the 19th century the principality was languishing in economic misery, but clever Grimaldis took advantage of its independent status to make it a centre for gambling and casinos and later for rich tax exiles and high society types. Today Monaco is one of the richest nations in the world on a per capita basis, with a flourishing economy and the highest population density of any country in the world.

The artful ruse that secured Monaco for the Grimaldis is today commemorated in the ruling family's coat of arms, which is supported by the figures of two monks bearing swords, and by the Grimaldi motto *Deo Juvante*: 'With God's help.'

The father of modern magic and the Algerian rebellion that never was: 1856

The land-grabbing of the colonial era often led to vicious revolutions, rebellions and insurrections of the native peoples against the occupying imperial powers. These conflicts were generally characterised by shocking violence, brutal suppression, appalling injustice and a terrible cost in lives and livelihoods. In one notable case, however, the clever use of deception and illusion by a master of these arts helped to defuse a rebellion before it could begin, in the remarkable story of Robert-Houdin's magical duel with the Marabouts.

Among the most prized and hard-won jewels in the French imperial crown was Algeria. The French conquest had begun in 1830 but the country was not properly subdued until the 1840s. By the 1850s, trouble was brewing once again. A religious sect known as the Marabouts were stirring up the population, using their powers of 'magic' to incite fear and respect. The Marabouts employed conjuring tricks of the sort well known to illusionists and sideshow artists today, such as eating glass without suffering injury or healing wounds by laying on hands. Under their leader Zoras al Khatim they were enthralling increasing numbers of Algerians, who would respond to their call to arms.

Rather than launching an expensive and bloody military response that would simply escalate matters, the French decided to play the Marabouts at their own game. Emperor Napoleon III commissioned Jean-Eugène Robert-Houdin, the greatest magician of his age, to travel to Algeria and engage in magical combat with the Marabouts – or at least to impress the natives with a display that would put the indigenous wizards in the shade.

Robert-Houdin is a seminal figure in the history of magic. His influence was such that he is now accorded the moniker 'The Father of Modern Magic'. Born in 1805 (as plain Jean-Eugène Robert – he acquired the Houdin from his wife) to a clockmaker, young Jean-Eugène followed in his father's footsteps and became an expert manipulator of mechanisms. At the same time he nurtured an interest in magic, conjuring and illusionism, finally giving up his trade at the age of forty to become a full-time performer. As a magician he was noted for making magic respectable, taking it off the streets and out of the travelling fairs and onto the theatre stage. He dressed in black tie rather than outlandish robes and despite performing for only a decade, devised many new tricks using technologies old and modern. His expertise with clockwork led him to build ingenious automata, while a keen interest in science meant that he was able to develop tricks based on new technologies such as electromagnetism. He would need his full arsenal of tricks and devices to head off the incipient Algerian revolution.

In 1856 Robert-Houdin arrived in Algiers and was booked into a local theatre. Extensive PR by the French authorities ensured that all the most influential natives would attend, along with as many of the common people as could fit into the overcrowded auditorium, all eager to see the great French magus. Robert-Houdin had carefully planned his act to include a series of tricks that would play on the imagination of any Algerians who were contemplating insurrection. In his own account of the Algerian expedition he described how he began with the standard materialisation of coins from an empty hand, but quickly moved on to producing a cannon ball from a top hat. He then played a variant of one of his signature tricks, the inexhaustible bottle – but with an inexhaustible bowl of sweetmeats, considered more appropriate for a teeto-tal Muslim audience. In another trick he called one of the rebel leaders on stage and made his shadow bleed.

But his piece de resistance was a trick he called 'the Light and Heavy Chest'. Inviting the strongest man in the audience on to the stage, Robert-Houdin asked him to lift a wooden box small enough for the weakest man to shift. He then claimed to have hypnotised the man, and instructed him to try again. To his horror, the strong man found that he could not budge the box, and was even forced to let go with a startled yell. According to Robert-Houdin, he fled the theatre in panic. The key to this trick was the little-known phenomenon of electro-magnetism. The wooden chest had a metal plate concealed in the base. At a signal from Robert-Houdin, a switch was flicked and an electromagnet below the stage was activated, causing the box to remain locked in place. As an additional touch, Robert-Houdin had electrified the brass handles of the box so that the victim could be given a shock.

Similar tricks amazed and astounded the audience as intended, and by the end of his run Robert-Houdin had attracted the attentions of a powerful local sheikh, Bou Allem ben Shenfa Bash Aga, who invited him to give a special performance. The Frenchman's success had already helped to dampen enthusiasm for a revolt, but he would still need to impress Sheikh Bou Allem and deflect the barbs of the Sheikh's antagonistic Marabout.

Robert-Houdin entertained the Sheikh and his minions with sleight-of-hand, but was accused of being a fraud by the Marabout. More sleight-of-hand and the earlier palming of the Marabout's watch allowed Robert-Houdin to make it look as if he had teleported a coin into his clothing and magically removed his timepiece. The indignant Marabout was humiliated and called the Frenchman out in a duel, claiming the right to fire first. Robert-Houdin agreed, but bought himself a little time to prepare by claiming that he needed to return to Algiers to reclaim a magical talisman.

The next morning the duel proceeded. The Marabout fired first, but was appalled to see Robert-Houdin apparently catch the bullet between his teeth. When it was the magician's turn to fire, he aimed his shot at a wall, which seemed to ooze blood. He had contrived to switch the real bullets for fake ones of his own devising.

The illusions succeeded, and the threat of an Algerian rebellion receded. The Marabouts found that their authority weakened in the face of the patently superior magic wielded by the colonial occupiers. Robert-Houdin was presented with an ornate scroll in recognition of his services in bloodlessly defusing a possible revolution. He returned to retirement and penned his memoirs, which subsequently inspired a new generation of conjurors, including an American-Hungarian named Erich Weiss, who later took the stage name Houdini to honour his hero.

Instead of contending with a rebellion, the French were able to strengthen their rule in Algeria, and eventually part of it became a Metropolitan district of France. The 'mother country' would not relinquish its grip on Algeria until the prolonged and bloody struggles of the post-war conflict.

The Luftwaffe's 'Potemkin village' ruse: 1936

Hitler himself described his reoccupation of the Rhineland, an area demilitarised under the Versailles Treaty of 1919, as the first and greatest risk that he took in the re-establishment of German military power and territorial stature, one of the key contributory processes in the build-up to World War II. Yet the German military of the time was as weak as a kitten and Hitler later admitted that the slightest hint of French reaction to the audacious move would have scuppered his plans. As part of the effort to discourage French intervention the German airforce, the Luftwaffe, resorted to a classic tactical deception, of the kind known as a *Potemkinsche Dörfer*, or 'Potemkin village', ruse.

The term 'Potemkin village' derives from the alleged activities of the Russian nobleman Prince Grigory Aleksandrovich Potemkin, a leading figure at the 18th-century court of Catherine the Great. Potemkin, a former lover of Catherine's, remained a favourite and was rewarded with a series of posts, culminating in his appointment as governor-general of 'New Russia', an area that included the recently annexed but desperately backwards Crimea. Potemkin was determined to make his tatty new realm a showpiece that would impress both his mistress and the assembled ambassadors of Europe's leading nations, improving Russia's standing in the courts of Europe and boosting his own stock with Catherine.

In 1787 Catherine began a grand tour of the region, mainly travelling by boat along the River Dnieper. Popular myth, probably initiated by the Saxon envoy to Russia, Georg von Helbig, an enemy of Potemkin, holds that the prince constructed entire fake villages out of pasteboard, displayed them on the banks of the river for the edification of the travelling imperial party, and then dismantled them and hurried them downstream to be erected again. In this fashion, it was alleged, Potemkin endeavoured to conceal the real poverty of the region and make it seem more prosperous and developed. In practice this story is almost certainly untrue, but the term *Potemkinsche Dörfer*, or Potemkin village, has come to mean a sham or hollow deception of this kind.

The Potemkin village type ruse has been employed by commanders in many different wars to help an inferior force create the impression of a more substantial one. A particularly notable example was the defence of the York-James peninsula by the Confederate general 'Prince' John Magruder. Magruder was known for his love of theatricals, but the task of holding off 120,000 Union soldiers with a force of just 8,000 men would call for a performance of rare wit. One of the deceptions Magruder mounted was to march a battalion along the defensive line in front of the Union force, keeping it under cover except where it passed through a small clearing in the woods, through which the marching soldiers would be clearly visible to their enemy. Magruder had the single battalion circle around the clearing for the entire day so that to the Union onlookers it seemed as if a constant train of soldiers was passing by, indicating a force of considerable size. The Union general McClellan was so taken in by this and other tricks that he delayed his attack for a month, giving the Confederates time to withdraw without losing a man.

In 1936 the German military was forced to rely on such devices to conceal its weakness, particularly when attempting something as potentially explosive as the remilitarisation of the

Rhineland. Both the emasculation of the German military and the demilitarisation of the Rhineland were terms of the Versailles Treaty devised by the vengeful Allies after World War I, aimed at shackling the German threat and preventing it from raising its head once more. These moves were led by the French, long the natural enemies of Germany in the European balance of power, who saw the Rhineland area as an essential buffer between the two countries. But the harsh terms of the Versailles settlement fostered bitterness and resentment in Germany, and a revisionist urge to roll back the insults of the treaty lent impetus to the rise of Hitler and his nationalist party. A key element in the nationalist agenda was the reclamation of Germany's former borders, and this included the military reoccupation of the Rhineland, despite what seemed to Hitler like the very real risk of a violent French reaction that might humiliate the resurgent nation and topple him from power.

The Rhineland reoccupation was probably in Hitler's mind for some time, but he was emboldened by the feeble response of the British and French to Italian transgressions in Africa in 1936 (ie the invasion of Ethiopia). On 7 March he ordered his troops to cross the Rhine, but he was terrified of what would happen if the French responded with force. The German detachment was feeble; as he later told Speer, 'If the French had taken any action we would have been easily defeated; our resistance would have been over in a few days.'

The weakest link in the German military was the Luftwaffe. Only two squadrons of aircraft could be mobilised, and only ten of the planes were armed. If the French got wind of the vulnerability of the German expeditionary force, they might overcome their political inertia and send in the troops. Deception was vital. The Luftwaffe resorted to the Potemkin village ruse to fool the chief of the French air force, who was touring the airfields. As he progressed from one airfield to the next, the few aircraft available went on ahead in secret, changing their markings each time and giving the impression that the Luftwaffe was much better equipped than it really was.

How much of a role this information played in French calculations is impossible to say, but it is true that the French did not have the appetite for the military risks that a counterattack would bring. Thanks, perhaps, to the Potemkin village ruse, they did not realise just how slight those risks actually were. Instead of marching their own forces into the Rhineland, which would have led to a speedy withdrawal by the Germans and sent Hitler scuttling back to Berlin with his tail between his legs, the French acquiesced to the new state of affairs.

In strategic terms, the reoccupation of the Rhineland was significant. The Germans were able to build a fortification line opposite France's Maginot Line, securing Germany's border with France and allowing Hitler to turn his attention to central Europe. Perhaps more significant was the effect on Hitler's thinking. According to Richard Overy's *The Road to War*: 'The Rhineland coup was a turning point. From 1936 Hitler began to take foreign policy more into his own hands. Success in the Rhineland fed his distorted belief that he had a pact with destiny. The bloodless victories fuelled nationalist enthusiasm and eroded the tactics of restraint.'

The Rhine was Hitler's Rubicon. Once he had crossed it his territorial ambitions escalated. His greed for land and his belief that the Allies would pursue a policy of appeasement would eventually lead to war.

The Battle of the River Plate: 1939

Deception, ruse and trickery have been an integral part of naval warfare since at least the great age of sail of the late 18th century. Ships routinely sent false signals, flew false colours, disguised themselves, feigned injury or otherwise practised to deceive. But naval commanders also followed strict rules of conduct – a ship's true colours, for instance, were always hoisted just before battle was joined. The Battle of the River Plate, in December 1939, illustrated both of these traditions. The British navy used a classic bluff to help win the first major naval battle of World War II, in the process convincing a German captain to scuttle his own ship in the face of inferior forces that he could easily have eluded or destroyed, before his own sense of honour sent him to a tragic end.

In the early months of World War II, the German navy seemed to have the upper hand. U-boats sank thousands of tons of Allied shipping, while an even greater threat was posed by the pocket battleship *Admiral Graf Spee*. Forbidden from building 'proper' battleships under the terms of the Treaty of Versailles, the Germans had produced an innovative and fearsome new type of ship – a heavy cruiser or pocket battleship. Faster than a full size battleship, this new ship had the firepower, range and armour of a much larger vessel, and was more than a match for British destroyers or cruisers of the time.

In three months of cruising in the Atlantic the *Graf Spee* had already sunk nine ships, totalling 50,000 tons, and threatened vital Allied shipping lines that affected theatres of operation from Egypt to Singapore. No less than nine Allied hunting groups were detailed to search for her, drawing ships from other areas. It was Hunting Group G, under Commodore Harwood, that finally tracked her down in the bay off the mouth of the River Plate, between Uruguay and Argentina, on 13 December 1939. Although there were three ships in his squadron, the *Exeter*, *Ajax* and *Achilles*, Harwood was outgunned – the *Graf Spee* could simply keep out of range of the smaller ships while pounding them with her heavy guns.

Disregarding orders, Captain Langsdorff of the *Graf Spee* decided to engage the enemy ships, and a fierce battle followed. The *Exeter* was badly mauled, with one gun turret destroyed, a direct hit to the bridge and the deck in flames, and had to retire from the battle. Both of the other Royal Navy ships also took hits, but Harwood's squadron had done enough damage to the

Graf Spee to convince Langsdorff that he needed to run for a neutral port, where he could repair the damage before attempting to break through the squadron and escape. On the morning of 14 December, the German ship headed for the Uruguayan port of Montevideo, with the two remaining Royal Navy ships shadowing her every move and taking up station in the estuary of the River Plate, patrolling back and forth to make sure their prey did not slip out unobserved. Harwood signalled for reinforcements to arrive as soon as humanly possible.

The British naval attaché in Montevideo was surprised to find the powerful German ship moored on his patch, but the world's media soon descended on the scene to broadcast every move to a fascinated world. This was the first major naval engagement of the war; in some ways it was the first time that the British and the Germans had been properly pitched against one another. Both sides had much to gain or lose in terms of prestige and morale.

Thinking that he was preventing the Germans from gaining any advantage, the British attaché, Henry McCall, asked the Uruguayans to invoke the rules applying to an undamaged ship in a neutral port: it would have 24 hours to leave or the crew would be interned. McCall soon realised his mistake – a short conversation with Commodore Harwood left him in no doubt that the two Royal Navy ships would be no match for the *Graf Spee* should Langsdorff decide to attempt a break out. It was vital to keep her in port as long as possible to give time for reinforcements to come up, but the nearest ships that could pose a threat to the pocket battleship were over 2,000 miles away. The only ship that could reach them in time was the light cruiser *Cumberland*, a ship too small to worry the *Graf Spee*. Somehow the British needed to convince the Germans, and especially Captain Langsdorff, that a much larger force was waiting for him, while keeping him in port for a period long enough to make the deception plausible. A combination of 'psy-ops' (ie propaganda) and diplomatic manoeuvring would be necessary.

To keep the *Graf Spee* in port, McCall made clever use of the Hague Convention governing the use of neutral ports in wartime. Under these rules, a warship had to give a departing enemy merchant ship 24 hours grace; ie if a British freighter left Montevideo, the *Graf Spee* would be bound to wait for 24 hours before sailing. Langsdorff was a sailor in the traditional mould, with little enthusiasm for the Nazis, and could be counted upon to do the honourable thing. McCall arranged for a series of British merchant ships to leave at intervals of a day, and the *Graf Spee* was duly immobilised.

Meanwhile the Admiralty launched a campaign of deception, masterminded by Winston Churchill, at this point still First Lord. Stories were planted in the British and neutral press claiming that the waiting British squadron included the *Renown*, a battleship, the *Ark Royal*, an aircraft carrier, and their associated escorts. The front-page of the *New York Times* carried headlines about a 'reinforced allied fleet'. Rumours planted in waterfront bars and diplomatic circles circulated the story that the *Renown* and *Ark Royal* had just refuelled in Rio de Janeiro, and the tale was backed up by ordering extra fuel from an Argentine naval base. Argentine newspapers, considered friendly to the Germans, quoted 'reliable sources' to the effect that 'more than five cruisers were waiting' for the *Graf Spee*. Even the BBC joined in, reporting a 'live' account of the non-existent fleet.

To back up the deception, Harwood had the *Achilles* signal to ships over the horizon, as if they were the *Renown* and her escort. When the *Cumberland* arrived, the German lookouts, expecting to see the bigger ship, reported her rigging as that of the *Renown*. Captain Langsdorff was completely taken in. He radioed his position back to Berlin:

Strategic position off Montevideo: Besides the cruisers and destroyers, Ark Royal and Renown. Close blockade at night; escape into open sea and break-through to home waters is hopeless ... request decision on whether the ship should be scuttled in spite of insufficient depth in the estuary of the Plate, or whether internment is preferred.

The reply was terse: 'No internment in Uruguay. Attempt effective destruction if ship is scuttled.' Langsdorff took what he believed was the only course available. On Sunday 18 December he sailed the *Graf Spee* out into the middle of the estuary and set off charges that scuttled and burned her. He and his men accepted internment in German-friendly Argentina, but when they arrived in Buenos Aires they discovered the deception. Langsdorff, honourable to the end, wrapped himself in the German naval ensign and shot himself. Pictures of the burning, sunken *Graf Spee* circled the world, as did news of the captain's suicide. It was a major propaganda coup for the British and a huge embarrassment for the Germans. More importantly, it helped to make the trans-Atlantic shipping lanes a lot safer for Allied traffic supporting far-flung theatres of war.

Bodyguard of lies – The D-Day deception: 1944

The D-Day landings of June 1944 were the culmination of Operation Overlord, the largest and most complex seaborne military operation ever seen. The future of Europe and the lives of over a million men were at stake. But success depended on another operation, one that took place behind the scenes, involving trickery, deceit, double agents, diversions and the utmost secrecy – Operation Bodyguard, the largest deception operation in history. This, then, is the secret history of the D-Day landings.

In 1944 continental Europe lay in the grip of the Nazis. Stalemated in the west, Hitler had turned his attention to Russia, where, after initial success, the German army had suffered some shocking defeats and was on the back foot. The war had reached a pivotal point. If the western Allies could pull off a successful invasion, the defeat of the Nazis was virtually assured. But to achieve such an undertaking they would have to overcome enormous odds. An amphibious assault on Hitler's Fortress Europe could easily come horribly unstuck if the Nazis knew where and when the blow would fall. The terrible consequences of failure were graphically illustrated in late April 1944, when American invasion training exercise Tiger went terribly wrong. A convoy of American ships was surrounded by German E-boats and torn to shreds. Even if the invasion forces could establish a successful beachhead, the Allied commanders knew that the true outcome would be decided by the subsequent race to build up forces in the focal area. The Germans, with reinforcements immediately on hand and dramatically simpler supply routes, might easily win the battle of the build-up and fling the invasion force back into the sea. Even in terms of sheer numbers the Germans had the upper hand, with many more divisions available in Western Europe than the Allies could muster, at that time, in Britain.

Thus the deception operation would need to work on three levels: the strategic level of large-scale disposition of armies around the continent; the operational level of divisions around the target area, and the tactical level of units around the actual invasion beaches. Allied planners needed somehow to prevent the Germans concentrating their armies in northwest France, to prevent those divisions already there from concentrating in Normandy and to protect the landing craft and airborne troops of the initial assault. Their response was the impressive Operation Bodyguard.

Operation Bodyguard took its name from a comment Churchill had made to Stalin at the Tehran Conference of 1943: 'In wartime, truth is so precious that she should always be attended by a bodyguard of lies.' It was a vast project involving six principal plans and 36 subordinate operations, with a scope that ranged from the broadest overview to the smallest detail.

Conceiving and orchestrating this complex plot was the motley crew of the London Controlling Section (LCS), a top-secret unit headed by former stockbroker Colonel John Bevan, which included among its staff an actor, a soap factory manager and the horror novelist Dennis Wheatley. Together they would help draw up a plan to fool the Germans on the strategic, operational and tactical levels.

Zeppelin and Fortitude North

Although the Germans were well aware that northwest France was probably the main target for an Allied invasion, the strategic elements of Operation Bodyguard aimed to make them think that invasions would be launched in other theatres of conflict. A plethora of diversionary fake operations were launched, intended to concentrate German attention on Spain, Turkey[1], Sweden and both the Atlantic and southern coasts of France, but the two primary strategic deception plans, Operation Zeppelin and Operation Fortitude North, targeted the Balkans and Norway respectively.

The Balkans made an obvious target for the Allies, since the area included vital oilfields, while Hitler placed great store in the support of his allies in the region. Operation Zeppelin included extensive efforts to make it seem that the Allies were close to 'turning' these Balkan states and getting them to switch sides or rebel against their Nazi-allied leaders. At the same time, bogus radio traffic and fake preparations made it look as though the Allies were getting ready to launch amphibious assaults and invasions from their bases in the Near East.

Zeppelin proved to be a major success. In March 1944 Hitler felt compelled to invade Hungary and threaten Romania to keep them in line, while important divisions were moved from

1. This operation, codenamed Royal Flush, recalled the Elizabethan diplomatic intrigues that induced the Ottoman Empire to threaten Philip of Spain's Mediterranean interests, forcing him to divert part of his navy away from the Armada invasion attempt.

France to the Balkans to secure the region. Among them were some of the best SS Panzer divisions, which were replaced in France by under-strength infantry divisions.

Operation Fortitude North was an elaborate plan to convince the Germans that an assault was planned on Norway, partly as a way of pressuring Sweden to cut off Germany's vital supply of special grade iron ore. The LCS planned as if launching a genuine operation, and drew up a detailed invasion scheme that involved an assault on a port and airfield, followed by movement against major towns. The attack was scheduled for after the real D-Day landings, so that German forces would be kept tied down in Scandinavia during the genuine invasion. As the obvious assembly point for a real Norwegian invasion was Scotland, this was also the centre for the fake operations.

A mixture of real and imaginary divisions were detailed to make up the fictional Fourth Army Group. For instance, the 3rd Infantry Division, a real unit, was sent to Scotland for training exercises that would prepare them for the real invasion, but their activities were given a Scandinavian spin with a mountain warfare element. The soldiers were given Norwegian lessons and even issued with 'Mountain'-labelled shoulder flashes. Real mountain warfare equipment, such as snow-ploughs, was mustered in Dundee harbour. All available ships were moored in the Firth of Forth and fake troop barges and landing craft were created, complete with the details required to make them seem genuine, such as lines of washing and smoke from funnels. Local newspapers joined in with the fiction, reporting Fourth Army football matches and weddings between local girls and imaginary troops.

Such activities were largely window dressing, for by this time German intelligence was severely hampered by Allied control of the skies. This meant that few reconnaissance flights were possible, so that German intelligence was forced to rely on two main methods of intelligence gathering – radio intercepts and secret agents. The crucial elements of both Fortitude North and South (see below) would be the deceivers' manipulation of these channels of information, by generating bogus radio traffic and by feeding disinformation through double agents.

In Scotland, the key element was radio deception. The man in charge of the Fortitude North deception, Colonel Roderick MacLeod, an authority on military deception, put together a team of radio technicians to simulate the volume and pattern of radio traffic that would be generated by such a large force. Fake signals had to be made not just for combat divisions, but also for all the support units that would be expected, such as the 87th Field Cash Office, or a special film and photographic section – both imaginary. Radio signals covered everything from fake assault exercises to fake orders for skis and snow boots. To gild the lily, double agents were given false information about the Forth Army Group to feed to their Nazi spymasters. For example, an agent codenamed Brutus described the insignia of the new army group, while another codenamed Hamlet 'discovered' that the Ministry of Economic Warfare had embargoed files relating to the Norwegian target towns.

A separate operation codenamed Graffham aimed to back up Nazi fears about the northern invasion route. Air Commodore Thornton was given the notional rank of air vice-marshal and sent to visit his old friend, the commander-in-chief of the Swedish Air Force. Thornton and the Swede discussed possible Swedish involvement in Norway but his real purpose was to be seen by German agents, who duly reported suspicious high level diplomatic contacts that seemed to confirm Allied intentions towards Scandinavia. Another element of Graffham was rigging the Swedish stock market to raise the value of Norwegian stocks as if anticipating that country's liberation.

Although the Germans never believed that a major invasion of Norway was likely, they did believe in the existence of the Fourth Army and the possibility of a minor landing, and maintained a force of eighteen divisions – 200,000 men, including a Panzer tank division – in Scandinavia throughout the

Normandy invasion. The immobilisation of such a force was a good return for the efforts of the 362 men who made up the Fourth Army.

Fortitude South

It was clear to both sides that the genuine invasion blow would have to fall on the northwest coast of France. Only the short hop across the Channel would allow for the logistical requirements of such an operation, with its attendant need for the transport of millions of men, thousands of machines and huge quantities of oil, supplies and ammo. Maintaining and defending lines of communication across more than a few miles would be impossible. So it was clear to Hitler, from as early as 1943, that the top priority for the defence of Fortress Europe should be northwest France, and clear to the Allied planners that their strategic deceptions could achieve only distractions at best. What they needed was deception at an operational level – a way of convincing Hitler and his generals that the blow would fall on a different part of north-west France, and at a later date, than the real effort. The result was Operation Fortitude South, the most important part of Operation Bodyguard.

Fortunately for the Allies, the most important condition for a successful deception was already in place – plausibility. For the most obvious invasion route was via the Pas de Calais area, which offered the shortest route across the Channel, access to a major port and the quickest way of reaching strategic objectives that Hitler was convinced must be uppermost in Allied plans, particularly the V-rocket launch sites and the major German industrial areas. This belief was backed up by the unsuccessful raid on Dieppe, which seemed to show that the Allies did indeed plan to seize a major port as the only logical means of facilitating the rapid build-up of forces that would be necessary for a successful invasion.

In practice, the Allies had drawn the opposite conclusion from the Dieppe debacle, which had shown that there was little chance of capturing a port intact, and in working condition. Instead, British and American ingenuity devised means of working without a port, thanks to the floating concrete harbours of the Mulberry project and the undersea oil pipeline project Pluto (see below). Allied planners were able to select an alternative invasion target, while arranging a massive deception based on the more obvious area. This deception would continue even after the D-Day landings and the invasion of Normandy, to pin down German forces in the Pas de Calais and prevent the arrival of reinforcements in the Normandy area.

As with the deception operation in Scotland, Fortitude South revolved around a fictitious army group – the First US Army Group, or FUSAG – that would muster in Southeast England. This notional army was under the 'command' of General George S Patton, a charismatic but unpredictable figure who had fallen from favour in Allied circles because of incidents of poor judgement, but who was very highly regarded by the Germans. They thought it entirely likely that he would be leading the assault forces, and were misled by his actions during the build-up to D-Day and by his absence from Normandy after the landings. They could not conceive that the Normandy invasion could be the main event if Patton was not present.

A leavening of real units was attached to FUSAG and stationed in the area to enhance the credibility of the ruse. As they transferred to Normandy after D-Day, they would be replaced by fictional units, many drawn from the fake Fourth Army Group in Scotland. In this way, FUSAG lived on for several months after the D-Day landings themselves.

Numerous sub-operations helped to ensure the plausibility of FUSAG and confirm German beliefs that Southeast England was to be the jumping off point for the main invasion. The main sub-plans were codenamed Quicksilver I–VI. Quicksilver I was the central deception that FUSAG would launch the major Allied invasion on the Pas de Calais, some weeks after the Normandy operation. Quicksilver II involved the generation of huge volumes of bogus radio traffic, created by special units, some equipped with transmitters that could multiply their signals so that one operator could appear to be six. Others were based in trucks that spent all day haring around the Kent countryside, broadcasting from as many different locations as possible to give the impression of multiple units.

The fake radio traffic was produced with incredible attention to detail and subtle touches. It reproduced the frequency and pattern of a real army group, and the operators replicated the individual broadcasting quirks and styles that the eavesdropping Germans would expect to hear from the signals men attached to each unit. The messages themselves came from a script book prepared by the planners at Supreme Headquarters Allied Expeditionary Force (SHAEF). This included the now celebrated message: '5th [Battalion] Queen's Royal Regiment report a number of civilian women, presumably unauthorised, in the baggage train. What are we going to do with them – take them to Calais?'

Other Quicksilver operations included arranging dummy landing craft and other craft around the coast of southeast England, and dummy aircraft on southeastern airfields, together with fake lighting schemes to add to the illusion of a build up, or help to divert enemy bombers attacking the real jumping off area. Such illusions had been perfected earlier in the war to deceive German bombers into getting lost, missing their target towns or aiming long or short. Set designers from Shepperton Film Studios were employed to create an impressive fake oil storage and docking facility near Dover. The king and General Montgomery paid highly publicised visits to the site and special effects, using smoke generators and flares, created a convincing response when the facility was hit by long-range German shells. The fake storage facility was a cover for the real operation, the Pipeline Under The Ocean – PLUTO.

The business end of this top-secret technology was concealed behind a number of innocent facades. For instance, one pumping station was disguised as a seaside ice-cream stall. Even Allied bombing raids on the Continent were carefully arranged to foster the impression that the Calais region was the primary target. For every bombing run on Normandy, there were two in the Calais region.

In May 1944, a high-ranking German prisoner of war, General Hans Cramer, was set to be repatriated on health grounds. LCS seized on the opportunity to have a trusted German pass on first-hand disinformation to his superiors. Cramer was taken from his camp in Wales to London and told he was being taken via the southeast, but was actually driven via the invasion build-up area in the southwest. On arrival in London he dined with Patton, who was introduced as the commander of FUSAG, and who managed to accidentally mention Calais. When Cramer got back to Berlin he duly reported the picture that LCS had so carefully painted for him.

The many disparate elements of Fortitude South, though impressive and extremely successful, mainly served to back up the picture that the Germans were receiving from their most highly valued sources of intelligence, their secret agents. Unbeknown to them most of these agents had in fact been 'turned' by British intelligence, and now operated under the auspices of the XX-Committee as double agents. It was these double agents who were to prove the most important and effective element of Operation Bodyguard. One agent in particular, known to the British as Garbo, made such an impact that he became known as 'the spy who saved D-Day'.

Garbo: The spy who saved D-Day

A combination of diligent counter-espionage work and the access to German radio traffic provided by the Ultra project (see page 114), meant that the domestic intelligence service, MI5, was able to intercept most of the German agents sent to Britain. Often these agents could be turned, making them into valuable tools for counter-espionage, and later deception, under the auspices of a special committee called the XX-, Double Cross or Twenty Committee (after the Roman numerals). According to JC Masterman, chairman of the Twenty Committee, 'we actively ran and controlled the German espionage system in [Britain].'

The Double Cross System overseen by the Twenty Committee helped with deception operations covering North African landings in 1943, the Balkan deceptions of Operation Zeppelin and others, but really came into its own with Operation Fortitude. Examples of double agents included Treasure, a Russian-born French journalist named Nathalie Sergueiew, who had been recruited by the Germans but then decided to offer her services to Britain. She convinced the Germans to send her to London, and once there was debriefed by MI5, revealed her cryptographic secrets and was used to pass misleading information back to her German controller. In 1944 she told him that she had a new boyfriend – a US soldier with the fictional Fourteenth Army, based in the Southeast and obviously preparing for the fake invasion aimed at the Pas de Calais. However, Treasure was unreliable and began to act up. After an angry showdown with her MI5 controllers, she was 'fired' and her employment as a double agent came to an end. She moved back to France and later wrote her memoirs, in which she lambasted her British controllers as 'gangsters'. Nonetheless, Treasure had done her part to further the D-Day deception plans.

The greatest of the double agents was undoubtedly Garbo, the code name given to a Spaniard named Juan Pujol. So effective was he that he became probably the only man in history to have been awarded both the Iron Cross and the MBE. Pujol had served under Franco during the Spanish Civil War, an experience that convinced him that neither the Fascists nor

Communists had the answer, and that only Britain could safeguard liberal principles in Europe. In 1940 he approached the
British in Madrid to offer his services as a spy but was turned
down. He then approached the Germans and was taken on by
the *Abwehr*, the German military intelligence agency, given the
code name Cato (later changed to Arabal), and tasked to spy
on the British. Thus armed, he once again approached the
British but was again turned down. Nothing daunted, Pujol
simply set up as a sort of freelance double agent, settling in
Lisbon, in neutral Portugal, but pretending to his German controllers that he was actually in Britain. Finally, in 1942, the
British relented and Pujol moved to England, under the code
name Garbo.

While in Lisbon Garbo had started to use imaginary sub-
agents to help extend his notional intelligence gathering abili-
ties. These fictional people had supposedly been recruited by
Garbo, and often subsequently recruited mini-networks of
their own. Working with his British controllers, Garbo eventually extended his fake network to include 24 fictitious sub-
agents, often inventing colourful back-stories for them and
even subjecting them to intelligence tests, which they sometimes failed. They ranged from a Gibraltarian ex-waiter to a
group of disgruntled Welsh nationalists who had banded
together with an Indian to form 'Brothers in the Aryan World
Order'. Garbo described their activities to his German controller as 'very limited and rather ridiculous'. Apparently they
spent most of their time making lists of Communists and Jews
who would be executed when the Aryan World Order was
declared.

Information gathered by this network of imaginary agents
was passed on to Berlin, via Garbo's controller in Madrid, in an
endless stream of messages – sometimes several each day –
building for the Germans a picture of FUSAG's fictional activities. Occasionally the disinformation was bolstered with reports
on real units from Montgomery's Twenty-first Army Group,

preparing for the Normandy invasion. When these units were subsequently recognised in France, Garbo's credibility with the Germans was enormously enhanced. Garbo's reports also helped to head off German suspicions about troop concentrations in the southwest. By May 1944, the German's had bought the Fortitude order of battle almost to the last detail.

In one daring move it was decided that in order not to undermine Garbo's credibility he would have to pass on a message alerting the Germans to the launch of Operation Neptune (the D-Day amphibious assault). By sending the message just before the troops hit the beaches, it was assumed that no serious harm could be done to the landings, and Garbo's communications regarding Neptune always carried the implicit assumption that it was simply a precursor to the main event. As it turned out, the Germans were not listening and Garbo was able to pass on a detailed message that impressed the Germans (when they eventually received it, too late to make any difference) while also berating them for their laxness.

After the landings on 6 June, Garbo's deception entered a new phase, if anything more important than before. One crucial intervention in particular earned him the sobriquet, 'the spy who saved D-Day'. Immediately after the landings, the German command on the ground in Normandy pleaded with the High Command to release armoured divisions that were, thanks to the success of the operational deception, being held in reserve to cover the expected main attack on the Pas de Calais. These units, including an SS Panzer division, had the potential to shatter the fragile Allied foothold.

On the evening of 8 June, with the vital divisions already on their way towards Normandy, Garbo sent a now celebrated message to his German contacts:

After personal consultation on 8 June with my agents [...] whose reports I sent today I am of the opinion [...] that these operations are a diversionary manoeuvre designed to

draw off enemy reserves in order to make an attack at
another place ... it may very probably take place in the Pas
de Calais area ...

After the war, Allied intelligence recovered the actual teleprinted
message that had been received in Berlin. The military's chief of
intelligence, Krumacher, had underlined in red the part about
the 'diversionary manoeuvre designed to draw off enemy
reserves in order to make an attack at another place', and had
pencilled in a comment of his own: 'confirms the view already
held by us that a further attack is to be expected in another place
(Belgium?).' This message was subsequently shown to Hitler.

The results were dramatic. The SS Panzer divisions advancing on Normandy were stopped in their tracks and sent back to
Belgium, where they sat out the desperate battle for Normandy
until it was too late. According to the official historian of
Fortitude, Roger Hesketh, senior intelligence personnel were
'convinced ... that it was Garbo's message [of] the 8th June,
1944, which changed the course of the battle in Normandy.'

Garbo continued to send his poisoned chalices to Berlin
until the last days of the war, when a defecting German intelligence agent in Madrid, eager to save his own skin, offered to
reveal to the British the existence of a super-spy network in
Britain. Obviously this would compromise Garbo in the eyes of
German intelligence, since they would expect the British to
arrest him. A story was concocted whereby Garbo allegedly fled
to south Wales, to hole up with his Welsh Nationalist contacts
and a Belgian (a fellow fugitive), and he wrote suitably desolate
letters to his German controller describing the boredom and
isolation and complaining that the Belgian 'is a man who is a
little simple. I do not know whether his brains are atrophied.'

Finally, in May 1945, Garbo and his German controller
agreed that he should try to escape to Spain, and arranged a
meeting at a café in Madrid, where he was to signal his identity by carrying the *London News*. In this way, just after the end

of the war, Garbo was able to finally meet the *Abwehr* controller, Kuehlenthal, who had been his conduit for so much disinformation. According to Hesketh, the German was delighted to finally meet one he regarded as 'a superman', and keen to ask this master spy for help in escaping Allied justice. Garbo said that he would see what he could do, but now he was leaving for Portugal. 'How do you propose to get from Spain to Portugal?' asked Kuehlenthal. Garbo replied: 'Clandestinely.'

There was no doubt in the minds of the Allied planners that the Double Cross System was the key element in the success of the strategic and operational deceptions practised on the Germans. In the official history of the operation, Roger Hesketh commented: 'There is only one method which combines the qualities of precision, certainty and speed necessary for the conduct of strategic deception at long range and over an extended period, and that is the double cross agent ... by setting up [the Double Cross System] the British Security Service laid the foundation for all that Fortitude achieved.'

So what exactly had Fortitude achieved? At strategic and operational levels it had been a resounding success. Major German forces had been decoyed to the Balkans or pinned down in Scandinavia, while in northwest France the main bulk of the German forces, the Fifteenth Army, were concentrated around the Pas de Calais. Even the formidable coastal defences of Hitler's much-vaunted Atlantic Wall were concentrated in the decoy area, while the German High Command was so in the dark about the timing of the operation that many senior officers, including the well-respected Rommel, went on leave the day before the invasion.

Most crucially of all, Fortitude succeeded in convincing the Germans that the Normandy landings were just a sideshow, a curtain raiser for the main event. According to General Omar Bradley, General Patton's superior and commander of US First Army during the landings, writing in his memoirs:

While the enemy's Seventh Army, overworked and under strength, struggled to pin us down in the beachhead ... the German High Command declined to reinforce it with troops from the Pas de Calais. There, for seven decisive weeks, the Fifteenth Army waited for an invasion that never came, convinced beyond all reasonable doubt that Patton would lead the main Allied assault across the narrow neck of the Channel. Thus ... the enemy immobilized nineteen divisions and played into our hands in the biggest single hoax of the war.

Battlefield deceptions on D-Day

The use of deception did not stop at the strategic and operational levels. To help protect the invasion fleet and the paratroops dropping in ahead of it, and sow confusion among the defending forces, a battery of tactical deception methods were employed. For instance, it was important to cover the approach of the Neptune fleet from detection by German radar stations, which might then scramble aircraft or alert German naval patrols. The first step was air attacks on many radar installations, which succeeded in destroying the most dangerous ones, but left operable those stations that could pick up decoy fleets.

The fake fleets were created using ingenious radar deception technologies; the forerunners of today's ultra-hi-tech electronic warfare gadgets and stealth technology. To give the illusion of a fleet approaching Le Havre, to the east of the actual target beaches, the 'Dambusters' 617 Squadron RAF flew a complex and dangerous mission called Taxable. This involved flights of aircraft dropping clouds of aluminium foil strips in carefully coordinated sequence. The clouds of foil, called Window, created the illusory radar profile of a fleet of ships. As the groups of aircraft advanced, making new drops, so the illusory fleet seemed to advance. In practice, this required the bombers to execute a rigid pattern of turns for several hours while flying in a crowded sky during a moonless night. Miraculously there were no collisions.

To back up the Taxable deception, small ships towing radar-reflecting balloons and equipped with radar reflectors and loudspeakers recreating the noise of a huge fleet, advanced up the Channel, past Le Havre and away from the actual invasion fleet. The Germans were fooled – aircraft, ships and shore batteries were turned on the decoy fleet, but the real fleet sailed unmolested and the German emplacements guarding the target beaches received no warning of the approaching onslaught.

More Window was dropped by a small group of bombers over the Somme. This had the effect of creating the radar profile of a massive bombing raid. Luftwaffe night fighters were scrambled to chase the non-existent bombing fleet, allowing the vulnerable transport planes carrying paratroops to slip through and release their loads.

Among the first wave of drops was Operation Titanic. This involved dummy parachutists being dropped outside the main target areas, along with a few SAS paratroops, equipped with gramophones to help them simulate the sounds of entire battalions and battle noises. Titanic worked brilliantly, helping to thoroughly confuse the German divisions guarding the Normandy area. Reserve units that should have been defending the beaches or dealing with real paratroops were instead led on wild goose chases around the countryside. One of the main successes of Titanic was in helping to relieve the disastrous landing at 'Omaha' beach. Here the Americans had run afoul of a series of unfortunate mistakes, and thousands of them were pinned down on the beach. However, the defending forces lacked the reserves they needed to properly counter-attack because they had been dispersed through the countryside to hunt down bogus paratroops. Instead of visiting a terrible massacre on the Americans, and opening a dangerous gap in the Allied lines, the German defenders were eventually forced back.

The success of Operation Bodyguard

Operation Bodyguard succeeded at every level, helping to ensure the success of the initial landings and the subsequent 'battle of the build-up', and making the breakout possible. What followed was the rapid liberation of most of France and the beginning of the end for the Nazis. But the true success of Bodyguard can perhaps best be assessed by looking at the 'what if?' scenario. If the operation had failed the D-Day landings might well have been rebuffed by superior German forces. The Allies would have found it extremely difficult to attempt another invasion, and the Nazi's Western Front would have been secure for years to come. Hitler could have consolidated his grip on Europe and turned his full attention to staving off the Russian threat, while the secret weapons being developed by the Germans, in which Hitler put so much faith, might successfully have been brought into proper use. The western Allies might even have been forced to seek some sort of accommodation with the Nazi regime. These were the true stakes for Operation Bodyguard. Without it, what might Europe look like today?

The Hail Mary Play and the invasion of Kuwait: 1991

Nearly 50 years after the grand deceptions of D-Day, another Allied commander planned an invasion deception on a massive scale. This time a coalition of nearly 20 countries aimed to drive the Iraqi army out of Kuwait, after its 1990 invasion of the oil-rich kingdom. Under the leadership of American general Norman Schwarzkopf, this complex alliance had to defeat an army of 1.2 million troops and over 10,000 armoured vehicles well entrenched and confident of the effect of its massed firepower. At the time the Iraqi army was said to be one of the world's largest and, after a brutal war with Iran during the 1980s, toughest. General Schwarzkopf was keenly aware of the potential cost in lives a massive amphibious assault on occupied Kuwait might incur, and wanted to do everything in his power to minimise Allied casualties.

For an American general in the post-Vietnam era, with its pervasive media coverage and fear of the 'bodybag' syndrome (the massive swing in domestic public opinion that could be produced by images of American dead), such concerns were only politically expedient. Part of the modern general's remit is to manage the political as well as military aspects of war; a defeat on the battlefield might not be the only way to lose the Gulf War. With the goal of minimal casualties in mind, Schwarzkopf formulated a daring plan based on a huge operational deception, a plan he called 'the Hail Mary Play', after an American Football play in which all is staked on a single long pass to the end zone. Its dramatic success would determine the course of the first Gulf War and inform American attitudes towards future military operations, with consequences being felt today.

The Iraqis had based their deployment on what seemed like the most obvious route of attack for the coalition. Infantry and armour were arranged along the border between Kuwait and Saudi Arabia (where coalition forces were massing) and around the angle where these borders met with Iraq's. They were also dug in along the Kuwaiti coast. In Kuwait City buildings along the shore had been evacuated and prepared as defensive emplacements. Reserve divisions were mustered to the north of Kuwait, protecting the Iraqi oilfields. The Iraqis were ready for the expected combination of an amphibious assault and a push from Saudi into Kuwait.

Schwarzkopf and his planners were aware that Iraqi intelligence capabilities were largely limited to what they could learn from the media (CNN being a favourite source of info), and they made skilful use of the media to reinforce Iraqi beliefs. President Bush and other leaders emphasised the limits of their UN mandate to liberate Kuwait, which made no mention of invading Iraq. The initial American force was organised around a Marine Expeditionary Brigade and Amphibious Task Groups, and television news crews were given access to amphibious assault exercises by the Marines. Press briefings revolved around the sort of tactics that would be important to an amphibious assault. The Americans also used 'Psy-ops', by dropping leaflets on Iraqi troops in Kuwait showing stylised Marines smashing down on the shore, with terrified Iraqis fleeing before them.

Everything was geared to give the impression that a huge amphibious assault was in the offing. In practice, however, Schwarzkopf was planning a daring ground offensive that would simply skirt the Iraqi troop concentrations by striking deep into the heart of Iraq, encircling the bulk of the forces and entirely sidestepping their laboriously prepared defences. Success depended on surprise, so it was essential to cover the movement of armoured divisions and their massive logistical support.

The first step in this operational deception was to build up the ground forces where the Iraqis would expect them. In mid-January 1991, all the coalition forces were arranged near or to the east of the tri-border junction between Kuwait, Iraq and Saudi Arabia. Extensive air attacks destroyed Iraqi air capability, and with it reconnaissance capability. What followed was an audacious redeployment, as the two key US formations, the VII and XVIII Corps, along with some coalition adjuncts, swapped places with Saudi and Kuwaiti forces in the east, and moved even further westwards to take up starting positions hundreds of miles further along the Iraqi–Saudi border. Over 100,000 men and 1,200 tanks were moved.

This redeployment, together with huge accompanying traffic in supplies, took place well back from the border so that the Iraqis would not be aware of it. To fool their limited electronic eavesdropping capability, deception cells were left behind to fake the electronic 'footprint' of the redeployed units, and a decoy military base, complete with fake missiles, fuel dumps and radio traffic, was created at the former VII Corps base. British units also practised deception, with fake radio traffic and a television report that showed an artillery unit practising by the sea, without mentioning that it was shortly to be redeployed inland.

When the invasion began on 24 February, it seemed initially to follow the pattern expected by the Iraqis. Marine units demonstrated (ie made a show of preparing to attack) off the coast of Iraq, and Radio Free Kuwait reported that Marines had landed on one of the islands just off the coast. Meanwhile the first land attacks were made by units to the eastern end of the coalition line. But the main thrust of the invasion was the land assault to the west, where the armoured corps drove deep into Iraqi territory without encountering significant resistance. Thanks to the success of the coalition air campaign, the Iraqis were unable to redeploy to meet the genuine threat, and the invasion was so successful that President Bush unilaterally declared a cease-fire on 28 February, just four days after it had begun.

In immediate terms Schwarzkopf's successful plan of attack secured the liberation of Kuwait with minimal coalition casualties. Arguably its longer term impact was more significant. The combination of the air campaign, which allowed the prosecution of war from a distance, and the successful deception, which sidestepped large-scale American casualties, meant that the American public could be served up a war without the messy consequences of the Vietnam era. War was once again a politically feasible option for America's leaders, a consideration that arguably informed the decision to pursue a second Gulf War.

The Iraq War and the WMD that never were: 2003

One of the central planks of the case for war with Iraq and the ousting of Saddam Hussein was the allegation that he was trying to develop weapons of mass destruction (WMD), including nuclear, biological and chemical weapons. It is now widely accepted that the intelligence that gave rise to this claim was faulty, but recent developments in the Middle East and Washington have raised the possibility that there was much more to this 'failure of intelligence' than an honest mistake. According to sources close to the US State Department and the CIA, America may have been tricked into going to war with Saddam Hussein by Iranian intelligence, in what Larry Johnson, a former senior counter-terrorist official at the State Department, has called 'one of the most masterful intelligence operations in history. [Iran] persuaded the US and Britain to dispose of its greatest enemy.'

At the heart of this murky story is Ahmad Chalabi, head of the Iraqi National Congress, an influential group of anti-Saddam Iraqi exiles who have gained positions of power in the post-Saddam, US-led regime. Chalabi had the ear of top Bush administration policy makers and, according to some, important US newspapers. His contacts with defectors from the Saddam regime and his intelligence from within Iraq were crucial to building the case for war, but he is now accused of being an Iranian intelligence plant who fed American hawks what they wanted to hear while bilking them for millions of dollars. Chalabi's defenders, however, insist that he is simply a pawn in an internecine conflict between neoconservatives based at the Pentagon, and their opponents in the CIA and State Department. Some even conclude that he has been smeared as part of US attempts to cosy up to the UN by suppressing evidence of a huge UN fraud during the oil-for-aid programme in the 1990s.

Chalabi's involvement with US intelligence dates back to the first Gulf War. At this time he was head of Jordan's Petra Bank and in close contact with CIA officials in Amman, supplying them with high-class intelligence from within Iraq. The Jordanian bank subsequently collapsed, almost taking the rest of the country's economy with it – according to Jordan, because Chalabi had systematically embezzled millions of dollars. He escaped from the country hidden in the trunk of a car, and now cannot visit most countries in the region for fear of being extradited back to face charges. Chalabi insists that the accusations of embezzlement are politically motivated.

Chalabi allegedly realised that America would fund anyone who could set up as a credible anti-Saddam opposition, and started to draw huge sums of money for his INC group – over $40 million over the last 13 years, according to some. He set up shop in the Kurdish-controlled region of Iraq, taking CIA money while providing intelligence and plotting various schemes.

However, Chalabi's involvement with Iranian intelligence dates back much further than his contact with the Americans. Allegedly he had a close personal relationship with Ayatollah Khomeini and helped Iranian intelligence during the Iraq–Iran War of the 1980s. He is even said to have used his CIA funding to pay for an Iranian intelligence office next to his own HQ. As head of the INC's own intelligence operation he employed a Shia Kurd named Arras Karim Habib, who the CIA knew to be an Iranian intelligence operative. In fact the CIA knew about Chalabi's own involvement with the Iranians, but while their aims coincided no one was bothered. He fell out of favour with them in 1995 when he allegedly forged a document that suggested the US was going to assassinate Saddam and then let Iranian intelligence see it. The incident triggered an FBI investigation.

New opportunities for Chalabi arose in 2000, with the election of George Bush and the accession of a new breed of conservatives to power in Washington. Led by the vice-president, Dick Cheney and the defence secretary, Donald Rumsfeld, these neoconservatives, as they are widely known, took an aggressive stance on foreign policy, and were particularly keen to finish what Bush Sr had started with the Gulf War by getting rid of Saddam Hussein. Both before and after the 9/11 attacks these neoconservative hawks were gathering evidence against Saddam and drawing up plans for an invasion. Working against them were more cautious heads at the State Department and the CIA. In this power struggle for the direction of American policy, the ear of the president and the backing of US public opinion, Chalabi was a key weapon.

In order to circumvent the CIA's control of intelligence gathering duties, Rumsfeld set up something called the Office of Special Plans (OSP) – essentially an in-house intelligence agency for the Pentagon, with the specific remit of gathering evidence to back up neoconservative aims. Rumsfeld felt that the CIA's own assessments were too cautious; his outfit would be much more aggressive. Much of the OSP's best material came via Chalabi and his man Arras Habib. They 'uncovered' a stream of defectors from the Saddam regime who told the hawks just what they wanted to hear – Iraq was pursuing WMD and had developed a range of capabilities. Chalabi assured the hawks that the Iraqi people would welcome US troops as liberators and that his INC could easily become the nucleus of a new, democratic, US-friendly regime. Chalabi also provided the source material for a number of important articles in major newspapers such as *The New York Times*, which helped to swing public opinion behind the war. It is now widely acknowledged that most of this information was groundless and misleading. So where did it come from?

The CIA insists that it warned the Pentagon about Chalabi's untrustworthiness and Iranian links right from the start, but that they did not want to hear about it. Instead Chalabi's INC was generously funded to the tune of $335,000 a month, and he and a small INC militia were spirited into Iraq almost as soon as US troops secured an airbase. Although the INC failed to receive the heroes' welcome they had led the Americans to expect, Chalabi and his cronies were nonetheless given prominent positions in the occupation administration. Chalabi was made head of the de-Ba'athification programme and one of his allies was put in charge of the currency changing operation to replace Saddam dinars with new dinars. It was widely suggested that the Pentagon saw Chalabi as a president-elect for Iraq.

But still he was dogged by doubts and detractors. Some Iraqis warned that what was needed was a de-Chalabification policy. Weapons inspectors failed to uncover any evidence for WMDs, and doubts were cast on INC intelligence. The currency changeover operation became mired in accusations of massive fraud. There were suggestions that the US was cooling on Chalabi.

Then, in May 2004, things seemed to fall apart all at once. Chalabi was accused of implication in the currency changeover problems. The US National Security Agency, the agency that deals with signals intelligence, apparently intercepted an Iranian intelligence message about US decryption of its codes, which gave Chalabi as the source for the information. In other words Chalabi had told Iranian intelligence that the NSA had cracked their codes and were reading their communications.

Defense Department funding of the INC was suspended and Chalabi's villa in Iraq was raided. A warrant was issued for the arrest of Arras Habib, who promptly disappeared. CIA and State Department sources in Washington started to brief journalists that, just as they had warned, Chalabi was a double agent and that the intelligence he had provided to the OSP in the run-up to the war was deliberate Iranian intelligence disinformation. The CIA have asked the FBI to start an investigation into how Chalabi might have acquired the sensitive information; it is assumed that one of his Pentagon supporters must have shown him something they shouldn't have. There is talk of lie detector tests, and a number of high-profile neoconservatives have already publicly distanced themselves from Chalabi.

Certainly it would make sense for Iran to want to lure the US into toppling Saddam. Hatred for Saddam is understandably deep-seated in Iran – he started the war in the 1980s and allegedly used chemical weapons on Iranian troops. Iraq was also the region's only genuine strategic counterbalance to Iran and its massive army. A new regime in Iraq would be much more likely to give the Shia majority a prominent role, and to include many Shia power brokers with close ties to Iran. Getting America bogged down in the morass that the occupation has become would also be a good way of deflecting attention from Iran's own nuclear weapons programme and discouraging neo-conservative zeal for regime change operations against Iran. There can be little doubt that the realities of the Iraq war have strengthened Iran's position considerably.

According to some in the American intelligence community, it is now obvious what's been going on. The *Guardian* newspaper quotes 'an intelligence source in Washington' as saying: 'It's pretty clear that [the] Iranians had us for breakfast, lunch and dinner. Iranian intelligence has been manipulating the US for several years through Chalabi.' Others aren't so sure. Some argue that Chalabi is simply being smeared as part of the power struggle between the CIA/State Department and the Pentagon, in particular because of CIA chagrin at Rumsfeld's setting up of the OSP. There are even some suggestions that this argument is partisan in nature, with the CIA/State camp being essentially anti-Bush and anti-Republican. Certainly the US military has recently come out in favour of the quality of much of the intelligence passed on by the INC, saying that it has helped to save US lives during operations against rebels and terrorists, while allegations about Chalabi's involvement in a currency scandal have been put down to complaints made by a disgruntled Iraqi Finance Ministry employee who is now in jail.

There are even suggestions that the US government as a whole is happy to smear Chalabi in an attempt to butter up the UN. When the Saddam regime was first toppled the INC were given access to the regime's intelligence files. They soon discovered evidence of massive fraud during the UN administration of the oil-for-aid programme in the 1990s, including allegations that Saddam had paid millions of dollars in kickbacks and bribes to UN officials. At the time of writing the US is desperate to secure UN backing for its plans for handing over sovereignty to a new Iraqi government. Perhaps smearing Chalabi is part of an attempt to suppress evidence of colossal UN corruption.

Chalabi's supporters point to one obvious flaw in the CIA/State accusations. According to the CIA/State story, the Iranian reaction to learning that their codes had been cracked and that the NSA was eavesdropping on them was to use the same codes to send a message on the subject. This seems like the height of stupidity. Surely the story cannot be true? Unless Iranian intelligence is engaged in a game of Byzantine complexity. John Brady Kiesling, a former US Embassy political counsellor, suggests that the Iranians knew exactly what they were doing, and wanted to get rid of Chalabi, who had outlived his usefulness:

> It is safest to assume that this gaffe was deliberate ... The leak ended a disastrous 18-month stalemate during which Paul Bremer, the US administrator, had been unable to impose a coherent Iraqi reconstruction policy, because Mr Chalabi had the Washington connections to thwart most concessions to Iraqi reality ... Iranians enjoyed America's floundering in Iraq, but only up to a point. Mr Chalabi may have promised the Iranians the moon, but the Iranians knew he was no more trustworthy as their partner than as the US's.

Deliberately accidentally unmasking Chalabi may simply be the endgame in Iran's deft manipulation of the US.

Despite the apparent reversal of his fortunes, Chalabi may not suffer too badly in the long run. In recent months he had started to bite the hand that fed him, denouncing US policy in Iraq. In the context of the raid on his villa and his new role as an enemy of the US he has become even more vocal, casting himself as an Iraqi hero standing up to the occupying infidels and playing up his Iranian connections. Given the poor image of America among Iraqis and the popularity of Iran, Chalabi may still be in the game.

5

Secret Rulers

This chapter explores the secret lives of rulers, including some who ruled in secret. Most sovereigns leave covert missions to their agents or underlings, but in some notable cases, such as Alexander the Great's strange journey to a desert shrine or the undercover ops of the Caliph Haroun al-Rashid, they carry them out in person. Other sovereigns rule in name only, while the true power sits behind the throne; in this chapter we meet some unsung women who wielded power in secret, and the archetype of the shadow ruler – Cardinal Richelieu.

Alexander the Great's strange pilgrimage: 331 BCE

Alexander the Great had such astonishing success that he became a near-mythical figure in his own lifetime, while stories about his exploits went on to form a staple of regional literature and fable from Europe to the borders of China. By the age of just 33 he had conquered most of the known world and created an empire that would shape the cultures of the Mediterranean and the Near and Middle East for centuries to come. What motivated this prodigy? Where did he acquire the unshakeable self-belief that would propel him beyond the borders of the known and into the realm of legend? Perhaps the key moment in Alexander's career, the crucial encounter that was to guide his destiny, was his visit to the Oracle of Ammon at the Siwa Oasis, deep in the North African desert. Although the story of this visit has become a legend, it remains shrouded in mystery.

In 332 BCE Alexander 'invaded' Egypt. In practice he had already defeated the forces of Darius III, king of Persia, in the Near East, and Darius had fled back to Persia. Egypt, which had never been a willing subject of the Persian king, was left essentially unguarded and welcomed the arrival of Alexander as a redeemer and liberator. He was to spend several months in the country, and given his otherwise relentless programme of conquest this period has often been seen as a sort of holiday, or at best an eccentric sideshow to his main pursuit.

Egypt was logistically important for Alexander, securing him a strong coastal base and strengthening his communications with Greece. It was key to his strategy of wresting control of the Mediterranean trade routes from the Phoenicians. But the country also held a deeper appeal for Alexander, raised on tales of the old gods by his mother, Olympia, and educated by his tutor, Aristotle, to believe that Egypt was the cradle of civilisation and the birthplace of philosophy. As he progressed down the Nile towards the ancient capital at Memphis, Egypt's stunning temples, awesome pyramids and ancient religion exerted still greater fascination for him.

On 14 November 332 BCE, Alexander was crowned pharaoh and acclaimed as a living god. This was at odds with Greek tradition, which frowned on deification of the living, but might have chimed with Alexander's growing conviction that he was marked by the gods or in some way chosen for greatness. Did he have a divine mission? Was he, even, divine himself? His line traced their ancestry back to Hercules, a demi-god and the son of Zeus. Perhaps Alexander already believed the connection might be more direct. The Egyptians had proclaimed him to be a son of the gods and the greatest of the Egyptian gods, Amun-Ra, was considered to be simply another name for Zeus. Over the next two months Alexander spent a great deal of money refurbishing Egyptian temples and doing honour to their divine patrons. He also studied Egyptian customs and tradition.

At the start of 331 BCE Alexander left Memphis and travelled back north to the coast, where he founded Alexandria, strategically placing it to become a great trading centre. He then travelled east along the coast of what the ancients called Libya, receiving tributes, before turning south and, accompanied only by a small escort and some guides, striking deep into the hostile desert. His target was the Oasis of Siwa, home of the oracle of the god Ammon (the Libyan form of Amun-Ra). The journey was difficult and dangerous. Two centuries earlier the Persian king Cambyses had sent an army to conquer Siwa, but it vanished into the desert and was never heard of again. No pharaoh had ever been. Alexander's companions tried to persuade him not to risk the journey, but he would not listen. He was a great fan of oracles and had absolute faith in their utterances. After his visit to Siwa, for instance, he would continue to consult the oracle for the rest of his life, sending questions back over vast distances from his camps in the heart of Asia.

As they struggled through the desert Alexander's party were assailed by near disaster on more than one occasion. First they ran out of water, but were saved by a sudden rainstorm. Then they became lost in a massive sandstorm, but were apparently led out of trouble by a pair of ravens. Was Alexander's divinity asserting itself?

Finally, exhausted and bedraggled, the party reached the Oasis at Siwa. Alexander did not wait to rest or recuperate, but immediately made his way to the temple of Ammon, the Ammoneion, home of the oracle. Here the high priest greeted him with the Greek words '*O, pai dios*' – 'Oh, son of god' –

exactly what the young conqueror wished to hear, although the Graeco-Roman historian Plutarch later suggested that the priest had actually mispronounced the phrase '*O, paidion*' – 'Oh, my son'.

Alexander was then accorded the rare honour of being invited into the *adyton*, the inner sanctum or holy-of-holies, to question the oracle. Exactly what was asked, and how it was answered, will never be known. On re-emerging into the temple forecourt Alexander would only tell his companions that he had received the answer he sought, and that he would only tell the 'secret prophecies' to his mother, and only face to face on his return to Macedon. However, it is generally assumed that Alexander asked about his paternity – specifically, whether or not he was of divine paternity. According to various ancient historians, Alexander first asked whether any of the assassins who had murdered his father, Philip, were still alive. Supposedly he was told to rephrase his question, because, in fact, his father was not mortal. He then asked a more direct question, and was told that yes, he was the son of Ammon (which, to Alexander, would have meant Zeus).

Let us assume that this is what really happened. Possibly Alexander was simply being told what he expected to hear by canny priests who wished to ensure the good will of a powerful patron (if so, it worked; Alexander made magnificent offerings to the oracle). Possibly it was a genuine revelation to him to learn that he was the son of a god, a semi-divine being fit for some awesome destiny.

Whatever he heard within the shady, incense-heavy inner sanctum of the ancient temple hidden deep within the desert, it had a profound effect on Alexander. Over the next eight years he was to drive his army across the empire of Persia and deep into uncharted territory, conquering nations to the borders of China and into India, crossing huge mountain ranges and 'impassable' deserts, overcoming all odds to become the richest man in the world and the greatest conqueror in history.

Only the mutiny of his army in the far eastern lands prevented him from going ever further. It is hard not to see these as the actions of one who believes he is something more than a man. Certainly in coins that were later minted bearing his likeness, he wears the horns of Zeus-Ammon, the mark of the god, while in his own lifetime he proclaimed his own divinity and ordered that he be worshipped as a god.

The conquests of Alexander created a vast Hellenic empire, which, although it broke up into smaller kingdoms shortly after his death, profoundly influenced the history and culture of the Near and Middle East for centuries to come. Was all this driven by the secret revelation vouchsafed in that mysterious temple? Alexander's attraction to the Ammoneion transcended death, for he asked to be buried there. His body *was* brought back to Egypt, but his tomb has never been found. Most scholars expect to find it in Alexandria, but some believe that they have located it already, near Siwa. The desert sands hide many mysteries.

Livia, First Lady of Rome: 58 BCE – 29 CE

Perhaps the most significant chapter in Roman history is the establishment of the empire under Augustus, whose long reign as absolute ruler transformed Rome and set the course for the next thousand years of European history. Standing by Augustus' side and according to many behind his throne was his wife Livia Drusilla, the most powerful woman in Roman history. Livia shared and guided the careers of two emperors, steering the ship of Rome in secret for more than 50 years. She is also accused of plotting and even carrying out the murder of no less than ten members of her own family in her ruthless drive to secure the succession for her son.

Livia's political career started when she married Octavian (later to become Augustus) in 38 BCE. The fact that she was heavily pregnant with her second son by her current husband, while Octavian's wife was also pregnant, caused no small measure of scandal at the time. This is particularly ironic given that the defining features of Livia's public persona in the long years to come would be her traditional virtues of rectitude and matronly modesty. The long-enduring success of Livia and Octavian's partnership suggests that they married for love, but some experts argue that it was a political match from the start. Livia and her existing family had supported the wrong side in the civil wars of the preceding years, and were thus in danger from Octavian, while Octavian needed the support that the aristocratic family of Livia could bring.

As Octavian rose to absolute power, becoming Augustus in 27 BCE, he and Livia worked to create a public personae as a couple, and in particular to foster her image as an archetype of traditional female values. She was associated with the spirits of motherhood, marriage and femininity, and was always portrayed with a traditional hairstyle, little jewellery and conservative attire, wearing the *stola*, a matronly gown. Augustus would boast that she weaved the cloth for their own clothes. They lived together in the same modest townhouse throughout his reign, a period during which they were one of the most powerful couples in history. It seems likely that Livia played as much of a role as Augustus in orchestrating all this.

Together they also ensured that she was awarded unusual official power for a Roman woman. Her person was made sacrosanct – given the official protection of the state – and she was given personal control of her own finances, eventually becoming fabulously wealthy. She was awarded honours and was allowed to commission and dedicate public buildings (the first woman to do so). She received embassies and clients, which meant that she was officially involved in the administration of the empire. Augustus was referred to as *princeps* – ruler – in respect for his authority; Ovid referred to Livia as *princeps femina*. Above all she was Augustus' counsellor and trusted ally. When he travelled abroad he would leave his personal seal in her hands; in his absence she was ruler of Rome. Her shrewd guidance and careful diplomacy helped Augustus to overcome centuries of entrenched traditions and cliques, forge a new ruling system and extend Roman hegemony over a still greater area.

But there was also a darker side to her reputation, with later Roman historians such as Suetonius and Plutarch suggesting dark plots and conspiracies. It is this image that was popularised in Robert Graves' epic *I, Claudius*, subsequently a popular television mini-series, in which Livia is portrayed as an arch-schemer who coldly disposes of anyone who stands in the way of her plans to make Tiberius, her first son emperor after Augustus.

Augustus was much concerned with the succession, which was a thorny problem because he and Livia never had any children together. He favoured the children of his daughter Julia (from his first marriage) and their offspring, adopting a succession of them as his heirs, but they had a habit of dying. While there is no proof that Livia was responsible, she made no secret of her prominent role in securing the crown for Tiberius, constantly reminding him that she was responsible for his accession to the throne. She probably had a network of agents, and many men owed their careers to her patronage; men who would later prove to be quite capable of conspiracy and murder in the turbulent history of late 1st-century Rome. Her grandson Caligula, later to win infamy as the mad emperor, allegedly called her '*Ulixes stolatus*' – 'Ulysses in a dress' – after the legendary Greek famous for his schemes and plots.

In Augustus' twilight years Livia constantly pushed him to acknowledge Tiberius as his heir. His more favoured candidate, Postumus (his grandson), had been exiled to a tiny island after charges of rape, which may have been orchestrated by Livia. In Graves' *I, Claudius* Livia tricks a Vestal Virgin into showing her a copy of Augustus' revised will, realises that he intends to pardon Postumus and reinstate him as heir, and poisons her own husband before he can publicise his intentions. The will is suppressed, and Postumus and anyone in the know are then murdered. Tiberius becomes emperor.

Whether this lurid tale is anything more than far-fetched fantasy will never be known, but after the accession of Tiberius, he and his mother ruled as virtual co-emperors. He tried never to cross her and made the senate award her honours – for instance, it was made treason to speak against her. When her grandson Germanicus, a former favourite of Augustus and rival claimant to the imperial throne, started to gain popularity, both mother and son became alarmed. Germanicus promptly met a mysterious and untimely death. Although there was no proof that Livia or Tiberius were responsible, they were openly delighted.

Eventually Livia's hand on his shoulder became burdensome for Tiberius and he moved to Capri, never to return to Rome. He also had her stripped of many of her privileges, and, when she eventually died in 29 CE at the age of 86, he vetoed the honours voted to her and refused to attend her funeral. It wasn't until the accession of her grandson Claudius to the throne that she was deified (as she and Augustus had intended).

Despite the later damage done to her reputation by Roman historians uneasy with her unusual combination of power and virtue, Livia was popular and respected during and after her lifetime. She had played a vital role in creating and consolidating the Roman Empire, an entity that was to last for centuries. What was all the more remarkable was that, because of the limitations placed on her by a chauvinistic society, she had to do it from behind the scenes.

The Pornocracy: c900–964 CE

For centuries to come, Livia would be the role model for Roman women seeking to wield the power that a chauvinist society denied them. Some 900 years after her era, a new generation of *princeps femina* would arise in Rome – Theodora and Marozia Theophylactus – but these women would prove to be the antithesis of Livia, epitome of virtue. Theodora and her daughter Marozia were members of the Theophylact family, a powerful Roman clan. Most historians describe them as prostitutes, though whether this simply reflects misogyny towards powerful women is not clear. They and their descendants fought for control of the papacy for much of the 10th century; a period sometimes referred to as the 'Pornocracy' because of the shocking immorality of papal life. Through a vicious tangle of intrigue, betrayal and murder they exerted their influence over local and European politics from behind the scenes, ruling through puppet popes and the princes and kings they seduced.

By the beginning of the 10th century, Theophylactus, count of Tusculum, had become de facto ruler of Rome, largely due to the beauty and cunning of his wife Theodora. Between them, the Theophylacts controlled the papacy and with their backing Sergius III gained office in 904. He seduced, or was seduced by, Theodora's daughter Marozia, a young girl of just 15 (13 according to some sources!). She became his mistress and bore him a son, who she was determined to place on the papal throne when he came of age. Marriage alliances with powerful noblemen consolidated her influence and power in Rome, and during the reign of John X (who owed his election to the influence of Theodora) she was effectively ruler of Rome. He acknowledged her power by granting her the titles *Senatrix* and *Patricia*.

In 927 John made the mistake of allying himself with Hugh of France, an enemy of Marozia. She had him arrested, blinded and thrown into a dungeon beneath the Castel Sant'Angelo. It was still too early to place her son on the papal throne, however, so Marozia installed a couple of 'caretaker' popes – Leo VI, who died after within a year, and then Stephen VIII. Concerned that John X might still present a threat, Marozia had him suffocated. When Stephen died in 931, Marozia's son by Sergius III was duly installed as Pope John XI. Her control of Rome was supreme.

Marozia continued to jockey for power through advantageous marriages, but made some fatal errors. First she tried to set up her daughter Bertha with one of the sons of Romanus, the eastern emperor, and then she got her son to officiate at her own wedding to Hugh of Provence, at that time king of Italy. Both moves displeased the people of Rome, especially her son from her first marriage, Alberic II of Spoleto. The eastern empire was Rome's rival, while Hugh was the half-brother of her deceased second husband (a match with her own brother-in-law was considered incestuous and thus frowned upon). Alberic probably resented the threats to his own ambitions to control Rome, while there was bad blood between him and Hugh.

In 932, supported by a wave of popular Roman sentiment, Alberic stormed Marozia's palace and took her and Pope John XI captive, assuming the titles 'Prince and Senator of the Romans'. Now Alberic was in charge. His half-brother John lived on as a puppet pope under house arrest in the Lateran until 935, while Marozia is thought to have died the following year. Alberic then placed a series of puppet popes on the throne, happily deposing and murdering them if they displeased him (as he did with Stephen VIII). Alberic's son, Octavian, Marozia's grandson, succeeded him as prince of Rome in 954, and Alberic's lingering influence ensured that he was elected pope as John XII (he was the first pope to change his name on acceding to office) in 955.

John XII won notoriety as the most immoral pope of all time, taking numerous mistresses, raping female pilgrims and turning the Vatican into a brothel, according to contemporary chroniclers. He was even accused of stealing money from collection boxes to finance his excesses.

Like his ancestors, John also sought to bolster his own authority by playing off his local rivals against powerful

outsiders. Threatened by the intrigues of Berengar II of northern Italy, he called in Otto the Great of Germany. In return for
his protection, John bestowed the crown of holy roman emper-
or on Otto. He soon realised, however, that Otto's new authority threatened his own, and promptly started to intrigue against
him with the very Berengar he had previously feared. This was
to lead to the eventual downfall of the House of Theophylact
and the end of the Pornocracy, as Otto marched into Rome and
deposed him. He died shortly afterwards, according to one
source while making love to a married woman.

One of the most notorious episodes in the history of the
papacy was over, but the influence of this catalogue of duplicity and immorality was twofold. Firstly, John had inadvertent-
ly reinvigorated the role of holy roman emperor, helping to
start a line that was to last for 900 years. Secondly, the
Pornocracy had seriously undermined the moral authority of
the pope and set unfortunate precedents for papal behaviour.
Many of the popes that succeeded John over the next few centuries would be lascivious hedonists, and as a result alternative
creeds, decried by the papacy as heresies, gathered followers.
Among the most important of these would be the Bogomils of
the Balkan region and the Cathars of southern France. Popes
such as Alexander III and Innocent III would sanction terrible
programmes of extermination against these and other heresies,
culminating in the formal institution of the dreaded
Inquisition by Pope Gregory IX in 1231.

Going incognito – Undercover rulers: 800/1697

While hidden powers sometimes rule in secret, acknowledged
rulers sometimes choose to hide their power and go undercover. Known instances of this are rare, but there are two from
widely different cultures that stand out.

Haroun al-Rashid (c763–809 CE) was the greatest of the
Abbasid caliphs. He ruled an Islamic empire that stretched

from Persia to Egypt and from Yemen to the Black Sea, and the fabulous splendour of his court and of his capital, Baghdad, is immortalised in *The Book of the Thousand and One Nights*, in which he features frequently. Haroun, whose title translates into the rather less romantic sounding 'Aaron the Upright', became caliph at the young age of 21 but was shrewd enough to appoint good ministers. One of the most notable features of his enlightened reign was the effort he made to improve the quality of life in Baghdad. Numerous hospitals, amounting to a sort of medieval health system, were set up, as were temples, schools and a postal system. Security was improved with a kind of municipal police force. Legal reforms were instituted to ensure just treatment for all citizens (although slavery was also a major feature of life).

Nevertheless, Haroun's life of luxury and splendour in his fabulous palace was still very far removed from the difficult daily lot of his subjects. Perhaps he realised this, because his concern for their welfare drove him to take the unusual step of going among them. At night he would disguise himself, slip out of the palace and wander the streets and bazaars, listening to conversations and talking to ordinary people. In this way he could discover grievances, find out what was unpopular and learn whether his administration was dealing justly with the common people.

How much impact Haroun's incognito adventures had is impossible to say, but he was a very successful ruler. In international terms his influence was felt from China to Europe, where he made alliance with Charlemagne against their common foe, the Byzantines. More relevantly, in domestic terms Haroun's rule encouraged a secure and tolerant culture in which arts, learning, science and the trade and industry that made Baghdad and his court so fabulously wealthy could flourish.

Some 900 years later another ruler would go 'undercover' to try to improve the lot of his people. Peter I (1672–1725), was the tsar who made Russia a Great Power and a military force to be

reckoned with, starting the long, painful process of western-
ising and modernising the country. He was successful enough
to be called 'the Great'. One of the key episodes of his reign was
the Grand Embassy of 1697–1698, during which the Tsar travelled incognito.

As a youth growing up in Russia, Peter had spent much time
in and around the enclave where the European traders and
workers were based. Here he had learnt much about the
'advanced' science and technology of the West, especially his
favourite topic shipbuilding, and had grown accustomed to the
informality of life among the Europeans. This was in stark
contrast to the regimented life he was expected to lead as tsar.

In 1694 Peter attained full control of the country and immediately started a limited programme of shipbuilding. He also
launched campaigns against the Ottoman Turks to the south,
in an attempt to secure access to the sea for his then land-
locked country. After early reverses, Peter's drive and ingenuity
won through, but the Russian military was weak and old-fash-
ioned and eventually these gains had to be surrendered. His
experiences against the Turks probably helped to convince
Peter that Russia desperately needed Western technology,
innovation and support if she was to become a significant
power.

In 1697 Peter organised a delegation of 250 Russian officials
and some of their European advisors to tour a number of
European countries. It was to be known as the Grand Embassy.
Led by one of Peter's best friends, Admiral Francois Lefort, a
Swiss, the group would travel to the West to try and win support for a Grand Alliance against the Turks and also to see for
themselves, first-hand, some of the latest European science,
technologies and industry. Such a delegation was not unheard
of, but unusually Peter decided to join the Embassy himself.
Even more unusually, he would travel incognito, under the
name Sergeant Peter Michailov. To address him by his true
name or title was punishable by death.

In practice it was hard for Peter to travel incognito, partly because he was six feet seven inches tall. Probably everyone in the Embassy knew who he was and he often attracted large crowds as he and his companions travelled. Undaunted, Peter arranged for members of the delegation, including himself, to get work at some of the shipwrights' yards they visited. Peter worked for four months as a ship's carpenter at the Dutch East India Company's yard in Saardam, in the Netherlands, and later at the Royal Navy dockyard in Deptford when the Embassy visited England. He and other delegates visited factories and observatories, the Royal Mint and the Royal Society. Peter inspected ships and troops, visited Parliament and met with Quakers for informal religious discussions.

It was this informality that marked his visit, and helped him to engage with people from a variety of backgrounds. Although in political terms the Embassy was a failure (European countries were more concerned with matters closer to home and had no interest in an alliance against the Turks), Peter's skill at learning from his surroundings meant that it was a cultural, technical and economic success. Many Europeans were engaged to come back to Russia, to work and to train other Russians. Their impact helped Peter modernise Russia's outdated military institutions, create a formidable navy from scratch and bring Russia onto the world stage for the first time. He may have failed in his bid to remain incognito, but his 'undercover' policy helped begin the transformation of Russia.

Cardinal Richelieu: 1585–1642

The name of Cardinal Richelieu, prime minister of France under Louis XIII, has become synonymous with the figure, 'the power behind the throne'. Thanks mainly to Alexandre Dumas' *The Three Musketeers*, and its subsequent film adaptations, the image of Cardinal Richelieu held by most people today is of a cynical, corrupt old man, hungry for power for its own sake. Perhaps his most famous quote is: 'If you give me six lines written by the most honest man, I will find something in them to hang him.' But what is the truth about this enigmatic figure?

He was born Armand-Jean du Plessis, the third son of the lord of Richelieu, the ancestral estate. Originally he intended to pursue a career in the military, but when his older brother resigned the family bishopric of Luçon, Armand changed his professional direction. He studied theology and was made bishop at just 21. Here his career should have stopped. The Richelieux were a minor noble family, and Luçon a minor provincial diocese. Yet he rose to become the effective ruler of France and one of the most important statesmen in French history.

Richelieu was both ambitious and talented. He worked hard to make a success of the Luçon diocese and spoke well in the states-general, the French equivalent of Parliament. To his growing reputation as a capable administrator he allied political savvy, becoming known as a *dévot*, a staunch Catholic with pro-Spanish views. Handily this was also the faction of the French regent Marie de Medici, who ruled France in the minority of her son, Louis XIII.

Richelieu came to court in 1615 and soon caught the eye of Marie's favourite, Concini, who recognised his talents and had him appointed secretary of state for war and foreign affairs. His star was rising, but in 1617 it seemed likely to be extinguished. Concini was assassinated by rivals jealous of his power and that of the regency, and Richelieu was forced to follow Marie into exile in the country. For years he languished in the political wilderness, but after Marie's escape from her imprisonment he was instrumental in negotiating a reconciliation between Louis and his mother, and in 1622 was rewarded by being made a cardinal. At this time Louis was seeking a new chief minister, and with Marie's recommendation he chose Richelieu, making him prime minister in August 1624.

Once in a position of power, Richelieu spent the rest of his career relentlessly pursuing his philosophy of proper governance. The power of the king, who embodied France, was all-important, and all other considerations were secondary to the welfare of the state. Richelieu was a firm believer that the end justified the means; he insisted that 'harshness towards individuals who flout the laws and commands of the state is for the public good; no greater crime against the public interest is possible than to show leniency to those who violate it'. This philosophy essentially made him a nationalist, since he vigorously opposed anything that detracted from the interests of France and the crown. It also made him numerous enemies at every level, from the aristocrats to the peasantry.

To enforce this ruthless pragmatism Richelieu used means fair and foul. He defeated the strong French Protestant faction, the Huguenots, and reduced their stronghold at La Rochelle. He tore down the castles and fortresses of regional princes and nobles to weaken their ability to oppose the crown. He changed his foreign policy to the opposite of his previous *dévot* stance, making alliances with Protestant nations against Catholic Spain and Austria. For this he earned the enmity of the queen mother. Domestically he replaced the corrupt system of government administration with intendants – agents of the crown. He also instituted an extensive network of spies and informers.

Thanks to these spies he was able to defeat the constant stream of conspiracies aimed at him by disgruntled aristocrats, including Marie de Medici. He had several rivals executed. In general, the king was happy to let Richelieu rule the country in his stead, but in later life the cardinal grew worried that he might lose influence and attempted to bolster his position by introducing an attractive young man to the court. As Richelieu hoped, Henri Coiffier de Ruzé, marquis de Cinq-Mars, became Louis' lover and favourite. Expecting to be able to control Cinq-Mars as his puppet, Richelieu was dismayed to find that the marquis was actually trying to turn Louis against him, urging the king to have him executed. Richelieu was not to be beaten at his own game, however, and it was Cinq-Mars who lost his head.

Richelieu's influence on the king held up from beyond the grave. As he felt the icy hand of death approaching, he picked Cardinal Mazarin as his successor and Louis acquiesced. When Louis died in 1643, just six months after Richelieu had passed away, his will stipulated that the regents who watched over his infant son must follow Richelieu's disposition for the governance of France, and Mazarin governed as prime minister for many years, continuing his predecessor's policies.

Richelieu had ruled France from behind the throne for 18 years, and as he neared death was able to write to his king: 'I have the consolation of leaving your kingdom in the highest degree of glory and of reputation.' Although he was a schemer and a plotter, he was not motivated by the pursuit of power for its own sake, only for the sake of France: 'I have never had any [enemies], other than those of the state.'

6

~❧~

Secret Projects

~❧~

We tend to think of 'secret projects' as something futuristic, with a tinge of science-fiction, but men have long counted on scientific and technological breakthroughs to give them the edge they needed. In this chapter we look at some of the greatest undercover projects that have made the biggest impact on history, from ancient Greek super-weapons to the covert operation that touched off the space race. These projects show that a combination of ingenuity, diligent research and secrecy has often been the deciding factor in a conflict or the guiding factor in historical development. Oddly enough, the science and discovery element of an important secret project often takes a back seat to the clandestine element. This is because the true value of undercover research is surprise. Once a weapon has been used or a discovery divulged, the value of surprise is lost and, as often as not, the other side catches up, as for instance the Manhattan Project demonstrates.

Also, secret projects do not exist in isolation. Research, discoveries and inventions can only flourish if given the proper context of support. For instance, the Nazis developed a number of advanced weapons during the closing stages of World

War II, but despite Hitler's conviction that these would win the war for Germany, lack of training, fuel, materials, manpower and, crucially, time, meant that their impact was extremely limited. As the investigation of Operation Paperclip shows, one of the most important results of the Nazi super-weapon programme was to kickstart Western development of advanced military technology – hardly the outcome that Hitler intended.

Lastly, care needs to be taken that the very secrecy surrounding a covert project does not become its undoing. The story of the archetypal secret weapon – the Greek fire of the Byzantines – illustrates this danger only too well, while in the case of the ultimate secret project – The Manhattan Project – concealment helped to transform a tool of peace into an instrument of repression.

Archimedes and the defence of Syracuse: 212 BCE

Ancient sources record a variety of secret weapons used to achieve victory in battle. The Israelites under Joshua used a god-powered sonic weapon, created by blowing their horns all at once, to shatter the walls of Jericho. Great Homeric warriors benefited from such divine weapons as the spear and aegis (impenetrable shield) of Athena or the winged sandals of Hermes (which helped Perseus to defeat the sea monster). But these weapons owed their special powers to the gods. One of the first recorded uses of human ingenuity to create super-weapons was the Siege of Syracuse, in 212 BCE, where one man's genius turned the tide of battle.

After the First Punic War, the Greek colony of Syracuse in Sicily, formerly aligned with the Carthaginians, made alliance with the Romans. But during the Second Punic War, the successes of Hannibal on the Italian peninsula led it to change sides once more, and a Roman army under Marcus Claudius Marcellus was sent to retake the city and punish the turncoats. Marcellus' first stop was the town of Leontini, which he sacked with horrible brutality. The citizens of Syracuse now knew what fate awaited them if they failed to resist the Roman attack.

In 213 BCE Marcellus moved against Syracuse itself. He could marshal 68 massive war galleys – ships known as quinqueremes, equipped with banks of oars, and filled, according to Polybius, the historian writing closest to the date of the battle, with 'archers, slingers and javelin-throwers'. Some of the galleys were roped together to form stable platforms upon which were raised siege engines known as *sambucae*. These were towers that could be brought up against the city walls to disgorge units of marines. Meanwhile Marcellus' co-commander, Appius Claudius Pulcher, led an army against the landward walls of the city. The Syracusans were massively outnumbered, and Marcellus assumed that the city would soon fall to the might of the Roman army. But, in the words of Polybius, 'in some cases the genius of one man is far more effective than superiority in numbers.'

That one man was Archimedes, the near legendary Greek mathematician and engineer. Generally regarded as the greatest mathematician of antiquity and one of the three greatest of all time, Archimedes was more interested in the pure delights of mathematics than the grubby realities of engineering, despite having invented such marvels as the planetarium, water organ and, according to legend, the water screw that still bears his name. But he was devoted to the king of Syracuse, Hiero II, and accordingly had set to work to surreptitiously strengthen the fortifications of the city and equip it with the most fearsome defensive arsenal ever seen. The attacking Romans were about to run into a battery of secret weapons the like of which they had never experienced.

The first weapons encountered by the advancing Romans were a series of fearsome catapults (probably actually mangonels, where the arm that tosses the projectile is powered by a dropping counterweight), which hurled huge boulders and lead weights. Archimedes had designed long, medium and short-range catapults, together with 'scorpions' – catapults that discharged iron darts; all were cunningly concealed behind the city walls. No matter how close the Romans pressed to the walls the defenders were able to fire at them, and to the terrified troops it appeared as if the stones were raining down from nowhere.

When the Roman galleys got too near for even the short-range catapults, the Syracusans deployed Archimedes' next innovation: extendable arms with weights on the end, which could be pushed forwards through specially designed embrasures in the walls until they projected directly over the enemy ships, whereupon the weights would be released to smash down onto the galleys and their siege engines.

Most fearsome of all was a war machine known as 'Archimedes' Claw'. This was a sort of grappling iron, sometimes described as an 'iron hand', on the end of a chain attached to a giant lever. The iron hand was tossed onto the prow of the enemy boat, seizing it fast. The lever was then depressed, so that the prow of the boat was elevated, standing the vessel on its stern. When the lever was released, the boat would crash back down, heeling over, capsizing or simply sinking, spilling the crew and marines into the sea. Similar devices were employed against the Roman soldiers advancing by land – the 'claw' engines seized handfuls of troops and flung them about.

These impressive and ingenious military innovations were recorded by a number of Greek and Roman historians, including Polybius, who lived shortly after the Second Punic War and might have had access to survivors. Later sources record the most startling and futuristic sounding of Archimedes' weapons – the Burning Mirror. The exact form given depends on the sources. According to the 12th-century Byzantine historian John Tzetzes, supposedly paraphrasing the Roman historian Dio Cassius (155–235 CE), it was a hexagonal mirror (probably of polished bronze), surrounded by smaller square mirrors, the whole assemblage fixed to an armature. The mirrors gathered the rays of the sun and concentrated them into a laser-like beam, which ignited the Roman galleys from a distance, reducing them to ashes.

Today Archimedes' Burning Mirror is generally considered to be a myth, but early European scientists had mixed feelings about the tale. In the 13th century, Franciscan monk Roger Bacon warned Pope Clement IV that '[the Muslims] will use these mirrors to burn up cities, camps and weapons' in their conflict with the crusaders, although he was apparently slung in jail for even suggesting such a heretical notion. In the 17th century Descartes dismissed the story as fantasy, but in 1747 George Louis LeClerc, comte de Buffon, claimed to have ignited a pine plank from 150 feet (45 metres), using an array of 128 mirrors. More recently in 1975, Greek scientist Dr Ioannis Sakkas claimed to have used 60 mirrors held up by sailors to ignite a wooden ship from 160 feet (48 metres), while in 2002 a German experiment using 500 people with mirrors supposedly had similar success. Even if the technology is feasible, this does not mean the story of Archimedes' Burning Mirror is true, but perhaps it should not be dismissed out of hand.

With or without the Burning Mirror, the genius of Archimedes was too much for Marcellus and the Roman army. In the words of Polybius, 'the Romans ... had every hope of capturing the city immediately if only one old man out of all the Syracusans could have been removed; but so long as he was present they did not dare even to attempt an attack ...' Beaten back with heavy losses, the Romans were forced to abandon their assault. Instead they opted to starve the city into submission, and launched an eight-month siege. Finally, in 212 BCE, Marcellus was able to take advantage of a Greek festival in the city to sneak past the defences and breach the inland walls.

Thus the immediate consequences of Archimedes' genius may have been slight, merely delaying the fall of Syracuse for a year. But his legacy to science has been considerable; even that of his perhaps-mythical Burning Mirror, which helped to inspire the research into parabolic dishes that has led to today's radio telescopes and satellite TV antennae. Whether fact or fiction, it has also left a more direct legacy as the forebear of the directed-energy weapons of the 'Star Wars' missile defence programme.

Archimedes himself had little regard for the concrete but transitory products of his fertile genius. He preferred the realm of mathematics, where truth is eternal. Accounts of his death relate that, as the Romans poured into Syracuse and sacked the city, a soldier broke into Archimedes' house and ordered him to report to Marcellus, but that he was too preoccupied with a mathematical problem and refused to come until it was completed, whereupon the soldier ran him through.

The lost secret of Byzantium – Greek fire: 675–950 CE

The archetypal secret weapon also remains one of the most mysterious. Greek fire was a napalm-like incendiary substance used by the Byzantines in the defence of their ancient but crumbling empire. Its technology was a closely-guarded enigma known only to the imperial family and associates, and remains a mystery to this day. In its own time it was sparingly used, and the obsessive secrecy that surrounded it ultimately led to its loss; nonetheless it is one of the best examples of a secret that changed the course of history.

In 673 CE the Byzantine Empire was the sole remnant of the glory that was Rome and last bulwark of European civilisation. After three centuries of vying with foes from east and west, it faced a new threat – the deadliest yet. The Arabs, fired with zeal for their new religion Islam, had overrun the Persian Empire and now assailed the great walls of Constantinople itself, threatening to utterly extinguish the Eastern Empire. Byzantium was outnumbered by land and by sea, and although the mighty defences of the capital could not be breached by the military technology of the time, the city could be starved into submission if the Arab fleet could wrest control of the seas.

In the amazing success of the Arab expansion, however, lay the seeds of their defeat. When their armies overran Christian Syria, refugees flocked to the safety of Constantinople. Among them was a Syrian Greek called Kallinikos, who brought with him the recipe for a weapon that would become known as 'Greek fire', in reference to his ethnicity, although it is also variously known as 'liquid fire', 'sea fire' or 'Persian fire'. The last of these is a possible reference to its true origin, for some sources claim that Kallinikos had previously been in the employ of the Muslim military. Incendiary weapons based on petroleum products, such as pitch or naptha, were part of the Arab arsenal; in fact they were probably known in one form or another to the Romans and Persians before them. What distinguished the new 'Greek' fire was its advanced composition and, crucially, the 'delivery' technology – the apparatus that was used to spray the flaming liquid.

Kallinikos is said to have been paid a fortune for the new technology, which thereafter remained a closely guarded mystery. Even today it is only possible to speculate on the composition of Greek fire, but it is generally thought to have included sulphur, quicklime, liquid petroleum and perhaps even magnesium (a constituent of modern incendiary weapons). Magnesium is a highly reactive metal that will even burn underwater, one of the characteristics attributed to Greek fire, which helped to make it such a fearsome weapon. To spray this liquid death, the Byzantines invented an ingenious siphon device. The Greek fire would be heated in a cauldron and then pumped through a system of pipes that heated and pressurised the mixture further, before spraying it out of a nozzle with an attached lamp for igniting the fluid. Greek fire thus involved a whole set of technologies and the related engineering and chemical skills to make them work. This complexity helped to keep the technology a secret, since only a few top officials would have all the pieces of the puzzle.

The effects of Greek fire were devastating to the enemies of Byzantium. The Byzantine navy used special war galleys known as *dromons*, which had wide, flat decks upon which could be mounted structures such as towers and castles, as well as the Greek fire siphons. These would spew their contents onto the decks of the enemy ships, where the crew and marines were very exposed and the wooden ships would burn easily. In 678 the Arabs would experience this first hand. The deployment of Greek fire dramatically turned the tide of battle. Where, a few years earlier, the Arabs had destroyed hundreds of Byzantine ships, now it was their navy that was shattered, with the loss of thousands of men. The siege was broken and the Arabs were forced to sue for peace. When they attacked again, in 717, Greek fire once again played a pivotal role in the defence of the city and the Arabs were again beaten back with severe losses.

The importance of Greek fire was obvious to the Byzantines, as was the need to guard its mysteries. It was used as little as possible, to help prevent the siphon apparatus falling into enemy hands, while prohibitions and legends grew up around its mysterious recipe. Writing to his son, Emperor Constantine VII Porphyrogennetos stressed that the secret must not be revealed even to allies, and explained:

> ... *the ingredients were disclosed by an angel to the first great Christian emperor, Constantine ... and that great emperor, wishing to secure the secret for his successors, ordained that they should curse, in writing and on the Holy Altar of the Church of God, any who should dare to give this fire to another nation, that he should not be counted amongst the Christians, neither should he hold any rank or honour and if he happens to have one already, let him be deposed and paraded like a common criminal throughout*

*the centuries, whether he be an emperor, a patriarch or any
other lord or subject; whosoever should attempt to disobey
this order.*

Over the next three centuries the Byzantine Empire contended
with enemies in all directions. Sometimes it expanded, recon-
quering territories possessed during the days of Rome; often,
however, it was on the back foot, and in defence of the empire
Greek fire was invaluable. (The difficulties of using it and
reluctance to expose the secret to capture limited its offensive
role.) But by 1204 the secret had somehow been lost.
Incendiary weapons were still used (and still referred to as
'Greek fire'), but the package of technology that made Greek
fire so formidable was no longer available. It seems likely that
the mystery surrounding the weapon was its own undoing.
The deadly politics of Byzantium meant that power was con-
tested through an endless series of coups, intrigues and assassinations. It is easy to see how the chain of transmission of the
knowledge was broken. The empire struggled on for another
five centuries, but grew steadily smaller as other powers
encroached. Finally, in 1453, the Ottoman Turks were able to
breach the defences of Constantinople using gunpowder, a
technology that would in any case have superseded Greek fire.

But Greek fire had already made its impact on history. By
checking the hitherto unstoppable spread of Muslim armies
and holding back the forces of Islam in the Eastern
Mediterranean for hundreds of years, the successful Byzantine
resistance gave the rest of Europe a centuries-long breathing
space. In this time, European nations grew strong, while
European military technology and tactics advanced to the
extent that they could hold their own. The success of the
Muslim advance across North Africa and Spain and into
Southern France showed the extent of their reach. If they had
overrun the Byzantine Empire in the 7th century and flooded
into the disorganised lands of Eastern Europe, how far might

they have penetrated? The shape of Europe and the direction of world history might have turned out very differently without the secret of Greek fire.

Captain Cook's secret search for the Southern Continent: 1768–1771

On 26 August 1768, James Cook (then only a lieutenant) set sail from Plymouth in the bark *Endeavour* on a mission that today is often compared to a voyage to outer space. Together with a small team of scientists and a crew of less than a hundred men, Cook would sail to the far side of the world and into the midst of a vast ocean of unknown limits and uncertain geography. Ostensibly his mission was to visit Tahiti where his passengers would undertake astronomical observations of the transit of Venus across the sun. But Cook had also been issued secret instructions by his masters at the Admiralty – instructions for a covert mission that would change the shape of the world and determine the course of history in the Pacific.

By the mid-18th century a number of European explorers had visited the Pacific and the seas of the Southern Ocean with one object uppermost in their minds. Learned opinion agreed that there must exist to the south a great landmass, a huge continent that would counterbalance the northern continents. It was assumed that this *Terra Australis Incognito*, or 'Unknown Southern Land', must be as rich in potential for exploitation and colonisation as the Americas had proved to be. Furthermore, it might be uninhabited, or inhabited only by the sorts of natives who had been so easily brushed aside in the New World. Whichever (necessarily European) nation could claim this territory first could reap great benefits and steal a march on its rivals. There would be untold advantages for science, mineral and agricultural wealth and trade.

Thus when a chance arose to dispatch a mission to discover, chart, explore and, if possible, claim this mystery land, the

British Admiralty seized upon it. That chance was offered by a scientific expedition planned by the Royal Society. Earlier in the 18th century the astronomer Edmond Halley had predicted that Venus would transit across the face of the sun in 1761 and then again in 1769. Observing and measuring the transit from two widely spaced points on the earth's surface would allow astronomers to calculate the distance from the earth to the sun, gaining one of the first elements of empirical evidence as to the size of the universe. An expedition to observe the transit from St Helena in 1761 had failed when low cloud obscured the sun. Now the Royal Society planned another, bolder expedition to the far side of the world. Observations garnered there could be compared to measurements taken at Greenwich, and used to calculate the earth–sun distance.

Previous such expeditions under the control of scientists had not gone well – one led by Halley himself decades earlier had nearly ended in mutiny. The admiralty insisted that this time the expedition be led by a navy man. Cook, having proved his credentials in surveys of North America's eastern seaboard, was selected. The Royal Society put about news of the voyage, which was to be bankrolled by the king, a keen astronomer. The cover story was in place, its credibility boosted by its veracity.

On 30 July, Cook was given his commission and issued with orders to go to Tahiti. Within the orders was a sealed packet of Secret Instructions. These made very clear the nature of his true mission:

> *Whereas there is reason to imagine that a Continent or Land of great extent, may be found to the South ... You are to proceed to the southward in order to make discovery of the Continent above-mentioned ... You are to employ yourself diligently in exploring as great an Extent of the Coast as you can ... to observe the Nature of the Soil, and the Products thereof; the Beasts and Fowls that inhabit or*

frequent it, the fishes that are to be found in the Rivers or upon the Coast and in what Plenty; and in case you find any Mines, Minerals or valuable stones you are to bring home Specimens of each, as also such Specimens of the Seeds of the Trees, Fruits and Grains as you may be able to collect ... You are likewise to observe the Genius, Temper, Disposition and Number of the Natives ... You are also with the Consent of the Natives to take possession of Convenient Situations in the Country in the name of the King of Great Britain; or, if you find the Country uninhabited take Possession for his Majesty by setting up Proper Marks and inscriptions, as first discoverers and possessors.

If he could not find the fabled *Terra Australis*, Cook was to explore instead lands already 'discovered' by Europeans, such as New Zealand and New Holland (as what little of Australia had then been sighted was known).

The voyage of the *Endeavour* fulfilled most of its instigators' dreams, except of course the discovery of the Great Southern Continent. Cook came within a few hundred miles of discovering Antarctica, but the Counterweight Continent as envisaged by Europeans did not exist. Instead the doughty navigator charted the coastlines of New Zealand and eastern Australia, claiming the latter for crown and country (despite the obvious signs of habitation). The *Endeavour* also visited and charted numerous Pacific islands and gathered a huge wealth of biological and geological specimens and data, not to mention successfully observing the transit.

The longer-term consequences of Cook's secret mission were profound. Australia and New Zealand became British colonies and were extensively settled by Europeans to the detriment of their indigenous inhabitants. Today they are successful, prosperous democracies. The other lands touched by Cook were also altered for better and worse, ending their isolation and incorporating them into the wider world. Disease, war, trade and colonisation killed many natives and transformed their cultures and societies. Bernard Smith, professor of History at Melbourne University, describes Cook as 'unquestionably one of the great formative agents in the creation of the modern world. His ships, you might say, began the process of making the world a global village.' His was a secret mission that genuinely changed the world.

Radar – The technology that won the war: 1940

Radar – radio direction and range-finding – was one of the key advances that made World War II a conflict of technology and science as much as men and bullets. It has been variously described as 'the weapon that won World War II' and 'the invention that changed the world'. During the 1930s the Germans and the British were engaged in a race to develop radar, and it was British superiority at the start of the war that helped to win the Battle of Britain. Key to this superiority was a clandestine mission to America undertaken by Britain's top scientists, to exchange technological secrets with the Americans and secure American help in getting an edge on the Germans.

The idea of using radio wave echoes reflected off distant objects as a means of detecting them – the basis of radar – had been suggested long before the 1930s. In particular, after the *Titanic* disaster of 1912, there was widespread interest in potential collision avoidance techniques, and German engineer Christian Huelsmeyer suggested using radio echoes for this purpose. In 1924 the British physicist Edward Appleton successfully used radar reflection to measure the height of the ionosphere. Both British and American scientists had been made further aware of the potential of radio waves by the disruption to radio signals caused by passing aircraft and ships. But it wasn't until Britain started to gear up for a potential war that attention was focused on the need to develop some sort of early-warning system for airborne attacks.

An early candidate for such a system used giant concrete acoustic mirrors to try to pick up the noise of approaching aircraft, but when a demonstration of the system was ruined by a passing milk cart the Air Ministry realised that something new was desperately needed. A committee under Henry Tizard was set up to examine the problem, and in late 1934 this in turn commissioned Robert Watson-Watt of the Radio Research Station to look at how radio waves might be used. He and his assistant AF Wilkins came up with the idea of firing out pulses of radio waves and detecting the echoes that bounced off approaching aircraft. Watson-Watt patented the idea in 1935, and by 1936 there was a chain of radar stations along the south and east coasts, forming the Chain Home (CH) early warning system.

The CH system, together with other radar technologies dreamt up by the scientists such as friend-or-foe identification technology, was to prove its worth during the Battle of Britain in 1940. Masses of German planes stretched the meagre resources of the RAF to breaking point, but thanks to radar the few planes available could be used to maximum effect. But the truth was that German radar was at least as good as, if not better than, British.

British radar was limited by the wavelength that British transmitters and receivers could use and the power they could manage. Overly long radio waves limited the resolution of radar, while low power meant that the range and accuracy suffered. The key to better radar was the ability to generate and detect microwaves – radio waves with very small wavelengths. In 1940 physicist Henry Boot and biophysicist John T Randall invented a device called the resonant-cavity magnetron, capable of generating high-energy pulses of microwaves. It was years ahead of its time, and exactly what Britain needed to gain the upper hand in the technology war with the Germans. The magnetron was small enough to fit into the palm of a hand, the perfect size to be fitted into aircraft, ships and land vehicles, making extremely high-resolution, highly accurate radar a possibility in all theatres of conflict. The Germans would have paid a king's ransom simply to learn of its existence. It was, in the words of radar historian Robert Buderi, 'Britain's most closely guarded secret.'

But there was a problem. Britain did not have the scientific or manufacturing might to put the magnetron to best use. British factories could not turn out enough of the magnetrons to the right specifications, while the associated technology of receivers and power supply was not adequate. Churchill hoped that the Americans, known to be pursuing their own radar researches but formally still neutral, could be convinced to exchange technological secrets and offer help. Tizard was commissioned to gather up the nation's top scientific and technological secrets, together with a crack team of scientists, and travel to America to meet his US counterpart. The brightest jewel in this treasure trove of technological marvels was the magnetron. James Phinney Baxter III, official historian of the US Office of Scientific Research and Development, later wrote: 'When the members of the Tizard Mission brought one to America in 1940, they carried the most valuable cargo ever brought to our shores.'

The initial reception for the Tizard Mission was frosty – some senior American officials didn't feel the British had much to offer in return for their state secrets – and since America was officially neutral both sides had to tread carefully, meeting behind closed doors and in confidence. When the British delegation unveiled the magnetron, however, a full and frank exchange began. The Americans had also been developing radar, and although they had not been able to crack the problem of generating high power microwave bursts, their associated technology and crucially their ability to mass produce were ahead of the British.

The collaboration that ensued was based around a new Radiation Lab (known as RadLab) at the Massachusetts

Institute of Technology. This grew into a huge research effort that eventually employed over 4,000 people on several continents, and designed half of the radar systems deployed during the war. Allied radar technology quickly outstripped German capabilities, with important consequences for the conduct of the war – for instance, night bombing became more effective and air fleets were able to operate in a wider range of weather conditions. The RadLab project has been described as 'one of the most significant, massive, secret, and outstandingly successful technological efforts' of the war.

Radar was just one of a host of technologies that made World War II a conflict of technology. Both sides pursued covert projects and German backroom scientists came up with as many incredible advances as Allied ones. But German 'super-weapons', upon which Hitler pinned so much hope in the closing stages of the war, failed to make a significant impact partly because the resources, training and tactics needed to back them up were not available. The Allies, on the other hand, were able to harness their inventiveness to logistical realities and realise the full benefit of their research. Clandestine missions like Tizard's made this possible.

The Manhattan Project: 1942–1945

The greatest secret project of all time was the Manhattan Project or, to give it its full title, the Manhattan Engineering District Project: the effort to develop a nuclear bomb. The Manhattan Project broke all records for its scale, cost and ambition. It was arguably the greatest scientific endeavour of the age, while also being one of the greatest civil engineering and industrial feats. Incredibly, it also managed to remain almost entirely secret, to the extent that many of its thousands of workers only figured out what they had been working on when news of the attacks on Hiroshima and Nagasaki was released. It wasn't until after the war that it was discovered that in fact there had been information leaks, with results that would change the world as much as the nuclear bomb itself.

The 1930s were years of great advances in nuclear physics, culminating in 1938 and 1939 with the discovery of nuclear fission and the realisation that it could produce vast quantities of energy. As a result of Nazi persecution, many of Europe's greatest physicists moved to the US to join the heavyweights already there. With them they brought disturbing news – the Germans had taken the first steps along the road to turning theory into devastating practice and had started to investigate the potential for a nuclear bomb. Aware that the warnings of foreign scientists might go unheeded, the leading émigrés, such as Leo Szilard and Edward Teller, approached the most famous scientist in America, Albert Einstein, and solicited his support. Einstein's 2 August 1939 letter to President Roosevelt triggered the start of America's attempt to develop 'the bomb'.

At first research was carried out piecemeal, at institutions around the country. There were two main strands of research. The first was the effort to work out the theory and practice of the bomb itself. What were the physics of nuclear fission? How would a chain reaction work? How could it be started? The second strand was the question of the fissile material itself – the radioactive material that would be needed to make the bomb. Danish physicist Niels Bohr had suggested uranium-235, a rare isotope of the element uranium that had to be separated from the much more common isotope uranium-238. Unfortunately no one was sure how to do this, particularly in the quantities and at the speed that would be necessary. American physicist Glenn Seaborg came up with another candidate, plutonium-239, and worked out that it could be created by exposing uranium-238 to neutrons in a nuclear reactor. Again, this had never been done.

While the scientists were formulating and theorising, the official status of the project was evolving. The initial research grant had come from the navy, and further research had been done under the auspices of the National Bureau of Standards. In 1940 President Roosevelt and Vannevar Bush, head of the Carnegie Institution, and destined to become the most powerful man in American science and research during the war, created the Office of Scientific Research to move nuclear research forwards. In 1941, word came that physicists in Britain had mathematically demonstrated the massive destructive potential of a fission bomb. Bush instituted a special committee to accelerate nuclear research. Soon afterwards the Japanese bombed Pearl Harbour and America was at war. As the country mobilised for a total war effort, the nuclear programme would change from a disparate group of independent researchers into the most focused, single-minded research effort in history.

The first step was, innocuously enough, an academic summer conference. Organised by J Robert Oppenheimer, a University of California scientist who had been working on the theory behind the bomb, the conference brought together many of the leading nuclear fission researchers. Together they thrashed out the basic design of a nuclear fission bomb. The conference also highlighted the need for a single laboratory where all the research efforts could be combined and coordinated, while it became clear to Vannevar Bush and other notables that the lack of fissile materials – the uranium and plutonium isotopes – was an even more serious problem.

In September 1942, Bush asked Roosevelt to combine the disparate research efforts under the command of the military. The project was given to the Army Corps of Engineers, who named it 'the Development of Substitute Materials' and assigned Colonel James Marshall to take charge. The first priority was to get started on the huge plants that would be needed to produce adequate quantities of fissile material, but at the time only one method had moved beyond the theoretical stage, and even that was riddled with problems.

Marshall was beset with difficulties. Project scientists criticised him for not getting started on the plants, but he was unwilling to move until designs had been finalised, while squabbling between the scientists made it hard to decide which research paths to pursue. He also struggled because the project had insufficient priority to allow him to requisition materials that were reserved for other war efforts, such as steel for the plant construction. Even the name of the project was criticised for giving too much away.

A new man was selected to take charge. Colonel Leslie Groves, almost immediately promoted to brigadier-general in order to impress the scientists he would have to command, had impeccable credentials, having just overseen the construction of the world's biggest office building – the Pentagon. Despite his desire to be posted to a combat theatre, he found himself in charge of a crisis-hit project at home. His first step was to rechristen the project, following the convention of naming Engineer Corps projects after the district of the project's headquarters; in this case, Manhattan.

Groves quickly got the Manhattan Project moving, settling disputes and making bold decisions. His aggressive and forceful management style would be key to the amazing success of the project. Groves purchased a site in Knoxville, Tennessee, later to be known as Oak Ridge, and ordered work to start on the uranium separation plant, even though the designs could not be finalised.

Meanwhile, in December 1942, Enrico Fermi, a Nobel Prize-winning émigré physicist, had made a major breakthrough. In his laboratory beneath an old playing field at the University of Chicago, Fermi had built a small nuclear reactor, and achieved the first self-sustaining nuclear chain reaction. Using scaled-up versions of his methods, it would be possible to make plutonium-239. Groves now selected another site, at Hanford in Washington State, for a huge plant that would produce plutonium.

The scale of the two plants, at Oak Ridge and Hanford, was breathtaking. Residents living in the areas were evacuated en masse, and entire towns built from scratch for the tens of thousands of workers. At Oak Ridge, for instance, by the end of 1942, there were plans for 13,000 people to live; by March 1943 this had been revised to 45,000 people. By the end of the war, Oak Ridge was the fifth largest town in Tennessee, and the uranium plant was consuming one-seventh of all the power being produced in the nation. Just one of the uranium separation factories, the Y-12 plant, required 38 million feet of lumber, and 15,000 tons of silver borrowed from the US Treasury (because there wasn't enough copper available), for making electrical components. All of this effort was directed according to plans that changed as construction proceeded, with all the glitches that might be expected in trying to transfer a process from lab to full-scale industry without any of the usual proving stages. Meanwhile, over in New Mexico, a small town had been built on the site of an old ranch. This was the Los Alamos research site, an 'intellectual boomtown' where J. Robert Oppenheimer led a team of scientists and engineers as they attempted to overcome immense theoretical and practical difficulties to design an atom bomb.

As well as the incredible size and speed of the project, Groves had to ensure its total secrecy. To achieve this he instituted a culture of absolute secrecy, following the dogma of compartmentalisation, where the left hand does not know what the right hand is doing: '... compartmentalization of knowledge, to me, was the very heart of security. My rule was simple and not capable of misinterpretation – each man should know everything he needed to know [to] do his job and nothing else.' Concealment extended to the smallest detail, though not always displaying great imagination – when Enrico Fermi visited the Hanford plutonium processing site his ID badge gave a fake name: 'Henry Farmer'.

The surreptitious nature of the project meant that Groves was able to circumvent political considerations of cost, safety or morality. There was effectively a blank chequebook for the

Manhattan Project, and its progress was not hampered or hamstrung by governmental oversight. This may have been justified at the time, but many feel that the Manhattan Project became the prototype for massive covert projects operating without proper civil or democratic oversight, a clandestine crop that would bear fruit in Eisenhower's warnings about the growing power of the military-industrial complex and operations like the Iran–Contra affair.

Under Groves' relentless driving, the Manhattan Project met its impossible deadlines. In less than three years, the fissile material production effort had gone from virgin ground to huge industrial plants, producing enough material for three bombs. One, codenamed Gadget, would be used as a test device. The other two, Little Boy and Fat Man, uranium and plutonium bombs respectively, would be used in anger.

By the summer of 1945, the Manhattan Project was ready to test Gadget. A test site in the Jornada del Muerto Valley in New Mexico was selected and codenamed Trinity. Harry Truman, who had recently become president on the death of Roosevelt, wanted to know the results before he attended the Potsdam Conference with Churchill and Stalin at the end of July. On 16 July 1945, Gadget was detonated at Trinity. The effects were awesome, as hundreds of thousands of Japanese would shortly discover. The Manhattan Project had succeeded.

By the end of the war the project had cost around $2 billion – over $25 billion in today's money. The cost in Japanese lives was probably around 400,000, but most historians agree that by shortening the war and avoiding the planned invasion of Japan, the bombs may have saved more than a million lives. The consequences for world history were profound and would last for decades. Despite the amazing success of the domestic security operation around the Manhattan Project, communist spies had succeeded in smuggling many of the secrets of the atom bomb to Soviet Russia, including details of research into the much more powerful hydrogen bomb. The discovery of this treachery led to a huge panic about the Soviets having the bomb and an escalation of nuclear weapon research and manufacture. To the dismay of many of the scientists who had originated and led the Manhattan research effort, the Project spawned a global arms race and a terrifying nuclear stand off that still bears fruit today, as unstable nations, rogue states and terrorists pursue nuclear projects of their own.

Operation Paperclip: 1945–1957

Perhaps the brightest episode in post-war American history was the successful moon landings. Underpinning this incredible achievement, however, was one of the darkest episodes of that history; a massive covert operation, codenamed Paperclip, to secure the technological and human riches of Nazi science for American ends and in the process helping hundreds of the Third Reich's worst war criminals to escape justice. Paperclip was just one facet of a wider American strategy of plundering the material and human assets of Germany, partly as a form of war reparation and partly to prepare for what many Americans already foresaw: the coming clash with the communists.

Operation Paperclip started life in 1945 as Operation Overcast, changing its name in 1946. The curious name derived from the practice of marking with a paperclip the files of those detainees who were selected for transfer to America. The aim of Operation Paperclip was to get hold of useful German science and technology before the Russians did. This included personnel. American teams from an agency known as Field Intelligence Agency Technical scoured the country looking for everything from chemical weapons and rockets to scientists and technicians. The whole operation was wrapped in secrecy from the outset. No media contact was allowed and no one else in the military was allowed to interrogate the chosen Germans. In all communications, care was taken to refer to them as 'German civilians' rather than scientists.

President Truman had signed on for Paperclip, but with the strict proviso that anyone found 'to have been a member of the Nazi party and more than a nominal participant in its activities, or an active supporter of Naziism or militarism' was excluded. Unfortunately this did not chime with the aims and intentions of those running the operation. When the War Department's Joint Intelligence Objectives Agency (JIOA) had finished compiling dossiers on the captured scientists, they were turned over to the State and Justice Departments for visa approval. The files revealed that all the scientists in question had been ardent Nazis, and their visas were denied. JIOA director Bosquet Wev complained: 'the best interests of the United States have been subjugated to the efforts expended in "beating a dead Nazi horse".' The files also suggested that the Nazi scientists would pose a threat to the security of the USA. Wev's response showed the thinking of the American intelligence community. Leaving these scientists in Germany where they might fall into the hands of the dreaded communists, he argued, was a 'far greater security threat to this country than any former Nazi affiliations which they may have had or even any Nazi sympathies that they may still have.'

The reaction of the JIOA and their colleagues in the CIA was to simply rewrite the offending profiles. Probably the most prominent Paperclip recruit was Wernher von Braun, architect of America's space programme, but previously mastermind of Germany's V-2 rocket programme. Von Braun's initial file labelled him 'a potential security threat'. The sanitised version, issued six months later, opined that 'he may not constitute a security threat to the United States.'

In fact von Braun's story illustrates well the ambiguous and sometimes insidious nature of Operation Paperclip. A physicist with a fascination for rockets and a dream of interplanetary exploration, von Braun's early research was funded by the German Ordnance Department. By 1934, however, with the Nazis in control, military development was the only avenue open and he began work at the notorious Peenemünde base, developing anti-aircraft and long-range ballistic missiles, culminating in the development of the A-4. In 1943, ignoring objections that it was an inefficient way of delivering explosives and an unconscionable drain on resources, Hitler decided that the A-4 would be a 'vengeance weapon', and it was pressed into service as the V-2. Hundreds were launched at London (where the authorities launched a concerted campaign to make it look as though the missiles were overshooting, to try to fool the Germans into aiming short), raining death and destruction with little strategic rationale.

The extent of von Braun's complicity is hard to gauge. His official biography, pushed to an American public ready to make allowances for their space hero, carefully paints the picture of a reluctant Nazi, concerned only with his dreams of interplanetary exploration and motivated only by his desire to build bigger and better rockets, and maybe it's the truth. According to this biography, von Braun was arrested by the Gestapo and charged by the SS with being too interested in space rocketry and insufficiently devoted to the cause of the Fuhrer. Supposedly he had been opposed to the use of the rockets to attack England. His military colleague at Peenemünde had to intercede with Hitler to get him released on the basis that the V-2 programme would cease to exist without him.

Not long after his return to the base, von Braun called together his team and they agreed to try to surrender to the Americans, reasoning that they alone would be able to afford to continue the rocket programme. Von Braun led a bold dash to safety through SS and Gestapo checkpoints, commandeering trains and trucks to carry 500 people and all their equipment, bluffing with forged papers where necessary. The boys from Operation Paperclip were already searching for them, so once contact was established the Americans were only too glad to take them into custody, and immediately dispatched a large team to loot Peenemünde and bring back 300 train carloads of

V-2 parts. Hitler's secret weapons would now serve a new master. Eventually (after suitable reworking of his dossier) von Braun and 132 members of his team were brought to America, to form the nucleus of the nascent US missile programme. In 1960 he finally achieved his dream of heading an interplanetary rocket research team, and masterminded the development of the Saturn rockets that would take man to the moon.

Von Braun's clashes with the SS and subsequent heroic, *Von Ryan's Express*-style exploits certainly made it easier for the American public to overlook his past, and the rehabilitation of his public persona was completed when he became an avuncular figure in a series of wildly popular Disney programmes. But question marks remained. How much of a Nazi was he? Hadn't he gone along with the use of slave labour at Peenemünde and masterminded a programme that brought death to hundreds of English civilians? His initial JIAO assessment was far from sanguine and not everyone was willing to forgive and forget. In later years von Braun found himself on a flight scheduled to touch down for refuelling in Britain, where he was still a wanted war criminal. A quiet word in the captain's ear ensured that the plane continued to a less inimical destination.

Many of the scientists recruited by Operation Paperclip were far less savoury than von Braun. For instance, Arthur Rudolph, another key member of the Saturn rocket team, had been operations director of a death camp factory that used slave labour who were starved, tortured and worked to death. His initial assessment labelled him '100% Nazi' and suggested internment. When his past was revealed in 1984 he fled to West Germany.

Even worse, Paperclip recruited many scientists who had been involved in the Nazi's notorious human experiments. Kurt Blome had experimented on concentration camp prisoners with plague vaccines and was accused of systematically murdering sick prisoners. He was recruited to work for the US Army Chemical Corps. Major General Walter Schreiber had overseen and directed experiments on concentration camp prisoners. He was recruited by the US Air Force School of Medicine. When his past was revealed in 1952 he was spirited out of America to live in Nazi-friendly Argentina. According to Linda Hunt, author of *Secret Agenda: The United States Government, Nazi Scientists and Project Paperclip, 1945–1990*, the true legacy of Paperclip was to inspire covert chemical warfare research on human subjects – *by the US army*. She alleges that US soldiers were exposed to nerve gas and psychoactive drugs at the US army chemical testing centre at Edgewood Arsenal, in a programme that involved Nazi scientists. More lurid conspiracy theories allege that this was just the start of a long-running programme of research into mind-control techniques, called Project MK-Ultra, but the credibility of this theory is undermined by its links to alien abduction and JFK assassination conspiracies.

According to official sources such as NASA, 642 'foreign technicians and specialists' came to the US under the auspices of Project Paperclip, of which von Braun's team of 132 was the largest single group. Paperclip was just one of a number of operations, however. The ultra-secret Operation Alsos was a similar project to retrieve nuclear secrets and scientists and prevent them from falling into Soviet hands. Beginning in 1947, Operation National Interest broadened the remit of Paperclip to bring over scientists to work for American industry or academia, and not just the military. Clandestinely, it also allowed the CIA to recruit intelligence and military assets who might be useful against the communist threat, opening another and even more shady chapter in the dark history of US involvement with post-war Nazis (see 'The real Odessa Conspiracy', page 37).

Whether you listen to the euphemisms of the official version or the accusations of the critics, questions over the morality of Operation Paperclip remain. The guiding principle for America's post-war treatment of potentially useful ex-Nazis was that the end justified the means. How many Third Reich criminals escaped justice as a result?

References

This is not an exhaustive list, but a brief resume of some of the more useful or interesting books, articles and websites I've used/referred to in the text. Each reference is only given once, but many of the books from the earlier chapters are also helpful for later ones.

Chapter 1

Aiuto, Russell (Accessed 13 May 2004) 'The First Crime Family', *Crime Library*, http://www.crimelibrary.com

Alder, Garrick (Jan 2001) 'The Pope Must Die', *Fortean Times*, 142

Bainton, Roy (July 2000) 'Mischief Myths', *Fortean Times*, 136

Barrett, David (Jan 2004) 'Plotting the Mason–Taxil line', *Fortean Times*, 179

Barrett, David V (1997) *Secret Societies*, Blandford, London

Bennett, Richard M (2003) *Conspiracy*, Virgin Books, London

Cornwell John (1989) *A Thief in the Night*, Simon and Schuster, New York

Cross, Suzanna (Accessed 5 May 2004) 'Julius Caesar, the Last Dictator', http://heraklia.fws1.com/conspiracy/index.html

Duffy, Jonathan (3 June 2004) 'Bilderberg: The ultimate conspiracy theory', *BBC News Online Magazine*,
http://news.bbc.co.uk/go/pr/fr/-/1/hi/magazine/3773019.stm

Farrell, Maureen (Accessed 25 June 2004) 'On a Mission from God: The Religious Right and the Emerging American Theocracy',
http://www.buzzflash.com/farrell/04/03/

Hunt, Linda (1992) *Secret Agenda: The United States Government, Nazi Scientists and Project Paperclip*, 1945–1990, St Martin's Press, New York

Kjeilen, Tore (Accessed 9 July 2004) 'Assassins', *Encyclopaedia of the Orient*, http://i-cias.com/e.o/assassins.htm

Ramsay, Robin (April 2004) 'Konspiracy Corner', *Fortean Times*, 182

Ramsay, Robin (Nov 2003) 'JFK-Case Closed', *Fortean Times*, 176

Rickard, Bob (July 2000) 'The Jewes shall be blamed', *Fortean Times*, 136

Rickard, Bob (Sept 1997) 'The Pope and the Virgin', *Fortean Times*, 102,

Ronson, Jon (2001) *Them: Adventures with Extremists*, Picador, London

Sharlet, Jeffrey (March 2003) 'Jesus Plus Nothing', *Harper's Magazine*

Sheldon, Rose Mary (Autumn 2000) 'Toga & Dagger: Espionage in Ancient Rome', *MHQ: The Quarterly Journal of Military History*

Simpson, Christopher (1988) *Blowback: America's Recruitment of Nazis and Its Effects on the Cold War*, Weidenfeld & Nicolson, New York

Stoneman, Richard (1991) *Greek Mythology*, HarperCollins, London

The Gunpowder Plot Society (Accessed 1 May 2004)
http://www.gunpowder-plot.org

Tobin , Paul (Accessed 20 May 2004) 'Popes Throughout History', *The Rejection of Pascal's Wager*,
http://www.geocities.com/paulntobin/index.html

Volkman, Ernest (1994) *Spies*, John Wiley and Sons, New York

Yallop, David (1984) *In God's Name*, Jonathan Cape, London

Chapter 2

'Spies', *Public Records Office*, (Accessed 1 July 2004)
http://www.pro.gov.uk/virtualmuseum/spies/

Bath, Alan Harris (1998) *Tracking the Axis Enemy: The Triumph of Anglo-American Naval Intelligence*, University Press of Kansas, Lawrence

Bennett, Richard M (2003) *Espionage*, Virgin, London

Durschmied, Erik (1999) *The Hinge Factor*, Coronet, London

Hollins, Dave (2001, Accessed 12 June 2004) 'The Hidden Hand –
    Espionage and Napoleon', Osprey Publishing,
    http://www.ospreypublishing.com/content4.php/cid=71

Momsen, Bill (1993, Accessed 29 May 2004) 'Codebreaking and Secret
    Weapons in World War II', *Nautical Brass Online*,
    home.earthlink.net/~nbrass1/enigma.htm

Overy, Richard with Wheatcroft, Andrew (1999) *The Road To War*,
    Penguin, Harmondsworth

Singh, Simon (1999) *The Code Book*, Fourth Estate, London

Vankin, Jonathan and Whalen, John (2004) *The 80 Greatest Conspiracies of
    All Time*, Citadel Press, New York

Chapter 3

'Documents in Law, History and Diplomacy', *The Avalon Project at Yale
    Law School* (1996–2003 Accessed 3 June 2004)
    http://www.yale.edu/lawweb/avalon/avalon.htm

Alexander, John K and Cooper, Richard T (December 19th 1998) 'The
    Impeachment Debate: "High Crimes, Misdemeanors": A Yardstick
    Whittled by History,' *Los Angeles Times*

O'Brien, Professor Joseph V (Accessed 9 June 2004) *Obee's History Page*,
    John Jay College of Criminal Justice,
    http://web.jjay.cuny.edu/~jobrien/reference/ob15.html

Society of American Historians (1991) *Reader's Companion to American
    History*, Houghton Mifflin Company, New York

Wetzel, David (2001) *A Duel of Giants: Bismarck, Napoleon III, and the
    Origins of the Franco-Prussian War*, University of Wisconsin Press,
    Madison

Chapter 4

'Sinon', *History of Espionage* (Accessed 30 May 2004)
    http://www.angelfire.com/dc/1spy/index.html

Borger, Julian (25 May 2004) 'US Intelligence Fears Iran Duped Hawks into Iraq War', *Guardian*

Carpenter, Ted Galen (9 June 2004) 'Did Iran use Chalabi to lure US into Iraq?', *Fox News Channel*

Cockburn, Andrew (26 May 2004) 'The Trail to Tehran', *Guardian*

Grove, Eric (2001) *The Price of Disobedience: The Battle of the Plate Reconsidered*, US Naval Institute, Bethesda

Hesketh, Roger (2002) *Fortitude: The D-Day Deception Campaign*, The Overlook Press, Woodstock

History of the Grimaldi family (Accessed 2 June 2004) http://www.grimaldi.org

Kiesling, John Brady (10 June 2004) 'Chalabi's Fall Shows that the US Cannot Match Mideast in the Art of Devious Diplomacy', *Financial Times*

Latimer, Jon (2001) *Deception in War*, John Murray Publishers, London

Neillands, Robin (1997) *In the Combat Zone: Special Forces Since 1945*, Orion, London

Parada, Carlos (Accessed 23 May 2004) *Greek Mythology Link*, http://homepage.mac.com/cparada/GML/

Rutter, Gordon (July 2004) 'Magic Goes to War', *Fortean Times*, 185

Society for Military History (1996) *Reader's Companion to Military History*, Houghton Mifflin Company, New York

Sutton, David (July 2004) 'Bodyguard of Lies', *Fortean Times*, 185

Chapter 5

'Fashionable Innovations of Tsar Peter the Great', *Hoogsteder Journal*, No 7, Sept 2004

Boardman, John, Griffin, Jasper and Murray, Oswyn (1986) *The Oxford History of Greece and the Hellenistic World*, Oxford University Press, Oxford

Cross, Suzanne (2004, Accessed 20 May 2004) *Feminae Romanae: The Women of Ancient Rome*, http://dominae.fws1.com/Influence/Livia%20Augusta/Index.htm

Fildes, Alan and Fletcher, Dr Joann (Accessed 13 June 2004) *Alexander in Egypt*, http://www.touregypt.net/featurestories/alexanderthegreat.htm

Goyau, Georges (1912) 'Armand-Jean du Plessis, Duke de Richelieu', *Catholic Encyclopaedia*, Vol XIII

Graves, Robert (1988) *I, Claudius*, Penguin, Harmondsworth

Kosmetatou, Elizabeth (Accessed 5 May 2004) 'Alexander's visit to the Oracle of Ammon', *Hellenic Electronic Centre*, http://www.greece.org/alexandria/alexander/Pages/siwa.html

Massie, Robert K (1981) *Peter the Great*, Ballantine, New York

Chapter 6

'Early Radar History – an Introduction', *Penley Radar Archives* (Accessed 1 July 2004)
http://www.penleyradararchives.org.uk/history/introduction.htm

'Operation Paperclip Dossier', Agent Orange, (8 August 1997, Accessed 24 June 2004)
http://www.conspiracyarchive.com/NWO/project_paperclip.htm

'The Culture of Secrecy and the Nuclear Age', *Women's International League for Peace and Freedom* (Accessed 27 May 2004)
http://www.reachingcriticalwill.org/technical/factsheets/secrecy.html

Bilstein, Professor Roger E (1979) *SP-4206 Stages to Saturn*, NASA

Buderi, Robert (1996) *The Invention That Changed the World*, Simon and Schuster, New York

Day, Dwayne A (Accessed 20 May 2004) 'Radar', *US Centennial of Flight Commission*,
http://www.centennialofflight.gov/essay/Evolution_of_Technology/radar/Tech39.htm

Dickinson, Michael (Accessed 23 May 2004) 'Captain Cook – The 1st Voyage', *Pacific Explorers Library*,
http://www.pacificislandtravel.com/books_and_maps/captain-cook1.html

Lahanas, Michael (Accessed 20 May 2004) 'Burning Mirrors', *Hellas: Ancient Greece: Science, Technology and other Interesting Stories*,
http://www.mlahanas.de/Greeks/Mirrors.htm

'Manhattan Project', *National Atomic Museum* (2004, Accessed 27 May 2004) www.atomicmuseum.com/tour/manhattanproject.cfm

REFERENCES

Mann, Horace (Accessed 12 May 2004) *Medieval War, Warfare, Weapons, Armour and Castles,*
http://www.sfusd.k12.ca.us/schwww/sch618/War/FireWeapons.html

Pillinger, Colin (May 1 2004) 'To infinity, and beyond!', *The Times*

Rhodes, Richard (1995) *The Making of the Atomic Bomb,* Simon and Schuster, New York

Rossen, Erich (2000, Accessed 19 June 2004) *Heliostats as Death Rays,*
http://people.linux-gull.ch/rossen/solar/deathray.html

Santee, Casey (2004) 'Manhattan Project Developed Under Extraordinary Veil of Secrecy', *The Pocatello Idaho State Journal*

Silverstein, Ken (3 May 2000, Accessed 30 May 2004) 'Our Nazi Allies', *salon.com,* http://www.salon.com/news/feature/2000/05/03/nazi

Smith, Bernard (1985) 'Academic Perceptions of Cook's Role in the Opening of the Pacific', *Cook's Log,* vol 8, number 2

The Manhattan Project: Making the Atomic Bomb (1998), DVD, AJ Software and Multimedia, New York

Volti, Rudi (1999) 'Greek Fire', *The Facts On File Encyclopedia of Science, Technology, and Society,* Facts On File Inc, New York

Index

Jerusalem, Kingdom
of 14
Jesuits 29, 30, 31
Jews 71-74
JFK assassination 58-
65, 235
Johnson, Lyndon 59,
63-64
Kempai Tai 105
Kennedy, John F (see
JFK assassination)
Kennedy, Robert F 61,
63
KGB 55

Langsdorff, Captain
163-66
Laocoon 151
Lateran Treaty 46, 47
League of Nations 144
Leigh-Mallory,
Trafford 113
Leopold, of
Hohenzollern 131-
33
Lewis and Clark
Expedition 128
Litvinov, Maxim 144,
145
Livia Drusilla 197-
200, 201
Livingston, Robert
127-28
London Controlling
Section (LCS) 168,
174
Los Alamos research
site 229
Louis XIII 206-09
Louis XIV 123-24
Louisiana Purchase
125, 127-28
Louisiana territory
125-28
Luftwaffe 111, 113,
159, 161-62

Machiavelli, Niccolo
23
Mafia 41, 43, 47, 48,
50, 51, 57, 58, 59,
60, 61, 62, 63
magic 156-59

magnetron 223-24
Magruder, 'Prince'
John 160
Manhattan Project vii,
210, 211, 225-31
Marabouts 156, 158
Marcellus, Marcus
Claudius 211-12,
214, 215
Marcinkus,
Archbishop Paul
48, 50, 57
Marie de Medici 207,
208
Marlowe, Christopher
85, 89
Marmont, Marshal
97, 98
Marozia
Theophylactus 201-
02
Mary, Queen of Scots
86, 87-90
Masons (see
Freemasons)
Mazarin, Cardinal 209
McFarlane, Robert
118
Mendoza, Bernadino
de 87, 88
Metaurus, Battle of 81
MI5 174, 175
microwaves 223
Midway, Battle of 114
military-industrial
complex 61, 63, 230
mind control 64, 235
Mohamed, Mahathir
74
Molotov, Vyacheslav
143, 145
Monaco 148
conquest of 153-55
Monroe, James 127-
28
Monteagle, Lord 25,
27, 28, 29-30, 31
moon landings 231
Morgan, William 74
Moro, Aldo 41, 44-45,
58
Moscow, Battle of 105
Mulberry project 172

Munich Conference
145
Myceneans 153
Mystery religions 1, 2-
4

Napoleon III 130, 156
National Security
Agency (NSA) 189,
191
Nazi scientists 231-35
Nazis 37-40, 42, 104,
108, 142-47, 232
and secret weapons
210-11, 225, 231-32
Nazi-Soviet Non-
Aggression Pact
142, 144, 146-47
Nero, Caius Claudius
80-81
Nero, emperor 3
New Orleans 125, 126,
128
North Atlantic, Battle
of the 112, 115
North, Oliver 118,
119, 120
nuclear weapons 190,
225-31

Oak Ridge processing
plant 228-29
Oates, Titus 75, 124
Octavian 6, 8-10, 197-
98
Odessa (organisation
of former SS mem-
bers) 37
Odysseus 149-52, 199
Office of Special Plans
(OSP) 188, 189,
190
Operation Alsos 235
Operation Barbarossa
104, 105, 147
Operation Bodyguard
166-82
Operation Fortitude
175
North 168, 169-71
South 171-80
Operation Gladio 40,
43, 44

About the Author

Joel Levy is a writer on history and the paranormal, and the author of several books, including *Really Useful* – the history and science of everyday things; the *KISS Guide to the Unexplained* – a beginner's guide to historical secrets and mysteries, the paranormal and supernatural; *Scam: Secrets of the Con Artist* – an inside look at the world and history of the con artist and his scams; and *Fabulous Creatures* – about creatures of myth and folklore.